Clootie Dumpling

$\frac{1}{2}$ lb S.R. Flour.

$\frac{1}{2}$ lb Currants

$\frac{1}{2}$ lb Raisins

$\frac{1}{2}$ lb Sugar.

3 Table Spoons Treacle.

1 Table Spoon Syrup.

Mixed Spice

1 Pint Milk

$\frac{1}{4}$ Teaspoon Salt.

$\frac{1}{2}$ tsp Cinnamon

$\frac{1}{4}$ Tsp Ginger

8 oz suet.

Sheila Hutchins' GOOD COOKING

Sheila Hutchins'
GOOD COOKING

Collins Glasgow and London

© Sheila Hutchins 1978
First Published 1978
Published by William Collins Sons and Company Limited
Glasgow and London
ISBN 0 00 435115 0
Printed in Great Britain

Contents

Introduction

'Cookery, like every other Art, has been moving forward to Perfection by Slow Degrees;' as John Farley, formerly principal cook at the London Tavern, wrote in the preface to the *London Art of Cookery*, 1783 'and yet daily Improvements are still making, as must be the Case in every Art depending on Fancy and Taste. From the many Books of this Kind already published, it could hardly be supposed there would be Occasion for Another, yet we flatter ourselves that the Readers of this Work will find, from a candid Perusal, and an impartial Comparison, that our Pretensions to the Favours of the Public are not ill founded.

......'We shall only add, that neither Labour, Care nor Expense have been spared to make this Work worthy of the Patronage of the Public.'

Chapter 1
Breakfast and Supper Dishes

Many breakfast dishes, such as kedgeree, are now more frequently served for supper than for breakfast, bacon and eggs being especially popular. Some of the best English fish dishes were originally eaten for breakfast.

In Victorian England it was considered essentially a family occasion. No servants waited at table, though in India they often stood outside the dining-room door. People helped themselves and their fellow guests. On a side table there might have been curried eggs, or bacon and eggs in a silver entrée dish as well as porridge, hot muffins, devilled grouse or pheasant which, as an old cookery book says, were 'very acceptable breakfast dainties for the masculine portion of the household, much regarded by the Anglo-Indian military.' The old country-house breakfasts were enormous, but of course meals were at different times in the 19th century and breakfast was often taken after a cold bath and a brisk five-mile walk, or morning prayers, while dinner – the main meal – was eaten at about four o'clock. Chelsea buns, lightly boiled eggs in knitted egg cosies, a Melton Mowbray or a veal and ham pie were all popular: 'Let your sideboard – it is assumed you have a sideboard – sigh and lament its hard lot under its load of cold joints, game and pies – I am still harping on the country house; and if you have a York ham cut, it should be flanked by a Westphalian ditto. For the blend is a good one. And remember that no York ham under 20 lb weight is worth cutting. You need not put it all on the board at once. A capital adjunct to the breakfast-table, too is a reindeer's tongue, which, as you see it hung up in the shops, looks more like a policeman's truncheon in active employment than anything else; but when soaked and then properly treated in the boiling, is very tasty, and will melt like marrow in the mouth', as Edward Spencer wrote in 1897 in *Cakes and Ale*.

Breakfast dishes varied in different parts of the country and some of our best regional and village specialities were eaten in the great houses at breakfast, fortunately, for there might otherwise be no record of them. In East Anglia in winter there was often Norfolk Partridge Pot — a casserole of old partridge in red wine or port which was usually eaten cold for breakfast with brown bread and butter or hot dry toast. In summer there might be plates of radishes (some seedsmen still list a variety known as the "breakfast radish", though the custom has vanished).

There was often fresh-caught mackerel, brook trout, or, in Scotland, Arbroath Smokies and marmalades and honeys. In the North West they favoured black puddings, grilled kidneys, potato cakes, home-made brawn, faggots and soft herring roes on toast.

Near Worcester, in the 19th century, there were funeral breakfasts as well as wedding breakfasts. A small boiled turkey would sometimes be served with the other baked funeral meats; mourning hatbands and scarves were worn.

Though a recent survey showed that 82% of all British adults still eat "a proper breakfast" regardless of class or income differences, the large breakfast has almost vanished.

Butchers, fishmongers and those who have to be at the big wholesale markets such as Smithfield or Billingsgate by 6 a.m. often eat a large "second breakfast" of Victorian proportions at work, with beer, rumpsteak, chump chops and so on. Farm labourers go home also to a solid second breakfast after milking, while builders, decorators and others who begin work early often have a fairly solid meal, a "second breakfast", on the site.

Irish Buttered Eggs

Take the eggs fresh from the nest, wipe them lightly if stained but do not wash them. Smear your hands with butter and cover each egg completely in a thin coating of it. Store them pointed end down in an egg carton. Boiled or fried they have a most subtle buttery flavour.

Boiled Eggs

Lightly boiled eggs are especially good when eaten with sippets or "soldiers" of fresh bread, thickly buttered, such as one dipped into a soft boiled egg yolk in childhood. The sippets can also be toasted, but the contrast between crust and crumb is very pleasant. Extra butter can be put in the eggs as well, with pepper.

The main problem with the lightly boiled, shop-bought egg is to prevent the shell from cracking. Put the eggs in cold water which bring to boil. When it is just bubbling the egg will be perfectly done, the shell not cracked.

Do not keep eggs in the refrigerator, buy them fresh and use them rapidly. If put into hot water when frozen the shells will almost certainly crack. Very cold eggs are useless too for making Mayonnaise and the whites of these chilled eggs are impossible to whisk.

Coddled Eggs

The really new-laid egg straight from the nest and laid that morning should not be boiled but coddled, as the white may harden before the yolk has set.

Put the egg into boiling water, cover the pan and take it off the heat. Leave the egg in hot water for 5–6 minutes. It can be kept in the hot water for some little time before becoming hard.

The familiar Staffordshire pottery hens on pottery nests were designed originally as a sort of egg cosy. They were used for these coddled eggs. Hot water was poured into the base or pottery nest. The eggs were put in the water with the hen "lid" on top. This was thought more practical than the old knitted egg cosies, for it kept them not only hot but from becoming hard and dry while waiting on the breakfast table.

Scrambled Eggs

The famous Hildagonda J. Duckett describes them as "Scratched Eggs" 'a favourite Colonial breakfast dish' in her *Hilda's Where*

11

Is It? of recipes. First published in 1891 it ran into many editions and is a sort of gastronomic bible in South Africa and Rhodesia.

She cooks them in a little butter in a frying pan stirring briskly and serves them on hot buttered toast, with pepper and salt.

To cook scrambled eggs, beat 6 eggs with a little salt and pepper. Heat ½ pint of milk in a pan; when almost boiling add the beaten eggs and stir until they set and scramble. Serve at once on hot buttered toast.

At breakfast, scrambled eggs are often served with bloaters or kippers hot and grilled, on the same plate.

Mumbled Eggs
For rich scrambled eggs, or "mumbled eggs" as they were known in King George IV's day, melt 2 oz of butter, stir in 6 well beaten eggs, some salt, and pepper. Stir them over a low heat until the eggs begin to thicken. Then fork in 2 oz more butter cut in pieces and add ¼ pint of thick cream.

When delicately made with butter and cream and mixed with small pieces of thin, tender, but lightly cooked garden asparagus – what the old gardeners call "sprue grass" – they make a most appetizing breakfast dish for springtime and would be most acceptable at supper.

Mumbled Eggs with Fried Sippets
The scrambled or mumbled eggs may also be mixed with sippets of bread which have been diced and fried crisp in butter. This is pleasant to serve hot, in a silver entrée dish, at the beginning of an elegant meal.

Alternatively, some tiny rolls of crisp fried bacon are placed in the hot entrée dish. The scrambled or mumbled eggs are then poured on top. With a lid on the dish it may be left for some little time on the electric hot plate. Some cooks pour a little melted butter over the whole before it comes to table.

Mumbled Eggs with Smoked Salmon
They are remarkably good with the smoked salmon, either to

have side by side on separate plates, which prevents the buttery eggs becoming mixed with any lemon juice squeezed on the salmon, or with a thin slice of smoked salmon laid on a very slightly warmed plate and the eggs, when mumbled, heaped on top as if it were hot buttered toast.

The eggs can also be mumbled with haddock, or smoked fillet. Blanch, skin and bone a Finnan haddock, then flake it and toss it in melted butter. When hot add at least 2 tablespoons of thick cream. Serve it beside the mumbled eggs on a very hot plate, or stir it into them when mumbled.

Scotch Woodcock

The Scotch Woodcock was a favourite Edwardian savoury. It consists of hot buttered toast spread with anchovy paste and topped with scrambled or mumbled egg. It was served in small pieces, hot at the end of the meal, often in a silver entrée dish.

It might now be served before a meal as what, in the 18th century, was known as "a nice whet" as they whetted the appetite for the meal to come; Mrs. Raffald gives recipes for several good whets in her book *The Experienc'd English House-keeper*, published in 1769.

In larger portions the Scotch Woodcock makes an acceptable supper dish.

Curried Eggs

This is a favourite English dish which was very popular in Edwardian and Victorian kitchens. It has only a distant affinity to oriental cookery and is eaten hot or cold with various chutneys, such as those called after Major Grey or Colonel Skinner, two mysterious Anglo-Indian figures who have given their names, one to a mild and the other to a slightly hotter chutney, and then been forgotten.

Hard boil two eggs per person, for 10 minutes, then drop them into cold water. Shell and cut them in two lengthways. Fry one finely sliced onion and one small peeled, cored and chopped apple gently in oil and when they are just golden add 1 level tablespoon of curry powder, stir it well and add ¾ pint of water, a little salt, a bayleaf and after letting it simmer for a couple of minutes, stir in 1 teaspoon of sugar. Add the sliced eggs, turning them so they soak up the sauce and cook them for 5 minutes. Serve on hot, plain boiled, well drained Patna rice.

Various Eggs

A Duck's Egg is larger than a hen's egg, pale green and strongly flavoured. They are unsuitable for boiling but may be used in cooking. One duck egg equals two hen eggs. They are very good in puddings and make excellent cakes. They usually weigh just over 3 oz while a good hen egg weighs almost 2 oz.

A Goose Egg weighs about the same as four hen eggs and makes a very good omelette, full of flavour. Goose and duck eggs are sometimes sold in country markets, often at National Federation of Women's Institutes' produce stalls in springtime and at the farm gates.

The taste of a free-range egg may vary according to what the hen has been eating. When buying eggs at the farm gates it may be useful to note the type of poultry food used, and to choose accordingly. This is usually publicized on the "Fresh Brown Eggs" notice at the gate. Years ago, the old farmhouse hens used to be left free to range the woods and coppices. Sometimes in spring they fed on the wild garlic or ramson leaves, which used to flavour the eggs.

Breakfast Radishes

People often ask why packets of seeds should be labelled French Breakfast Radishes as no-one eats them for breakfast nowadays. It is one of those hangovers from the distant past, people used to have radishes for breakfast in Victorian England with boiled eggs and newly baked bread, thickly buttered. They are very good; large peppery radishes are especially nice if one dabs a little butter on them before putting them in one's mouth. Alexis Soyer, famous chef at the Reform Club, writing in 1850, not only commends hot buttery muffins, black puddings, bacon and sausages, but says there should be 'orange marmalade in its original pot, watercresses and a few nice radishes' on the breakfast table with the toast and coffee. Watercress is good too to nibble at breakfast with boiled eggs and buttered toast.

Bacon and Eggs
Some people put quantities of dripping or lard in the pan when frying bacon. This is unnecessary and makes the food greasy.

Bacon rashers can be fried just in their own fat with none added to the pan. Lay them in the hot pan with the lean over the fat. Turn them after a few moments and fry the other side. They take 3–4 minutes to cook. It is usual to remove the rind before cooking them. Remove the rashers and keep them hot. Drop the eggs one by one into the frying pan and baste them with the hot bacon fat. If there are more than six eggs drop them all at once into the pan, baste them once with bacon fat, cover the pan with a lid until done.

Bacon used to be thought best when cooked on the end of a toasting fork before the dining-room or the kitchen fire. For this it was cut in very thin rashers then divided into pieces convenient for serving. The rind was trimmed to prevent the bacon curling up and the bacon was toasted on a long wire fork.

Thin rashers of bacon, without the rind, can be grilled. They take 3–4 minutes to cook and should be turned once.

At breakfast time in Irish farmhouses there is generally a great "cake" of brown soda bread on the table, salty yellow butter, thick strong tea, rashers and eggs, porridge and cream, and perhaps a honey comb. The cream itself has a particularly pleasing flavour as much of the milk is unpasteurized.

Soyer's Patent Chops used to be cooked at the breakfast table in his Magic Stove – a patent chafing dish – together with eight pieces of very thin bacon, four sausages and a quantity of fried bread. This invention of the 1850s was considered 'the forefront of *bon ton*' in many of the best families. It ensured that the breakfasts were hot and sizzling when put on the plates, unlike the tepid bacon and eggs which had to be carried down endless stone flagged corridors from a distant kitchen.

Some Garnishes for Bacon, Egg and Sausages

Breakfast Pikelets These are very light and should be made just before breakfast and served at once. Mix 4 tablespoons of self-raising flour with pepper and salt and a little chopped parsley if available. Beat in enough milk to make a creamy batter. After frying the bacon or sausages drop a good teaspoon of the mixture at a time into the hot fat. It rises quickly. When cooked underneath turn it over with a fish slice and fry the other side.

Fried Bread Cut the bread in slices $\frac{1}{4}$ inch thick. Stale bread is best. Cut off the crusts. There should be enough fat from the breakfast bacon to fry the bread. If not lard or dripping could be added to it. Heat the fat in the frying pan. When it is fairly hot, dip both sides of the bread in it and then leave it to fry until crisp and golden-brown, turning it once.

Fried Tomatoes Heat the bacon fat and put the halved tomatoes in it in the frying pan, cut side up. The fat should be really hot but not smoking. Reduce the heat, fry the halved tomatoes gently until they are beginning to be soft, turning them over when almost done, in about 5 minutes. When both sides are done, drain the halved tomatoes and serve with cut side up.

Car-Cakes (Scotland) Sometimes fried in bacon fat with the breakfast rashers in Scotland. Mix 4 oz oatmeal, a pinch of salt, a dash of pepper, a pinch of cream of tartar, a pinch of bicarbonate of soda. Stir in enough milk to make a pouring batter. Fry this in spoonsful in the hot bacon fat. If there is not enough to cover turn them over when brown and fry the other side.

Cheshire Potato Cakes
These are the kind of potato cakes which used to be made in country kitchens in Cheshire in my childhood. Whey or buttermilk was used to mix them; this can now be bought from the milkman.

Mash 1 lb of warm boiled potatoes with about 6 oz of plain flour, a dessertspoon of butter and a good pinch of salt. Stir in just enough buttermilk to make a firm pastry dough, working it with a wooden spoon until it forms a ball in the basin and comes away from the sides. Roll out this dough about $\frac{1}{4}$ inch thick. Cut it in rounds with a teacup and fry these in hot frothing butter. Eat them as hot as possible, split and sandwiched with more butter. They may also be cooked in bacon fat and served with fried bacon.

Excellent potato cakes are made in Ireland and Scotland and cooked on an ungreased griddle. These are usually served hot at tea time rolled up with butter. Sometimes a glass of buttermilk is drunk with them.

Bacon
In Victorian households the very thin cut streaky bacon rashers were often dipped in beaten egg with a little pepper, and then in breadcrumbs. They were then fried crisp in a chip pan in deep hot fat or oil. They were used mostly as a garnish.

In Lancashire and the Midlands, they like long cut bacon rashers with the back and streaky in one piece. If left whole they are best done in a tin in the oven.

One still finds old fashioned country grocers and pork butchers who have sides of bacon in white knitted cheesecloth covers dangling from hooks in the ceiling, one of the advantages of these is that they will be sliced to order on a bacon machine in the shop at whatever thickness the customer prefers.

In Scotland one must distinguish between bacon which has been rolled Ayrshire style and bacon which is Ayrshire cured. Some Welsh bacon seems very salt but much of it is delicious and well worth buying from country butchers.

Black Puddings and Staffordshire Oatcakes
Black puddings can be heated through in hot water then served with mashed potatoes, or they can be sliced and fried in dripping or bacon fat. They are very good with bacon and eggs.

The delicious Bury puddings of Lancashire are small and round unlike other black puddings and are best cut in half for grilling or frying. They are always tied in bundles and in pork butchers' shops in the North West one sees bunches of them hung from the ceiling like huge black grapes. Lancashire children still get bread and bacon dip or dripping with their bacon and eggs and the Bury puddings are often eaten with big hot Staffordshire or Derbyshire oatcakes. These are as big as a frying pan, soft and floppy and more like a Breton pancake than Scots oatcakes. In the North West people often buy them from the baker to re-heat at home, but they are easy to make.

17

Warm 2 pints of water to blood heat, add ½ oz of salt, and 1 oz of crumbled bakers' yeast. Mix 1 lb of Scotch oatmeal with 8 oz of wholemeal flour and ½ oz of baking powder. Add this gradually to the yeast mixture, stirring and beating till it is like Yorkshire pudding batter. Let it stand in a warm place for 20 minutes to "work" stirring it up if it drops down.

If the mixture seems thin add a little oatmeal, if thick a little water. Grease an iron griddle or bakestone (or an ordinary big frying pan or cookie sheet), heat it, then pour a teacup of batter in the middle so it spreads evenly. Cook it 5 minutes, turn, cook the other side, then back to the first side for 2 minutes. Cool the oatcakes on a wire sieve.

In Lancashire there are sometimes "treacle butties" for breakfast too, made with the black treacle that has been so much used in the North West that it is virtually a regional speciality.

Gammon Rashers

Thick gammon rashers, or gammon "steaks", fried slowly in a pan and served with fried eggs and tomatoes are popular in Lancashire and Cheshire for breakfast or High Tea. Some Cheshire pubs make a speciality of them and though not at all cheap they are nevertheless excellent.

When the gammon rashers are more than ¾ inch thick they are best cooked in the oven. The huge thick rasher may be divided in half, like a rumpsteak, if it is wished to make two portions. To prevent the gammon rasher from curling in cooking, cut off the rind and snip the fat at intervals. Place the gammon rasher in a meat tin or fireproof dish, dot the top with pieces of butter, dripping or lard. Bake it in a moderate oven (350°F, 180°C, Mark 4) for 25 minutes or longer, depending on thickness, and turning it once. Sausages and mushrooms or black puddings may be cooked at the same time in the hot fat. Eggs are best cooked separately.

Mr Bloom's Breakfast Kidney

'Mr Leopold Bloom ate with relish the inner organs of the beasts and fowls. He liked thick giblet soup, nutty gizzards, fried hencod roes. Most of all he liked grilled mutton kidneys which gave to his palate a fine tang of faintly scented urine . . . "There's a smell of burn," she said. "Did you leave anything on the fire?"

' "The kidney!" he cried suddenly.

'He fitted the book roughly into his inner pocket and, stubbing his toes against the broken commode, hurried out towards the smell, stepping hastily down the stairs with a flurried stork's legs. Pungent smoke shot up in an angry jet from the side of the pan. By prodding a prong of the fork under the kidney he detached it and turned it turtle on its back. Only a little burned. He tossed it off the pan on to a plate and let the scanty brown gravy trickle over it.

'Cup of tea now. He sat down, cut and buttered a slice of the loaf. He shored away the burnt flesh and flung it to the cat. Then he put a forkful into his mouth, chewing with discernment the toothsome pliant meat. Done to a turn.'   From *Ulysses* by James Joyce.

Kidneys and Bacon
Split the lambs' or pigs' kidneys open lengthways without dividing them, strip off the fat and skin and run two parallel skewers through them to keep them flat in grilling. Lay them on the grill rack, cut side up, season them well with Cayenne and black pepper, but no salt till they are cooked. Grill them about 4 minutes per side and turn them immediately that side is done. Grill the other side and serve at once. The exact cooking time depends on the heat of the grill and size of the kidneys.

Old fashioned *Curly Bacon*, first blanched in boiling water then taken out and, when wet, curled – not too tight – was grilled before an open fire in the dining-room and served with the kidneys.

The rashers may also be done under the gas or electric griller. To curl well the bacon must be cut as thin as possible, preferably on the No 3 cutter. If somewhat thicker, the rinds should be cut off and the rashers stretched with a knife, they can then be rolled, fastened with a small skewer or toothpick and grilled.

A tablespoon of hot whisky may be poured over grilled kidneys as they come to table, then set on fire to flame them lightly.

If the griller is small, the split skewered kidneys may be laid in the bottom of the grill pan with the bacon uncurled and laid out above in rows, fat over lean, on the hot grid. It drips on to the kidneys and bastes them. When done remove the bacon, keep it hot and go on grilling the kidneys for 5 or 6 minutes, turning once, till done. Whole mushrooms without the stalks can be grilled under the bacon with the kidneys too.

Grilled Kidneys with Devil Butter

Allow 2 lamb's kidneys or 1 pig's kidney per person. Slit open on the plump side and skewer them flat on two parallel skewers. Dip them in melted butter. Grill them about 4 minutes per side and dish on very hot plates with a pat of Devil Butter on each.

Devil Butter Cream 4 oz of butter with a spoonful of curry paste, a few drops of tabasco and some chopped chives or parsley. The juices from the grill pan may be kept for making fried bread.

Soyer's Kidney and Mushroom Sandwich

An excellent dish, which appears to have been forgotten.
'Grill three plain kidneys speared *à la brochette* to keep them flat. Grill also six large mushroom heads, well season with salt and pepper — Cayenne if approved. A few minutes will do them. Then rub a little fresh butter inside the mushrooms. Dish up each kidney between two mushrooms while very hot and serve.

'If a large quantity is required proceed thus: Well butter a sauté pan, lay in 20 or more heads of large mushrooms just washed, season well with salt and pepper. Let them stew for twenty minutes gently in an oven or until done. Make your kidney sandwich as above, put a tablespoon of the kidney and mushroom gravy over, and serve. The same may be served on thin toast. The stems of the mushrooms may be stewed and served with the dish.'   From *The Culinary Campaign* by Alexis Soyer, 1857.

Thespian Dumplings

The Thespian or Kidney Dumpling recipe comes from a book of memoirs by a long-forgotten Edwardian actor. It was popular in theatrical lodging houses at the end of the last century.

Cut four large peeled Spanish onions in half, then take out the middles and substitute a lamb's kidney, cut in quarters, in each. Add pepper and salt before joining the two halves of the onions together.

Roll out about 8 oz of shortcrust pastry and divide it into four. Put one stuffed onion in each piece of pastry, moisten the edges of the pastry and bring them up round the onions, trimming off any extra bits of pastry. Press the edges together then turn your Thespian Dumplings the other way up. Put them in a greased baking tin with the join underneath. Brush the tops with milk and bake them for about 60 minutes in a moderate oven (350°F, 180°C, Mark 4).

Welsh Laver Bread – Bara Lawr

This is sometimes rolled in oatmeal, fried in bacon fat and eaten for breakfast with grilled gammon or with salty Welsh farmhouse bacon. In cooking it must be mixed with a wooden or silver spoon and cooked in either an enamelled or an aluminium pan, iron spoils it. It can be sprinkled with a little lemon juice.

The name is misleading, it is not like bread at all. Laver is a fine silky seaweed which grows on the rocks and is sometimes called sea spinach, or by small children, angels' hair. Much liked in Pembrokeshire and other parts of South Wales, it has to be cured in drying houses and boiled for a long time before it is used. It is sold ready prepared in Swansea Market and elsewhere when it is known as *Bara Lawr*, Laver Bread.

It may be cooked and eaten as above, it does not taste fishy, is really very pleasant though is perhaps an acquired taste like oysters. In the Hebrides and Ireland it is called sloke.

Finnan Haddock

Findon haddocks, or Finnan haddies, are called after a village in Kincardineshire about 6 miles south of Aberdeen where they used to be dried over smoking seaweed (and sprinkled continually with seawater) but this method is not always followed now. They must have been much saltier in the 19th century. 'We have to soak our Findon haddies in cold water all night, as the crofter said they were too strong in taste', as Lady Clark of

Tillypronie wrote, 'Sir Bartle Frere recommends buttermilk instead of plain water to soak them in.' The great matter, she went on nearly 100 years ago, is to get the skin off without breaking the flesh of the fish. To do this she suggests doubling the split haddock lengthways and clapping or slapping it sharply two or three times. 'This will loosen the skin, which must then be carefully removed. Then roast. That is, cook on a brander before the fire toasting the thin under boney side *first* and then the fleshy part (the side from which you have removed the skin) – last. Neither butter nor flour are wanted:

> "Roast my breist afore my back,
> And dinna burn my banes,
> An' I'll never be a stranger syne
> Fra yure hearth stanes."

In a footnote, the editor of her posthumous cookery book adds, 'Sir John Clark says the best Findon Haddies can hardly be had now. They used in old days to be smoked over birch logs which gave a special flavour not obtainable from other fuel.'

Finnan Haddock *An Edinburgh recipe*
Put the haddock skin side up under the hot griller for a few moments. Then lay the haddock – skin side up – flat on your left hand. Slap it hard with the right hand, beginning at the head. The skin will come off easily.

Turn the whole fish over into a pan and cook it gently with butter and a little pepper for nearly 10 minutes. Add about one third of a pint of milk towards the end. If liked, a poached egg and a piece of butter may be placed on each cooked haddock before serving.

Ham and Haddie *A Girvan Recipe*
A dish which is popular in Scotland for High Tea or supper.

Heat and skin the fish as in the Edinburgh recipe, line a well-buttered pudding basin with slices of cooked ham, and lay the fish on top. Add about half a pint of cream and a little pepper. Bake it in a moderate oven (350°F, 180°C, Mark 4) until the cream is bubbling hot, slightly thicker and brown on top.

Arbroath Smokies

Finnan haddies, like the very pale, smoked Moray Firths and Glasgow pales, are cold-smoked at under 85°F, therefore they are not cooked at all during smoking and this must be done before they are eaten. The small Arbroath Smokies, however, are lightly cooked in curing, and can be eaten as they are. They have a strong smoky flavour, and are a great delicacy. The best of all are from fish which have been line-caught.

One delicious way of preparing them is to remove the two "fillets" of flesh from the skin and bone. Then fry them lightly in butter with bacon and mushrooms. Some old cooks frizzled them on a toasting fork before a blazing fire then stuffed them with butter, which melted as they came to table.

'We breakfasted at Cullen. They set down dried haddocks along with our tea. I ate one; but Dr. Johnson was disgusted by the sight of them so they were removed.' From *A Tour to the Hebrides* by James Boswell, August 26th, 1773.

Smoked Haddock (*London*)

A smoked haddock was popularly known in Victorian England as a "Billingsgate pheasant". They are traditionally smoked in London as well as in Scotland, in the East and South East and in Deptford and Rotherhithe, by Cockney salmon smokers. Haddock-smoking in New Cross and district goes back at least to the 18th century; bloaters were another speciality.

There are many traditional smoke houses, some still using oak and red sawdust, which have been in the same family for generations. A London smoked haddock is easily recognizable as it is split from the head down and has the bone on the left, while a Scottish smoked haddock is split from the tail up and has the bone on the right. The large, brilliant yellow boneless smoked fillets are smoked cod that has been dyed as well as smoked. Small golden haddock fillets are now sold too.

Smoked London Haddock with Bacon

Lightly smoked haddock may be fried with bacon: cook 4 rashers of streaky bacon gently in 4 tablespoons of butter or bacon fat. Then, having cut up the haddock, put the pieces in the pan, skin side down, and baste them with the melted butter. Put a lid on the pan and let them cook gently for about 10 minutes. Serve the fish and bacon with plenty of hot toast and freshly made English mustard.

Various Names for Haddock

Speldings *Not* smoked, but left some hours in salt water and then dried on a wall, or rock-dried. 'You skin them carefully and broil (grill) them, and serve on a napkin. If too salt for your taste, steep them for a couple of minutes in hot water before broiling them.'   From *Lady Clark of Tillypronie*.

Wet-Fish 'Are merely salt watered and hung in the air, and cooked and eaten at once. They are better flavoured but they will not keep.'   From *Lady Clark of Tillypronie*.

Pipers 'Are small haddock. Clean and scale them, hang them in the air for two or three days, not too much in the sun. They require a little salt. Cook on the brander (griller) and serve very hot.'   From *Lady Clark of Tillypronie*.

They were often served for breakfast skinned, cleaned, but not split, the sides were slashed once or twice with a pointed knife, and stuffed with butter, then the fish was dusted over with flour and grilled very slowly. *An Elgin recipe*.

Blawn Fish Fish which is hung up in a breeze or a draught to mature and acquire flavour. "Blawn" — wind blown.   From *The Aberdeen Fish Market Association*.

Smoked Haddock Mousse
An elegant dish for a cold supper, the delicate smoky flavours combine perfectly with cream and aspic and it looks well in the traditional white fluted china soufflé dish.

Simmer 8 oz of smoked haddock, or smoked fillet in $\frac{3}{4}$ pint of milk. Shell and chop 2 hard boiled eggs roughly. Drain the fish, skin and flake it, but keep the milk. Melt 1 tablespoon of butter in another pan, stir in 1 tablespoon of flour, add most of the fish-milk, little by little, stirring and heating gently until the sauce is smooth and thick. Add a little white pepper, a pinch of nutmeg, the contents of a 5 oz carton of cream, the hard boiled eggs. Make up $\frac{1}{2}$ pint of aspic jelly, stir a couple of spoonsful into the fish mixture, then tip it into a white china soufflé dish. Chill, but do not chill the remaining aspic. When set, pour the rest of the now cold aspic jelly gently over the top. To do this pour it across the back of a tablespoon, as one pours the cream on top of Irish coffee. Chill and serve.

Arnold Bennett's Omelette

This was created specially for the author, Arnold Bennett, by the chef at the Savoy Grill, Jean Baptiste Virlogeux who was known as "Rocco" in Arnold Bennett's novel *Imperial Palace*. The omelette, much copied, has since become almost more famous than the book. This, says the Savoy Hotel, is the original recipe:

Mix 3 eggs with 1 tablespoon of Gruyère cheese cut in $\frac{1}{4}$ inch cubes. Add 2 tablespoons of smoked haddock cut in cubes, a little pepper, but no salt. Beat the mixture with a fork, then melt a little butter in a small frying pan. Turn the mixture into it, lifting the edges with a fork so that the runny top flows underneath and begins to set. The omelette should not be folded but, according to M. Virlogeux, the runny top may be browned under the grill. It should be rather fluid when served on a dish. Cover it with cheese sauce. Sprinkle grated cheese on top and brown it once more under the grill.

Bloaters

Bloaters are unsplit herrings with the hard or soft roes inside them. They are salted but only lightly smoked and, when freshly done, are delicious. They were once a great Cockney dish and in the 1860s Billingsgate Market, London, used to sell 265,000 baskets a year with 160 bloaters per basket. One seldom sees them now, fishmongers say they went out of fashion because they were too cheap. Any good fishmonger would order them however.

Small fish shops on the South Coast sometimes stock them in autumn, freshly smoked over oak sawdust and strung by the heads on a wooden stick outside the shop in the traditional way.

To Grill Bloaters first run the point of a knife down the back of the bloaters from head to tail making a cut about ¼ inch deep and stuff some butter into it. Line the grill rack with foil to stop it smelling of fish. Lay the bloaters on it and grill them for 6 or 7 minutes till the skins are all crunchy, turning them over with a fish slice to grill the other side. When done, put them on hot plates with mounds of mashed potato. Open the backs of the bloaters, stuff another pat of butter in each and close them again. Cooked in this way they are excellent especially when moist and freshly smoked. Ask your fishmonger to order some for you.

Some people cut them right open and grill them flat like kippers. They are then delicious laid crisp and hot on thin buttered toast with scrambled egg poured over.

A hot grilled bloater, all plump and juicy with the roes inside it, is also very good on hot toast with a layer of buttery mashed potato on top.

Kippers
The aristocrats of the kipper world are those from Loch Fyne. Though famous, until one tastes them it is difficult to realize how superb and succulent is the flavour. They are bigger and dearer than most kippers but well worth looking for.

In the South, however, people like dyed kippers and think the pale ones are anaemic looking, but in Lancashire they wouldn't give you 4d. for them. In Bolton and Liverpool and Bury, folks swear by the fat and juicy kippers from the Isle of Man. These are a pale lemon colour specially smoked over oak chippings but undyed because Manx law forbids it. Other delicious little succulent undyed kippers come from Craster in Northumberland, then there are special kippers from Whitby.

They may be grilled, fried or cooked by plunging them head down into a jug of very hot water deep enough for just the tails to stick out. Leave them for about 3 minutes, take them out, drain and eat them with knobs of butter on each.

They are superb with that kind of buttery mashed potato that the Scots and Irish call Champs or Colcannon (see page 188). The kippers should be served on side plates. Highland malt whisky goes well with them, though perhaps not at breakfast.

Grilled Herrings in Oatmeal (*Scotland*)

When fresh they are the most delicately flavoured fish, superb grilled and garnished with mustard butter to eat with Champs, stelk or Colcannon. When this is served the grilled herrings are best eaten, very hot, from side plates.

Before grilling the herrings should be split, cleaned and have the backbone removed, it lifts out easily. Sprinkle the fish with oatmeal and pepper, garnish each with a lump of butter before grilling five to six minutes on the cut side under a very hot grill. Turn them, add another small piece of butter, grill two to three minutes on the skin side. Turn them again and place a lump of Mustard Butter (see page 116) and a little salt on each before serving. Hot bannocks and a glass of buttermilk are sometimes taken with them.

Fresh caught brown trout may be similarly cooked and eaten.

Kedgeree

It was a popular Victorian breakfast dish which became fashionable in the 'twenties for Eaton Square luncheon parties, and is still much liked for supper and informal meals. Of Indian origin, it probably dates from the days of the East India Company.

Several of the old-established London wine merchants serve vintage champagne, kedgeree, small hot mince pies and tawny port at their pre-Christmas parties. Some families now abandon lunch on Christmas day and have a large late breakfast of kedgeree and Buck's Fizz at about 11 a.m., saving their appetites for the Roast Goose and Plum Pudding that night.

Smoked Haddock and Hard Boiled Egg Kedgeree, with plenty of butter, is very popular.

Poach 2 lb of smoked haddock or smoked fillet gently in milk for 7–10 minutes, adding a good pinch of English mustard powder. Then flake the fish, throwing away the skin and bones. Stir it into 8 oz of hot boiled Patna rice. Add 3 tablespoons of butter, a teaspoon of curry powder. Mix well and add three hard boiled eggs cut in quarters. Beat up one or two raw eggs in a teacup of the fish poaching milk, stir this into the kedgeree, warm it in the oven for a few minutes.

Cold Salmon Kedgeree

There are various kedgerees, some highly spiced. In Irish country houses, it is often made with cold salmon. Madame Cadec who had a famous saucepan shop for many years in Greek Street, Soho, used also to make kedgeree with cold salmon. She added hollandaise sauce instead of cream, and boiled the rice for it in the *court bouillon* in which the salmon had been cooked. Left-over kedgeree, she used to tell me, makes very good fish cakes. Eliza Acton, writing in 1845, described kedgeree, or "kidgeree", as 'an Indian breakfast dish', adding that a Mauritian chutney, or chatney, may be sent to table with it, and pointing out that 'cold turbot, brill, salmon, soles, John Dory and shrimps may all be served in this form.'

Mrs. Marshall's Kedgeree of fish *A Victorian recipe*

Put ¼ pint of thick cream in a pan with 1½ oz of butter and a pinch of salt and a few grains of Cayenne pepper. Bring it to the boil, add 6 tablespoons of any cold cooked fish, 2 large tablespoons of plain boiled rice, 4 hard boiled eggs cut in small pieces. Let it just boil up, turn it out in a heap on a hot dish. 'Serve for a breakfast dish.'

Blenheim Palace Cadgery

As made for the tenth Duke of Marlborough, the recipe was given to the author by Mr. Heintz, chef at Blenheim Palace, who explained that salmon or turbot or sometimes smoked haddock might be used. He added that, though many recipe books specify curry powder and a dry mixture with no sauce of any kind, His Grace liked it with sauce and without curry in it. The unusual spelling of the name is the one in use at Blenheim Palace.

Boil 6 oz of Patna rice for 15 minutes then drain it. Mix it with an equal quantity of flaked cooked salmon, without the bones. Add two chopped hard boiled eggs and a *sauce suprême*. For this stir 1 oz of flour into 1 oz of melted butter, gradually. Then little by little add 1 pint of stock heating and stirring until the sauce is smooth and thick, continue to heat and stir until the taste of flour has gone. Pour it into the top of a double saucepan and stir in 4 tablespoons of thick cream beaten up with three egg yolks. Heat the sauce, whipping with a piano wire egg whisk, and without letting either it or the water in the pan below, boil. When thick, mix it with the rice, salmon and chopped eggs until of the required consistency. Warm the cadgery gently.

At Blenheim, the estate cream which is what is used in the kitchen, is of a deep yellow and so thick as to appear clotted.

Fish Cakes

The best English fish cakes have always been made with tinned salmon, the dark red kind which is more expensive almost all the year round than fresh fish, and has been the great delicacy for High Tea in working-class homes for nearly 100 years.

Boil 12 oz of potatoes in salted water, drain and mash them with butter. Put them in a big mixing bowl with 1 tablespoon of parsley, an 8 oz tin of salmon, a little paprika pepper to give the fish cakes a pink colour.* Add a chopped hard boiled egg. Beat up a raw egg with a little milk. Stir in enough of this to mould the mixture into 1-inch thick flat fish cakes. This is best done with floured hands. Let them dry for an hour, if possible, before brushing them with the rest of the egg and milk. Have 2 oz fine white breadcrumbs on a plate, dip the fish cakes into them. Cook your fish cakes about 6 minutes per side in hot frothing butter in a frying pan. When golden brown, drain them and serve them, if liked, with Parsley Sauce (page 139).

* Excellent fish cakes can also be made with left-over Kedgeree (see page 27 and opposite).

Fried Hencod's Roes

This is a proletarian dish popular in big cities, an old Cockney favourite which was also well liked in James Joyce's Dublin. The hard roe of the female (or hen) cod, it is excellent fried with bacon but it has to be boiled first. This is often done by the fishmonger, but the roe soon becomes dry and unless freshly boiled will taste better if prepared at home.

Rinse it in cold water in a sieve. Have a pan of hot salted water, add a dessertspoon of vinegar. Lower the cod's roe into it gently, either on a strainer or in a cloth, without breaking the skin. Bring it to the boil and simmer for 15 minutes. Drain, then press it between two plates with a weight on top. Slice it when cold. Have a paper bag of seasoned flour. Shake the rounds of cod's roe in this, one at a time, and fry them in lard or bacon fat. Serve them with small crisp rolls of fried bacon. Cover the pan with a lid – for the hot fat splutters!

Potted Hencod's Roe
Having boiled the cod's roe as before, put it steaming hot into a hot basin and skin it quickly before it cools. Beat in about 2 oz of butter and 1 tablespoon of anchovy essence, 1 tablespoon of vinegar. Pot. When cold, run the pots over with melted butter or clarified butter to seal them from the air. Store them in the freezer or, for a short time, in the refrigerator.

Oysters on Toast
'Cut some pieces of bread the size of a half-crown, barely a quarter of an inch thick. After they are fried, cut out bacon the same size; very thinly fry. Put on bread anchovy and cayenne, then bacon, then a roasted oyster, a few grains of cayenne, and a little oyster liquor. N.B. Roasted oysters are really only made hot through.' From *Breakfast Dishes for Every Morning of Three Months* by Miss M. L. Allen, 1888.

The Sea Cook's Cheese Dish (*Royal Navy*)
Spread 2 oz of butter thickly over the bottom of a shallow baking tin or fireproof dish. Sprinkle 2 tablespoons of finely chopped onions over it. Then put in 8 oz of grated cheese.

Beat up 4 eggs lightly with pepper and salt. Pour them over the cheese and bake it in a hot oven (400°F, 200°C, Mark 6) for 15–20 minutes. Serve at once. It can also be made in smaller quantities in individual dishes.

Irish Crubin or Crubeen
In Ireland one finds these pigs' feet, or trotters, cooked, in the shops and in the pubs on Saturday evenings, ready to eat for sobering up. The famous Ballybunion "Grunters' Club" is well-

known for its beer and crubeen suppers after the Listowel Races.

The pigs' feet should be cut at the first joint before the hock; wash them well. Put 6 or 8 of them in a pan of boiling water. Add sliced carrot and onion, salt, pepper and herbs. Bring them to the boil and simmer for about 3 hours, until the meat is coming away from the bones.

Take them out of the stock and serve them steaming hot, to eat in the fingers with well-buttered soda bread and a glass of stout or whiskey.

The stock which sets in a jelly when cold can be used for Jellied Hen (see page 148), Pork Cheese (see page 105), and to add to soup.

Pigs' Feet in Batter

This is a North Country delicacy mostly eaten for High Tea, but in common with other Victorian books, *Warne's Model Cookery* published in 1869, lists them as a fashionable breakfast dish.

Boil the pigs' feet until tender, as in the previous recipe, and pour off the cooking liquor. Take all the bones out of the pigs' feet and mince or chop the flesh, adding salt and pepper and a little of the cooking liquor.

Pour this mixture on to a large meat dish to the thickness of about half an inch and leave it till cold.

Make a fritter batter with flour, egg and milk. Cut the now jellied meat in pieces. Dip these in the batter and fry them in shallow fat on both sides till brown. To be eaten hot.

Soyer's Mushrooms

'There is one dish which the Devonshire cottager can procure and enjoy better than even the most wealthy person. It is the mushroom. After having plucked them, perhaps on the road home for his breakfast, broiled them over a nice bright fire, seasoned with a little pepper and salt, and a small bit of butter placed inside them; the flavour is then pure and the aroma beautiful, but by accident I discovered a new and excellent way to cook them. Being in Devonshire, at the end of September, and walking across the fields before breakfast to a small farmhouse, I found three very fine mushrooms, which I thought would be a

31

treat, but on arriving at the house I found it had no oven, a bad gridiron, and a smoky coal fire. Necessity, they say, is the mother of invention . . . and the following was the result.

'I first cut two good slices of bread, half an inch thick, large enough to cover the bottom of a plate, toasted them and spread some Devonshire cream over the toast. I removed all the earthy part from the mushroom, and laid them gently on the toast, head downwards, slightly sprinkled them with salt and pepper, and placed in each a little of the clotted cream; I then put a tumbler over each and placed them on a stand before the fire, and kept turning them so as to prevent the glass breaking, and in ten to fifteen minutes the glass was filled with vapour, which is the essence of the mushroom; when it is taken up do not remove the glass for a few minutes by which time the vapour will have condensed and gone into the bread, but when it is, the aroma is so powerful as to pervade the whole apartment. The sight, when the glass is removed, is most inviting, its whiteness rivals the everlasting snows of Mont Blanc and the taste is worthy of Lucullus.'

'Mushrooms, or the Pearl of the Fields', from Alexis Soyer's *A Shilling Cookery Book for the People*, 1855.

Prunes and Other Breakfast Fruit

The poor relations of the fruit world, prunes should be rediscovered.

Soak 8 oz of prunes overnight in 1 pint of cold tea, or red wine, or in red wine with a little water. Next day add 1 tablespoon of sugar and simmer for a few minutes.

Stewed prunes are still served at breakfast in many Scottish hotels, they go well with the porridge, hot rolls and Dundee marmalade. Figs in syrup (nowadays often tinned) make an excellent Scottish breakfast, too, when followed perhaps by undyed oak-smoked kippers, hot puffy breakfast rolls, plenty of black coffee with cream and Demerara or cane sugar.

Nowadays tropical fruit, undreamed of a generation ago, is widely available in Britain and is delicious for a summer breakfast. Pawpaws, mangoes, melons and pineapples are on sale almost all the year round and can be found at oriental food

stores, if not at the average fruiterer's shop. The pawpaws should
be cut in two lengthways, have the black seeds removed and are
then eaten with a spoon after being sprinkled with lemon or
fresh lime juice. The mango is a very similar looking fruit.
Nowadays at least three types are available, yellow mangoes
from India, rosy "apple" mangoes from Africa and a very large
type of mango which comes from Kenya. They have a large
stone in the middle but, like pawpaws, are delicious with lime or
lemon juice, and perhaps a little sugar.

An 18th Century Scottish Breakfast
'He found Miss Bradwardine presiding over the tea and coffee,
the table loaded with warm bread, both of flour, oatmeal and
barley-meal in the shape of loaves, cakes, biscuits, and other
varieties, together with eggs, rein-deer ham, mutton and beef
ditto, smoked salmon marmalade and all other delicacies . . . A
mess of oatmeal porridge, flanked by a silver jug, which held an
equal mixture of cream and butter-milk, was placed for the
Baron's share of this repast . . .'   From *Waverley*, by Sir
Walter Scott.

Oatmeal Baps
In Scotland fine white buns or baps hot from the oven are still
commonly eaten for breakfast. Soak 4 oz of oatmeal in ½ pint of
sour milk overnight. Sift 4 oz of flour with a rounded teaspoon of
salt and a rounded teaspoon of baking powder. Stir it into the
soaked oatmeal adding more flour, if necessary, to make a fairly
stiff mixture. Knead the mixture, roll it into a round about 2
inches thick. Place it on a floured baking tray, mark it into sec-
tions or farls. Bake it in a fairly hot oven (375°F, 190°C, Mark
5) for 20 minutes or longer, till cooked through and lightly
browned.

   In Scotland a round flat "cake" made of dough, usually the
size of a meat plate and baked traditionally on the girdle or
griddle is known as a bannock. A "farl" is a section of a bannock
– an oat bannock – which is quartered before being cooked.
This quartering is like the cross made in Irish soda bread before
baking 'to let the devil out'.

Porridge

Present-day Scots have forgotten so much of their culinary heritage that very few have porridge at all; those who do, tend to use rolled oats and not the oatmeal which their grandfathers insisted on. Almost the only relic of the past they cherish is the custom of cooking porridge with rather more salt than is usual south of the border and of frowning on any form of top-dressing such as sugar, syrup or honey. Some people still remember that the dish used to be spoken of in the plural and referred to as "them" and that, in country houses and farms, the porridge was eaten standing up or walking round the dining-room.

As F. Marian McNeill points out in her admirable book *The Scots Kitchen* there is much more to porridge than that, not to mention all its relations, brose, gruel, crowdie, cranachan, etc.

'Bring the water to the boil and as soon as it reaches boiling-point add the oatmeal, letting it fall in a steady rain from the left hand and stirring it briskly the while with the right, sunwise, or the right-hand turn for luck – and convenience . . . When the porridge is boiling steadily, draw the mixture to the side and put on the lid. Let it cook for from twenty to thirty minutes according to the quality of the oatmeal, and do not add the salt, which has a tendency to harden the meal and prevent its swelling, until it has cooked for at least ten minutes. On the other hand, never cook porridge without salt. Ladle straight into cold porringers or soup-plates and serve with individual bowls of cream, or milk, or buttermilk. Each spoonful of porridge, which should be very hot, is dipped in the cream or milk, which should be quite cold, before it is conveyed to the mouth.'

Ale and Beer

Ale or beer was drunk at breakfast for centuries, farmers and country squires seem to have had ale at breakfast far on into the 18th century when others were perhaps drinking chocolate.

Of course Sherlock Holmes and Doctor Watson always had cocoa for breakfast when setting out on an expedition. It was probably a repulsive concoction for in those days it was usually made with cocoa nibs. These had to be boiled for five hours then strained. If they were left in the cocoa it became bitter.

Chapter 2
Overtures
and Soups

Overtures

Whets, Short Eats and Appetizers

A Whet was the 18th century name for a delicious trifle or dainty which whetted the appetite before meals. Short Eats was the name used to describe the little sausages and appetizers served at cocktail parties in Ceylon and other outposts of Empire at the beginning of the 20th century.

Cocktails were drunk by the Bright Young Things – with Short Eats – after the First World War. People who drank them were thought "rather fast". 'There was an age not so long ago', as Rebecca West wrote, 'when a cocktail was considered an immoral drink as different from sherry as concubinage is from marriage, and a cocktail party meant an assembly of people who had abandoned normal restraints.' There were hundreds of different cocktails, some with daring names such as Between the Sheets and Feathers Freezer. Most cocktails were based on gin. This had only recently become respectable, when "pink gin" (Plymouth gin mixed with Angostura bitters) began to be drunk by Naval officers. Distilled in London and Plymouth, with differing flavours, it has of course a tempestuous history. In 18th

THE

ECONOMICAL COOK

and

Frugal Housewife,

a New System of

DOMESTIC COOKERY,

BY

Mrs. MARY HOLLAND.

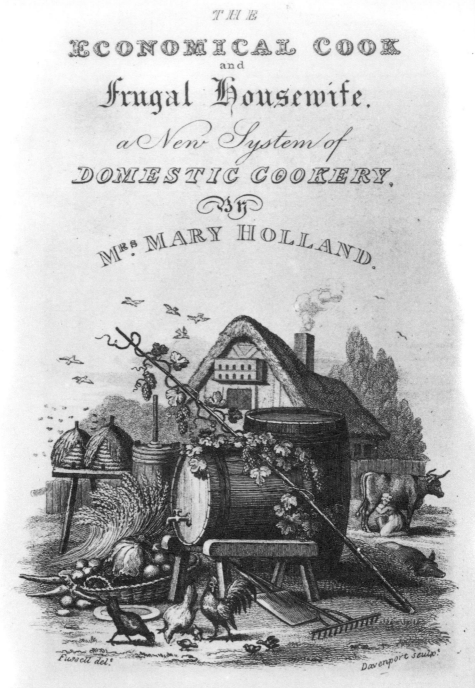

Fussell del.

Davenport sculp.

A NEW EDITION.

London.

Steel Plate

PRINTED FOR T. T. & J. TEGG, CHEAPSIDE,

R. GRIFFIN & Cº GLASGOW, & J. CUMMING, DUBLIN.

century London cheap and murderous gin was drunk in Ho-
garthian quantities while brandy, sometimes smuggled, was the
drink of the gentry. 'Drunk for 1d., dead drunk for 2d., clean
straw 3d.' was a familiar notice. Until the 20th century, gin or
"mother's ruin", was the drink of the poor. One of Grimaldi the
clown's most famous songs was about gin drinking:

'A little old woman her living she got
By selling hot codlings,* hot, hot, hot,
And this little old woman who codlings sold,
Though her codlings were hot, she felt herself cold,
So to keep herself warm she thought it no sin,
To fetch herself a quartern of . . .
Ri-tol-idd-iddy, ri-tol-iddy-iddy, ri-tol lay . . .'

* A codling is a variety of apple.

Mrs. Bradshaw's Bacon Savoury
Very thin rashers of bacon are to be dipped in beaten egg and
then rolled in fine white breadcrumbs mixed with grated cheese.
Fry them, until they are golden brown, in oil or frothing butter.
Drain and serve them hot.

At the turn of the century these appeared at the end of the
meal, before the coffee, but nowadays might be better liked
before the meal with drinks.

Mrs. Whitehead's Practical Cheese Puffs
These may be served, hot on a folded napkin, with clear soup.
Or with drinks before a meal, perhaps on cocktail sticks or
toothpicks.

Mix 8 oz of strong grated cheese with 2 heaped tablespoons
of soft white breadcrumbs, a pinch of salt and a good pinch of
dry mustard powder. Add a dash of Worcester sauce and the
yolk of an egg to moisten it. Then fold in the very stiffly beaten
white of egg and shape the mixture into small balls, a teaspoon at
a time.

Roll these in more breadcrumbs, fry them in a deep pan of
very hot oil till golden. Drain, serve hot.

37

Marrow Bones with Hot Toast and Brandy

The marrow found in the middle of beef shank bones is a delicacy when cooked and served piping hot. It was eaten in Georgian England at banquets and still appears at some dinners and in a few old fashioned public houses. The marrow bones are very cheap but it may be difficult to get them sawn in the requisite short lengths.

Wrap four pieces of marrow bone in kitchen foil. Bake them in a fireproof dish in a moderate oven (350°F, 180°C, Mark 4) for 45 minutes. Unwrap and serve them very hot, folded if liked in small hot napkins, and flanked by hot dry toast. Traditionally the marrow is scooped out with a long silver marrow spoon, well peppered, and eaten at once perhaps with a little coarse salt such as Maldon sea salt.

A glass of Cognac or Armagnac should be drunk with it to correct the richness of the marrow. In Denmark and Norway, where beef marrow and hot toast is now more popular than it is here, chilled Aquavit or vodka is drunk with it. A fine malt whisky such as a delicate 10-year-old Glenmorangie, from Ross and Cromarty, might be equally acceptable.

This is not a dish for everyone, people either dislike the hot marrow intensely and find it indigestible, or they like it very much.

Marrow Toast

In Victorian England the marrow bones were usually reserved for gentlemen while ladies had marrow toast. According to Francatelli, for some years Chief-Cook-in-Ordinary to Queen Victoria, 'Marrow toast used to be eaten every day at dinner at the time when I had the honour of waiting on Her Majesty.'

The marrow should be removed from the bones and cut in pieces 'the size of a filbert'. Cook them in boiling salted water for one minute then drain them at once on a sieve. Season with pepper, salt, lemon juice, a very little finely chopped shallot and chopped parsley. Toss it lightly together and spread on crisp hot dry toast. It should be eaten at once.

It is something that you either loathe or enjoy, like oysters, and only experience will tell you whether you wish to eat it.

Gulls' Eggs

In season in May, they make an elegant beginning to a meal.

Black-headed gulls' eggs are best, the huge eggs of the herring gull taste very fishy. Plovers' eggs are in season at the same time and were once similarly served. They are very rare now as the plover is a protected bird and the eggs will have, or should have, to come from abroad. It is an offence to collect them in Britain.

Gulls' eggs are always sold cooked by the dealers, who boil them hard then prick the shells. There should be a distinct bluish colour inside. They are served with seasoned or celery salt, or Oriental salt,* or simply with freshly ground black pepper, and with brown bread and butter. They are usually sent to table on a folded napkin or, more traditionally, nestling in a little punnet lined with moss.

The trade in gulls' eggs is a very specialized one, mostly to big hotels, luxury liners and to firms catering for banquets, though they are sometimes available from fishmongers or game-dealers to the general public. Towards the end of the season, when they are imported from Denmark, the prices drop.

* This is a highly flavoured and spicy salt mixture sold by its blenders in jars for use with gulls' eggs and so on.

Quails' Eggs

In season all the year round quails' eggs are no bigger than olives and have pretty speckled shells. They are served hard boiled, perhaps on a silver *tazza* or tray on the dining table, to precede an elegant luncheon. One cracks and nibbles them as one might radishes. Celery salt and so on might also be served with them.

Blue Bantam Eggs

Bantam eggs are to be had sometimes from farms in springtime. They look charming, when hard boiled, to serve in salads and also when pickled. Blue bantam eggs are laid by the Araucana hens, a breed which came originally from South America. The shell is a very pretty bright greenish-blue both inside and out. They may well be served instead of the very expensive quail eggs.

Salted Almonds
Salted almonds are often served in dishes on the dinner table.

Blanch the almonds by pouring boiling water over them and leaving them for about a minute. It will then be easy to squeeze off the brown skins between the finger and thumb. Put the almonds in a pan with a little hot oil over a gentle heat, shaking the pan so they are browned lightly all over. Drain them and dry them in a tea towel, sprinkling them with salt.

Toasted shredded almonds, or those browned lightly in oil or butter are sometimes used as a garnish for cream of chicken soup.

Crisped Bacon Rinds
These are a speciality of the tiny Glansevern Arms Hotel, Llangurig. Mrs. Joyce Edwards saves the bacon rinds from several breakfasts, puts them in a roasting tin a hot oven (400°F, 200°C, Mark 6) and cooks them till crisp. These are served in the public bar.

Mrs. Beeton's "Pastry Ramakins"
Excellent, hot with soup, though Mrs. Beeton suggests serving them 'with the cheese course'. They are good too with drinks before a meal.

'Ingredients — any pieces of very good light puff paste, Cheshire, Parmesan, or Stilton cheese. Mode — The remains of odd pieces of paste left from large tarts etc. answer for making these little dishes. Gather up the pieces of paste, roll it out evenly, and sprinkle it with grated cheese of a nice flavour. Fold the paste in three, roll it out again, and sprinkle more cheese over; fold the paste, roll it out, and with a paste cutter shape it in any way that may be desired. Bake the ramakins in a brisk oven from 10–15 minutes, dish them on a hot napkin, and serve quickly. The appearance of this dish may be very much improved by brushing the ramakins over with yolk of egg before they are placed in the oven. Where expense is not objected to, Parmesan is the best kind of cheese to use for making this dish.'
From Mrs. Isabella Beeton's *Book of Household Management*, 1861.
Note: Sam Beeton, owing to legal and copyright troubles was forced to make over all the rights of his wife's famous book to

Messrs. Ward Lock. They have been reprinting cookery books with her name on them at frequent intervals ever since, but revised and re-written over and over again. Modern ones bear no relation to the original work.

To Stew Cheese with Light Wigs

'Cut a plateful of cheese, pour on it a glass of red wine, stew it before the fire, toast a light wig [a small yeast bun something like a brioche]. Pour over it two or three spoonfuls of hot red wine. Put it in the middle of your dish, lay the cheese over it, and serve it up.' From Mrs. Elizabeth Raffald's, *The Experienced English Housekeeper*, 1769.

Angels on Horseback

A famous Victorian savoury, it consists in raw oysters each wrapped in a rasher of streaky bacon without the rind and fixed with a cocktail stick. Fry or grill the oysters briefly, a few at a time, in their bacon. Serve them very hot on their cocktail sticks on a hot dish with aperitifs before a meal. They are splendid with champagne but the ruination of a good red wine. As a savoury they were served on small pieces of fried bread or hot toast without the cocktail sticks.

Devils on Horseback

Soak 24 prunes in cold tea for 4 hours until they have swollen. Drain, dry and stone them, stuff each with a small piece of Cheddar cheese. Wrap a piece of streaky bacon round each prune, fasten it with a cocktail stick or toothpick. Cook them under a hot grill, turn once or twice until the bacon is crisp and frizzled. Serve at once.

Archangels on Horseback

For those people who think an oyster too good to eat in any way other than raw.

Cut the creamy white and orange part of some fresh raw scallops in chunks. Fry these gently in butter, then wrap each piece in a rasher of lightly fried bacon. Secure with a toothpick or cocktail stick. Serve very hot.

Note: Small pieces of chicken liver may be similarly wrapped, cooked and served. These are delicious for a cocktail party.

Hot Shrimp Pots

Butter some individual fireproof pots or ramekins thickly. Put 2 tablespoons of cooked, peeled shrimps in each. Add pepper, a good pinch of nutmeg and a pinch of salt to each. Cover them with cream, add a knob of butter and a few breadcrumbs to each shrimp pot. Bake them in a fairly hot oven (375°F, 190°C, Mark 5) until they are just beginning to brown on top. To be eaten hot and hot, with a spoon.

Soft Herring Roes, Baked and Hot, on Oatcakes

The milt or soft roes are thought best though others prefer the hard ones from the female herring. Wipe six soft roes, lay them in a large pie dish. Put 2 bayleaves, 6 white peppercorns, a pinch of salt, $\frac{1}{4}$ pint vinegar and $\frac{1}{4}$ pint water in a pan. Bring it to the boil and strain it over the roes. Bake them in a moderate oven (350°F, 180°C, Mark 4), covered, for 10 minutes.

Butter six small oatcakes, place a drained roe on each, dot with butter, grill for 2–3 minutes. Sprinkle with parsley and lemon. Serve hot and hot, as they used to say.

Soft Herring Roes, Devilled

These are to be served very hot – instead of pâté – with hot dry toast folded in a napkin.

Wash 2 oz of fresh soft herring roes in cold salted water and drain them well, patting them dry in a towel if necessary. Melt 1 oz of butter, add salt, black pepper and Cayenne pepper, or melt 1 oz of Devil Butter (see page 20). Add the roes, cook them gently with a lid on for 5–10 minutes stirring often. They used to appear on small squares of hot buttered toast in a silver dish as a savoury.

Soft Herring Roes in Hot Potatoes

Take the hot jacket potatoes out of the oven. Cut them in two and scoop out the floury potato with a spoon. Having rinsed and dried some soft herring roes, fry them gently in butter adding salt, pepper and then the hot potato. Pile this mixture back into the skins. Top them with grated cheese, a little butter. Brown them in the oven or under the grill. To be served hot with, if liked, a small jug of melted butter.

Soups

Chicken or Turkey Carcase Stock
A left-over chicken carcase and giblets, or the remains of a turkey carcase will make good stock, so will a duck or goose.

Wash the lot in cold water, breaking up the carcase with your hands so it will go into the pan. Add the giblets if any, cover it with cold water. Add 12 peppercorns, 2 cloves, 2 bayleaves and some mixed herbs, sliced carrot, turnip and onions as available. If the skins are left on the onions they darken the stock and improve the colour. Let it simmer for about 2 hours either in a pan on the stove or in a casserole in the oven, or cook it all in a pressure cooker for 30 minutes. Poultry stock should be strained through a fine sieve to get rid of bone splinters. It freezes well. The broth can also be cleared very easily with egg whites (see Hessian Soup, page 49).

Chicken and Sherry Soup
Beat up three eggs with ¼ pint of sherry and the strained juice of a lemon. Stir this into 1¾ pints of warm chicken stock, little by little. The stock could be made from a left-over chicken carcase and giblets. Heat it gently, stirring, to let the eggs thicken the soup slightly. Do not let it boil as they would scramble and curdle it.

Toasted and shredded almonds are sometimes added to these creamy chicken soups as they come to table, or sippets of crisp fried streaky bacon. Sometimes salted almonds are handed with the soup.

Soupe à la reine, or Lorraine Soup, popular in Scotland, is often said to be named after Mary of Guise (Mary Queen of Scots' mother) but according to *Larousse Gastronomique* it is really an old French soup. The broth is thickened with ground almonds, white breadcrumbs, cream, and mashed hard boiled egg yolks. *Feather Fowlie*, another old Scottish soup, is chicken broth thickened with raw egg yolks, cream and minced chicken. (For Cock-a-Leekie, see page 145.)

Crab Soup

This is the classic Partan Bree of Scotland. The word "bree" means pot liquor, broth or stock and is also used for salmon bree, the liquor in which the fish was cooked, and for Bawd Bree or hare broth (see opposite). Partan from the Gaelic is the old Scots word for a crab (as also in Partan "Pie", hot buttered crabs served roasted in their shells). In some parts of Scotland, as in Northumberland, only the claws of the partan or crab were eaten or thought edible until very recently.

Simmer 2 oz of rice gently in 1 pint of milk with a nut of butter to prevent it frothing up. Add ½ teaspoon of salt and ½ teaspoon of pepper. Meanwhile pick the meat from a large crab setting aside that from the large claws. Purée the crab meat and cooked rice in the electric mixer. Return it to the cooking milk and gradually stir in enough white stock, bouillon or fish bree (preferably from boiling the crab) to make it up to 2 pints. Heat, taste for seasoning, and add a little anchovy essence. Before serving add the claw meat and stir in 5 fl oz of thick cream.

Curry Soup with Cayenne Cheeses

Beat up an egg with a large teaspoon of curry powder. Heat 1¾ pints of chicken broth or stock to boiling point. Pour a little of it into the egg mixture, then stir this gently into the broth, heating it without letting it boil – for the egg would curdle.

Mrs. Beeton's Cayenne Cheeses, served hot, are very good with it: Rub 8 oz of butter into 8 oz of plain flour, adding 8 oz of grated cheese, ⅓ teaspoon of Cayenne pepper and some salt. Mix well, stirring in a little water, just enough to make a pastry dough. Chill it for one hour or longer. Roll it out on a floured surface, cut it in fingers about 4 inches long. Place these on a greased

44

baking sheet. Bake them in a moderate oven (350°F, 180°C, Mark 4) until they are a very light golden colour. They are to be served hot.

Game Stock
Good game stock can be made by boiling down the carcases and tougher left-over pieces of game which have been served roast. Tough old stewing birds, pieces of rabbit, the scrag end of venison, the legs of hare (when the saddle has been roast) all make excellent game broth, too. They may be simmered slowly or cooked in a pressure cooker. Sherry or Madeira are very good in thick brown meaty soups, such as game or oxtail soup. A glass of Madeira or Amontillado sherry may well be drunk with the soup also.

Lentil and Game Soup *Old Scottish recipe*
Cool the strained game stock, add 8 oz of lentils and a peeled, chopped onion to 2½ pints of game stock, with 12 peppercorns and a little salt. Let it simmer for about 2 hours until the lentils have "cooked down". Twenty minutes before it is ready, add a large grated carrot and a spoonful of chopped parsley. Taste for seasoning. Mash or press everything through a sieve, or purée in the mixer.

Bawd Bree *A Scottish country house soup*
The traditional Scottish Hare Soup, or Bawd Bree (from the Scottish *bawd* – a hare) is interesting in that it has a *liaison au sang*, i.e., it is thickened with blood in the French manner, with port added before serving. It is sometimes served with dumplings or small forcemeat balls in it.

Cut the hare in pieces keeping the blood. Put the pieces of hare in a large pan with two peeled sliced onions, two sticks of celery chopped, two or three scraped sliced carrots, a pot posy,* salt and pepper, and a piece of turnip. Add cold water to cover, bring it to the boil and simmer for 1½ hours.

Strain the blood through a sieve, add a little cold water, put it in a pan and stir one way over a gentle heat till it boils. Remove from the heat. Mince or purée the hare meat and veget-

45

ables. Put them back in a large pan, strain the liquor over them, add the boiled blood. Simmer for another hour. Then, mix 1 tablespoon of flour with a little cold water and 2 tablespoons of Worcester sauce. Add it to the soup and heat, stirring, until it comes to the boil.

* Pot posy is the English name for a *bouquet garni,* a bunch of kitchen herbs tied together with cotton and added to the pot (of soup, stew or whatever) to give flavour. They should be removed by means of the cotton before serving.

Ham, or Bacon, Stock
The stock left after boiling a bacon joint, piece of gammon or ham makes an excellent basis for soup. Slight saltiness can be corrected by boiling some potatoes in it – these absorb the salt and if mashed afterwards will thicken the soup. Dried beans, split peas, lentils and so on serve the same purpose. Pork butchers and grocers selling ham on the bone often sell ham bones cheaply to good customers. The ham bone makes excellent stock and may have a surprising amount of meat on it, some of which, chopped, may be served in the soup.

Lentil soup, watercress soup, pease soup and onion soup are all excellent when made with this kind of stock.

The stock from boiling salt silverside or brisket, or from an ox tongue can be treated in the same way. Plain or salted, pigs' trotters which do not in themselves make a strong stock for soup will, if cooked with the stock, give it a rich consistency and it will set in a jelly when cold. Pork tails – or "pork bones" as some call them – are used in the Midlands, traditionally, for making broth together with grated carrots and parsnips, peeled diced onions and a few lentils. They have been popular among local people for generations and are still sold, for instance in Gloucester Market, and by country butchers. Salt should not be added to these stocks until just before serving, and after tasting it.

Beans and Bacon Soup
Simmer 3 oz of white beans gently in 3 pints of bacon or ham stock until they are soft. Fry a peeled sliced onion in 3 oz of lard,

when it is soft and golden stir in 2 oz of flour. Add some chopped parsley and stir it into the soup together with some diced boiled bacon or ham.

Lentil soup could be made in the same way.

White Haddock Soup

This simple fish soup is popular in the West of Scotland. The recipe comes from Inveraray.

Poach about 1 lb of fresh haddock fillets in hot water. Drain, then purée the fish in the electric mixer. Add salt, pepper and a *roux* – made by melting 1 tablespoon of butter, then stirring in 1 tablespoon of flour. Now add enough hot fish stock, or boiling water and a cube, to make a soup of the right thickness. Heat it gently, stirring, until the flour in the *roux* is cooked. Beat in a little thick cream and sprinkle chopped parsley on top.

The soup can, in fact, be made with almost any fish. Smoked mackerel is very good and has a tang of its own. If a whole fresh haddock be used instead of fillets, poach it as before, then cut the flesh off the bones and keep it. Simmer the bones, head, etc. in the fish water or stock to increase the flavour. Of course this must be strained before it is used for soup. Then add the fish purée and the *roux*, etc. as before.

When the soup is made with smoked cod fillets, or with Finnan haddock, some Scottish cooks add two or three drops of bottled yellow colouring. Then they only half stir in the thick cream before serving. The yellow and white makes an attractive contrast. This is similar to Cullen Skink, or Smoked Haddock Soup, which originated on the Morayshire coast.

Bolting Lettuce Soup

This is an especially useful recipe if one has a quantity of gone-to-seed lettuce in the garden. The soup is a summer favourite in some country pubs and is especially nice when made with ham bone or bacon stock. The addition of a little watercress improves the colour.

Wash two or three lettuces in cold water pulling them apart and, if they have gone to seed, throwing away the stalks. Frizzle a large, peeled, chopped onion gently in 1 oz of butter with a lid

47

on the pan until it is limp and golden. Stir it occasionally. Add the well drained pieces of lettuce. Simmer, stirring for a couple of minutes. Moisten a dessertspoon of cornflour so that it is smooth and free of lumps, add this, then gradually stir in 2 pints of stock. Ham or bacon stock gives a good flavour. Let it simmer for about 10 minutes. Then purée the onion and lettuce and any pieces of ham in the electric mixer and re-heat them in the stock. Before serving, stir in 2 tablespoons of thick cream and a little chopped parsley or chopped watercress.

Mrs. Mercer's Bone Broth
Beef bones make quantities of good nourishing soup which usually sets in a jelly when cold. Your butcher will probably be glad to let you have them very cheaply, so few people ask for them now there is little sale for them. If you have bought a whole brisket or a forequarter of beef for the freezer you will have acquired some big bones with it, these make excellent soup. Ask the butcher to saw them small enough to go into your largest saucepan.

Put the bones in a pan with cold water to cover. Add 12 peppercorns, 2 cloves, a little allspice if available, some mixed herbs, a couple of onions with their skins. Then add whatever vegetables or vegetable trimmings come handy — leek tops, leafy celery tops, the thinner ends of some parsnips and so on. Add a little salt, 1 teaspoon of vinegar. I also strain in about a teacupful of cold milkless tea as some do in Ireland; it improves the colour. Left-over bones from a roast joint help to make well flavoured stock, so do game bones and carcases; 2–3 oz of cooked cowheel will also add body to the soup making the liquor more gelatinous.

Bring it all to the boil then let it simmer bubbling faintly for about 1½ hours either in the oven or on top of the stove. There will be a little fat that can be removed with a tablespoon, or you can let the soup get cold then lift it off in one piece. Take out the bones putting back any bits of meat. Discard any messy looking vegetables, they have served their purpose. Re-heat the soup, taste it for seasoning. Add a few spoonsful of red wine if available. It freezes well.

Oxcheek or Hessian Soup

A strong clear soup cooked on the same lines as a *pot-au-feu* but cleared with white of egg, it was fashionable in Victorian England; Francatelli used to prepare it for the Royal Household at Windsor, though there are many earlier recipes going back for several centuries.

It was made with beef bones as well as oxcheek, which when available is usually very cheap and makes excellent soup, so do the more expensive shin and leg beef. Follow the recipe for Mrs. Mercer's Bone Broth (see opposite), adding 1–1½ lb of oxcheek. One can also add a chicken carcase or chicken giblets when available. When cooked the oxcheek was pressed between two plates until cold, then cut into 'neat collops an inch square and half an inch thick' which were heated in the cleared soup with button onions, very small blanched Brussels sprouts and other vegetables.

To clear beef or chicken broth: When the soup is cold remove all the fat from the top wasting a little of the stock if necessary. Then strain it through a sieve into a pan. Add two lightly whisked egg whites and the crushed shells. Let it boil over a gentle heat for about 2 minutes whilst whisking to make it frothy. Then let it stand, covered and off the heat, for 10–15 minutes. Strain it into a jug through a Melitta coffee-filter paper – twice if not perfectly clear.

Clear Soup *A note*

A good clear soup made at home from shin of beef, soup vegetables, bones, sherry and a pig's foot, and cleared with white of egg, is served traditionally at the beginning of the Christmas dinner in Ireland. For details see Oxcheek or Hessian Soup (above), substituting shin of beef for oxcheek if liked and adding a pig's foot.

Clear soup is often garnished with chopped parsley or hot beef marrow or both just before serving. Hot cheese straws are sometimes served with it. In Bermuda thin slices of skinned and stoned avocadoes are sometimes dropped into the plates of hot clear soup instead of the beef marrow just before they come to table.

It is now unusual to have a special wine with the soup except at banquets. Sherry or Madeira used to be drunk with it but they are now mostly served beforehand as an aperitif. Either Sercial or Verdelho Madeira are, however, excellent to drink chilled with clear soup — turtle soup especially. Four to six tablespoons of soft smoky Verdelho Madeira or of brown sherry may be stirred into $1\frac{1}{2}$ pints of clear beef soup before serving.

Kidney Soup with Port, or Sherry *An Edwardian favourite*
Slice half an ox kidney weighing about 8 oz, then wash and dry it, throwing away the skin and core. Mix $1\frac{1}{2}$ oz of flour with salt, black pepper and $\frac{1}{2}$ teaspoon of allspice (Jamaica pepper) on a plate. Toss the kidney pieces in this.

Melt $1\frac{1}{2}$ oz of dripping or butter and in it fry a thinly sliced onion gently until golden, then add the sliced kidney and the flour. When browned, gradually stir in 3 pints of well flavoured stock, add a bunch of herbs tied together with cotton, some diced carrot and turnip. Bring it to the boil and let it simmer about 2 hours until the kidney is tender. Strain the stock, cut the kidney pieces in dice, return them to the soup adding 1 tablespoon of Mushroom Ketchup (see page 276) if available, and a little port or sherry. Taste for seasoning.

Mulligatawnay Soup
This is a thick or a clear "pepper water", or curry-flavoured soup of Anglo-Indian origin which was fashionable early in the 20th century.

Plain boiled rice, hot, is handed with it and added to each portion as helped.

Heat 2 pints of stock with 2 onions finely sliced in it, add 1 cored and chopped apple, 1 tablespoon desiccated coconut, 1 dessertspoon curry powder. Add some game bones, a chicken or rabbit carcase and some giblets. Simmer for 60 minutes, strain and re-heat it with pieces of game or chicken in it.

Mutton Broth
Delicious on a wet autumn night with the rain driving across the Welsh hills, in uphill farms they sometimes eat it with small

currant dumplings floating in it. Welsh mutton broth often has bacon in it as well as lamb or mutton, and is best made the day before it is wanted, then, when cold the fat can be taken off. Manx broth, traditional to the Isle of Man, is also made with lamb or mutton and in Ireland there are special cuts of mutton, such as the "Housekeeper's Cut" of Co. Cork, that make good broth.

Put 2 lb of scrag end or neck of lamb in a pan with a good 3 pints of water, adding a bacon hock or piece of streaky bacon if liked. Bring it to the boil adding chopped carrots, turnip, parsnips and onion. A large well washed leek, 2 oz of pearl barley and two peeled potatoes can be added. Bring it to the boil and simmer $1\frac{1}{2}$–2 hours. Taste for seasoning.

Remove the meat from the bones, chop it and add it to the soup. In Wales a handful of chopped parsley is placed in the bottom of the soup tureen and the broth is poured on top. In Scotland the chopped parsley is sprinkled on top of the soup. This is now served in a number of Welsh hotels, with or without grated cheese, as "Minestrone".

The old fashioned but practical soup kettle may still be used in parts of Wales and the West Country, but is rare. It has a stumpy wide mouthed spout through which the soup can be poured off easily leaving the meat and vegetables for another meal. The soup was then known as "Kettle" or "Kiddley Broth".

In Scotland people used to make the broth in quantities large enough for two days for a big family, sometimes with beef as well as mutton. Then it was re-heated on the second day when, tradition has it, the broth tasted even better than on the first. There is another excellent old Scottish soup made in late autumn with curly kale, when it has just been touched by the first frost. The stock for this is made with a cowheel and a piece of hough, or what in England is known as leg beef, rather than with mutton. It is thickened with oatmeal, hence the name brose – kail brose. In the Highlands and perhaps elsewhere in Scotland the broth, or brose, was cooked in a kail pot – a large cast iron pot which could be kept simmering above the fire, perhaps of peat. The word kale or kail is sometimes used in Scotland as a synonym for broth. The Welsh word *caul* or *cawl* for soup has a similar association, it comes from the Latin *caulis* – *colis, coulis* which means the stalk of a plant of the cabbage family. One finds the same root in *cauli*flower and broc*coli*, and the word *coulis* or *cullis* is used in very old English cookery books to denote a rich gravy or stock (not necessarily cooked with cabbage, however).

Oyster, or Cockle and Mussel, Soup
White Oyster Soup was a popular dish in Regency London. It was usually thickened with cream and arrowroot. Large quantities of what were then called "sauce" oysters – small family oysters rather than the best Whitstable or Colchester natives – were used and it was not unlike the oyster soups still enjoyed in the United States. Another and rather different oyster broth used, however, to be made in South Wales – generally a good mutton and barley broth served with oysters.

Mrs. Rundell's Oyster Mouth Soup from her *New System of Domestic Cookery*, 1806, is unbelievably lavish but was probably very good:

'Make a rich mutton broth with two large onions, three blades of mace and black pepper. When strained pour it on a hundred and fifty oysters, without the beards, and a bit of butter rolled in flour. Simmer gently a quarter of an hour, and serve.'

A mixture of cockles and mussels with perhaps a few of the small scallops or "queens" now fished off Devon, Wales and Scotland will make an excellent similar tasting soup at a fraction of the cost.

Some shellfish soups had mashed hard boiled egg yolks added and were then thickened with raw egg, like a custard. A very good soup used to be made in South Wales from Penclawdd cockles to which a little laver bread was often added, with good effect. There was even, it is said, a soup made from limpets. These are a totally forgotten delicacy in this country, but they are still pickled and sold in bottles in small shops in Funchal, Madeira, where they are eaten with great relish.

Another Cockle and Mussel Soup (*delicious*)
Make 2 pints of fish stock by simmering 1 lb of fishbones, sole

trimmings, etc. from the fishmonger in 1 quart of water with 6 white peppercorns, a small teaspoon of salt, 1 dessertspoon of lemon juice, a piece of lemon peel, a piece of mace, a bunch of thyme and parsley, a peeled chopped onion. Let it simmer bubbling gently for 30 minutes then strain the stock into a clean pan.

Meanwhile wash and scrape 1 pint of mussels, throwing away any that remain open after banging them on the table. Put the mussels into a frying pan with a knob of butter over a fierce heat for about 5 minutes, shaking and stirring until all are open. Strain their liquor into the fish stock. Shell and keep the mussels. Repeat with 1 pint of well washed cockles.

Put 1 lb of white fish fillet cut in chunks and without bones or skin into the pan with the stock. Add the shelled cockles and mussels with the white and yellow part of three ordinary large scallops. Or if available add 1 pint of "queens" or scallops opened as above, together with their strained liquor. Add 3 oz of butter and $\frac{3}{4}$ pint double cream and heat simmering gently for 15 minutes. Do not let it actually boil as it might curdle. The fish could be served in a shallow dish separately from the soup if liked. Hand a dish of small sippets of bread fried crisp in butter.

A few shelled oysters could be added, with their strained liquor together with the scallops, if they are available for this purpose.

Oxtail Soup
It is a dish which has been endlessly elaborated by chefs. There is both thick and thin, and also an Oxtail Soup Lady Curzon, with curry, egg and cream in it, popular in the Netherlands and the Scandinavian countries.

This is a simple but excellent household recipe by a professional family cook:

'Put the oxtail, cut in chunks, in a large saucepan with a good 2 quarts of water to simmer for 4 hours on a low heat. Take it off the heat and let it stand till morning, then skim off the fat.

'Take 4 large carrots, 4 large onions and turnips, if you can get them. Put all through a mincer. Then put it all into the soup and cook on a low heat. Salt and pepper.

'It is simply lovely and lasts us for 3 days. It sets like a jelly and is so good, better than the tinned soup one buys.'

Note: Alfred Suzanne chef at Woburn Abbey to a 19th century Duke of Bedford, maintained that Oxtail Soup was of French origin: 'At the time of the Revocation of the Edict of Nantes, there was a number of Huguenot refugees in London where they formed a sort of French colony in the quarter of the city occupied by the tanners' guild. The buyers of ox hides, having no use for the tails, gave them to the poor of the neighbourhood who made them into a sort of *pot au feu*. One day a rich and philanthropic gourmet visiting these poor exiles, was initiated into the mysteries of this excellent soup. He introduced it into high society where it immediately became fashionable under the name "tanners' soup".'

Pease Soup or The London Particular

Pease soup is probably the most popular of our old traditional soups. Thick and yellow it gave its name to the old London fogs, or "pea soupers" of the 19th and early 20th centuries. They were also known as the London Particular, a name which I gave half jokingly also to thick pease soup in a previous cookery book; it has since been much plagiarized.

Soak 8 oz of dried peas, whole or split, in tepid water for 2–3 hours adding a pinch of bicarbonate of soda if the water is hard as it is in London. Put them in a pan of cold water, adding a bacon hock or knuckle of pickled pork (previously soaked for 2 hours in tepid water). If liked a pig's foot, split in half, may be added too. A game carcase gives an excellent flavour.

Bring it all slowly to the boil and let it simmer gently with a lid on, either on top of the stove or in a slow oven (300°F, 150°C, Mark 2) for about 3 hours until the peas are tender and the meat is dropping off the bones. Stir occasionally. Thirty minutes before it is cooked add a large, peeled sliced onion, two sliced carrots, some diced celery. Simmer. Then purée the soup in the electric mixer or serve it as it is, garnished with chopped parsley and shreds of boiled bacon.

In Norfolk the soup is served with Norfolk Dumplings, or "Twenty-minute Floaters" (see page 122), made from bread dough, while in Holland where pease soup, or *snert* as they call it in the Dutch army, is almost a national dish, they chop Frankfurter sausages in chunks, then heat and serve them in the soup.

Salmon Broth

Once popular in small country hotels during the fly fishing season, salmon broth can be made from the head, bones and trimmings of a salmon or sea trout. They can usually be had cheaply in summer from fishmongers when the rest of the fish has been cut and sold in pieces.

The left-over bones, head, skin and so on, from a boiled or baked salmon or sea trout can also be used. If available add some of the cooking liquor.

Put the fish head, bones and trimmings into a large pan with cold water or the fish bree to cover. Add a large peeled sliced onion, two diced carrots, a heaped teaspoon of paprika pepper (not Cayenne pepper). Let it simmer for about 35 minutes. Strain the soup, pressing the vegetables through a sieve, thicken it with mashed potato, or with potato powder. Add some small pieces of flaked salmon from the head, a handful of soft brown breadcrumbs and, if possible, 2 tablespoons of whisky, a glass of white wine and a dash of Angostura bitters. Taste for seasoning, serve garnished with chopped parsley.

Shellfish Soup

Put the trimmings from 1 pint of cooked shrimps or prawns together with some sole trimmings in a pan with 2 pints of water, 1 peeled roughly chopped onion, salt, pepper, 1 clove, and a slice of bread and butter, and a little freshly grated nutmeg. Bring to the boil and simmer for 30 minutes, stir occasionally.

Strain the broth into another pan, and grind the prawn trimmings with a little of the broth to a purée in the electric mixer. Strain and add this purée to the broth stirring it in together with 1 heaped teaspoon of paprika (not Cayenne) pepper.

Bring the soup gently to the boil, adding a few peeled prawns, and if liked a small glass of sherry.

The shell, the pieces of left-over bone and the small legs of a fresh crab served at home can be simmered to make about 2 pints of good stock with a perceptible shellfish flavour, though they are usually too tough to grind afterwards in the mixer.

Turbot Soup

After cooking a turbot, brill, or other flatfish in milk (see recipe on page 222) keep the fish liquor and the discarded skin, bones and so on to make soup. They may be stored briefly in the refrigerator.

First simmer the bones, head, tail and so on in the milky turbot stock gently for 20 minutes adding a good pinch of nutmeg, some chopped parsley and a piece of lemon peel. Then strain it into another pan, adding a few pieces of cooked potatoes chopped up small if available, the pieces of fish, some chopped parsley and dessertspoon of pearl sago. Simmer for another 15–20 minutes and the soup is almost ready. Before serving, squeeze the juice of half a lemon into a cup and beat up an egg in it. Stir a little of the hot soup into the cup, then tip it all into the pan and heat gently, stirring and without letting it boil, so the soup thickens.

It could hardly be cheaper or easier.

Turtle Soup

For generations Turtle Soup, the great English speciality, was almost inevitable at ceremonial and diplomatic dinners and banquets and as indispensable as venison or whitebait. It is still one of the delicacies traditional to the Lord Mayor's banquet, though in recent years concern for the survival of the green turtle has caused the custom to lapse. During the Regency and for the best part of the 19th century the turtle was 'esteemed the greatest luxury which has been placed upon our tables' and at the Spanish Dinner at the London Tavern in 1808, when 400 guests attended, (according to *Bell's Weekly Magazine* of the day) 2,500 lb of turtle was consumed. Indeed the usual allowance at a Turtle Feast was then 6 lb live weight per head. In those days ships of the Royal Navy sailing in the Spanish Main used to catch turtles and keep them alive on board in barrels of sea water as a source of fresh meat. On returning to London any left-over turtles were presented 'to our Lords of the Admiralty.'

Some of these, it is presumed, were smuggled ashore and sold to good customers by master mariners. A hundred years ago the turtle trade was still largely based on these unofficial deals between individual seamen and the marine store dealers in Limehouse, most of whom carried a supply of live turtles as part of their regular stock.

According to Alexis Soyer, turtle soup and turtle meat was introduced to England in about 1710 but only at the tables of the large West Indian proprietors, from whom it progressed to those of the City companies.

'During the time of the South Sea Bubble, when the female aristocracy partook of the prevalent feature and flocked into the courts and alleys surrounding the Exchange, turtle soup was the height of fashion, the cost being one guinea per plate.'

But the green turtle is now threatened with extinction. This is not only because of rapacious soup-eaters but because the turtle eggs are poached and the female turtles are killed as they come ashore to lay, and also because the breeding beaches all over the tropics have been invaded by tourists and industrial development. Australian conservationists are now rearing turtles in hatcheries, and some turtle farming was begun on the Cayman Islands in the Caribbean a few years ago – mostly for soup though some were set free.

In any case the prospect of making soup from a live turtle, even if one were available, is not to be contemplated. Most people bought their turtle soup from the pastry cook and tavern keeper even a hundred years ago. Nowadays it is sold in tins ready made and more popular in the Scandinavian countries than in Britain.

It should be served hot, with a little Madeira or brown sherry poured into it. Tiny "eggs" (see below) are sometimes served in the soup and hot cheese straws are handed with it.

Egg Balls for Turtle Soup *A Victorian delicacy*
Press three hard boiled egg yolks through a sieve. Add one raw beaten egg yolk, a little flour, salt and curry powder, with a good pinch of freshly grated nutmeg. Mix well, roll it into little balls. Poach in boiling water before they are put into the hot soup.

The egg balls look well in any clear soup. The chopped hard-boiled egg whites are sometimes shredded into it too, or a little chopped parsley or some fresh coriander leaves may be chopped and added to a clear broth. For Hot Cheese Straws, see Mrs. Beeton's Cayenne Cheeses (page 44).

Watercress Soup

'Watercress pottage is a good remedy to cleanse the blood in spring', according to Thomas Culpeper in *The Compleat Herbal*, 1653, 'and help headaches, and consume the gross humours winter has left behind. Those that would live in health may use it as they please, if they will not, I cannot help it . . . if any fancy not pottage, they may eat the herb as sallet.' Nettle broth was made in some parts of the country from the young shoots in springtime for the same purpose.

Blanch two large bunches of watercress by plunging them into a pan of boiling salted water and letting it boil fiercely for three or four minutes. Then rinse the watercress under cold running water and dry it in a tea towel. Reduce it to a pulp in the electric mixer adding the yolk of an egg and 2 oz of butter. Heat the watercress mixture in a saucepan with a couple of spoonsful of cream. Then off the heat (and preferably using a balloon shaped wire egg whisk) gradually beat in the stock.

For this melt 3 tablespoons butter, stir in 3 tablespoons of flour and gradually, heating and stirring, add 2 pints of chicken stock, or ham or bacon stock if not too salty. Heat stirring till smooth and thick, simmer for 20 minutes.

Garnish with small bread sippets, fried crisp in butter.

Water Souchy

Water Souchy, Souchet or Waterzouchy was once a speciality of Greenwich. Until the 1890s it was fashionable to sail down the Thames to Greenwich for the whitebait dinners. The fish used to be caught in shoals off Greenwich and Blackwall in July and August and were crisp-fried and sold by the plateful. Water Souchy or Waterzouchy — pots of eel broth or fish stew — was served while the whitebait were being cooked, and was eaten with hot brown toast or bread and butter.

It was made from the many freshwater fish then caught in the Thames, some of the odd fish taken out of the whitebait nets, and with the eels for which the river Thames and the Lee and the Medway were then renowned. It seems to have had some affinity with the now better known Flemish *Waterzootje* or *Waterzoi* — a sort of thick freshwater fish and celery stew — still popular in Belgium.

Greenwich Water Souchy was cooked with Hamburg or turnip rooted parsley, the fleshy roots of which are eaten like celeriac and excellent for flavouring. Ordinary parsley does not have the same flavour.

Put three Hamburg parsley roots chopped in inch lengths then divided into match sticks in a pan with a little salt, 12 white peppercorns and a bunch of green parsley leaves. Add 3 pints of water or strained fish bone stock and bring it to the boil and simmer for 30–60 minutes until the roots are well cooked.

Meanwhile prepare about $2\frac{1}{2}$ lb of mixed fish — small flounders, perch, tench and eels were popular and sometimes mixed with small soles and pieces of salmon. But the selection really depends on what is available. Cut it in 2 inch chunks, freed of any dark skin. Add to these the parsley broth, bring it once more to the boil and then let it simmer for 8–12 minutes being careful not to let the fish break up from too fierce cooking and removing the rising scum with a slotted spoon. Two minutes before serving, sprinkle the Souchy with finely chopped parsley leaves and add the juice of half a lemon just before the pot is set on the table. Serve it with slices of brown and white bread and butter, or hot toast wrapped in a napkin.

Welsh Onion Soup with Milk and Cheese

Peel and dice $1\frac{1}{2}$ lb of onions. Put them in a pan with salt and pepper and enough water to cover. Bring it to the boil and then let the onions simmer gently, covered, until they are a pulp. Stir in 8 oz of grated cheese and a tablespoon of butter. Mix them well and then add 1 pint of milk. Bring it gently to the boil then season to taste.

It may be garnished with chopped parsley.

Welsh Leek Soup – Sŵp Cennin

Bacon or ham stock is particularly good for this soup, to which cheese is sometimes added. Alternatively a small piece of bacon, or a hock of bacon, might be cooked with the vegetables to make stock, it is then chopped and served with the soup.

Hot dinner rolls buttered, wrapped in foil and warmed in the oven are sometimes served with it in Welsh hotels as well as old fashioned *Bara Ceirch* – oatmeal bread (see below).

For the soup: Trim, cut up and wash two large leeks including the green part. Peel and chop 1 lb of potatoes. Add the bacon stock or water to cover amply and about 8 oz of diced belly bacon. Simmer with a lid on until the vegetables are soft. The potatoes should partly break up and thicken the soup. They may be squashed lightly with a fork. Add 1 pint of milk and 3 table-spoons of grated cheese. Heat without boiling as the milk may curdle. Serve garnished with chopped parsley.

When the soup is made with bacon stock or cubes, crumble a few rashers of crisply fried bacon into it before serving.

Bara Ceirch

This is made by mixing 4 oz of plain flour and 4 oz of medium oatmeal with ½ teaspoon salt and ½ teaspoon of bicarbonate of soda. Rub in a good tablespoon of lard and mix it all to a stiff dough with a little water. Having sprinkled a little oatmeal on the kitchen table roll the mixture out on it. Stamp it in rounds with a tumbler. Bake these on a greased baking sheet in a moderately hot oven (375°F, 190°C, Mark 5). Eat them hot from the oven and spread with butter.

Chapter 3

Meat

Beef

Cuts of Beef

The cuts of meat vary in Britain, as they always have done, according to what region one is in. They also vary in Scotland from one part of the country to another. Meat is cut differently for instance in the Glasgow area from the way it is done in Aberdeen. The Scottish flesher also cuts the meat differently from an English butcher who usually tries to produce more prime cuts from a beef carcase.

The Scottish cuts listed below are only approximately the same as the English ones listed opposite them.

Scottish Top Rump is similar to the English Topside/Silverside.

Scottish Pope's Eye Steak is similar to the English Rumpsteak.

Scottish Hough (Hok) is similar to the English Shin Beef, Leg Beef.

Scottish Shoulder Steak is similar to the English Clod and Sticking, Chuck Steak, Neck of Beef.

Scottish Nine Hole Cut is similar to the English Flank.

The Irish victualler, or butcher, cuts his meat differently again from a Scotsman or Englishman. For instance in Co. Cork and perhaps elsewhere, they commonly sell an enormous cut of grilling steak, commonly called rump, though very different from an English rumpsteak. It usually weighs about 3 lb and is

61

cut right across the whole top of the leg of beef, like a gammon steak or a Scottish gigot steak. Though the meat is excellent it is often insufficiently hung for English tastes, and may therefore appear tough to those unaccustomed to it. The butcher should be asked to hang it for the required time.

In England many of the frozen carcases supplied to freezer centres are cut up by a rotary saw, this produces some odd-looking cuts of meat unlike anything cut by conventional means in a butcher's shop, and for which there are no accepted names. Some thought is often required before cooking them successfully.

Roast Sirloin of Beef (also Wing Rib and Forerib)

The classic accompaniment to fine wines, this is of course one of the joints which looks like a giant cutlet. It should be left on the bone and at its best – and most expensive – also includes the undercut. It must be well hung, and to be worth the money should come from prime beef, not a dairying herd and be delicately marbled with fat. Ask the butcher how long it has been hung – 14 days is about the minimum, three weeks would be even better. If he does not know, do not buy it.

Wing rib and forerib are similar cuts to the sirloin, not quite so fine and without the undercut. They too should be left on the bone, both for flavour and because boning makes the meat shrink. The perfect accompaniment to a good claret, the meat is usually roasted on a rack in the tin. Put it in a hot oven (400°F, 200°C, Mark 6) and allow 15 minutes per lb and 15 minutes over, or 10 minutes per lb if liked rare. Baste it every 10 minutes or so with beef dripping. Season the beef after roasting and "rest" it for 15 minutes at the entrance to the oven with the heat switched off before carving it.

Joints on the bone cook more quickly than boned meat as the bone is a conductor of heat. Beef is particularly juicy when served slightly underdone; some prefer it served rare though it is often overcooked in Britain.

If Yorkshire pudding is cooked under the joint it should be raised on a rack for the last 30 minutes so the juices drop on the pudding below.

In England roast potatoes, buttered parsnips, Yorkshire

pudding, freshly mixed English mustard and freshly grated horseradish in sauce are traditionally served with roast beef. In Ireland (where they also make an excellent gravy for the joint by stirring cold milkless tea into the sediment in the roasting tin) Boxty Pudding (see page 136) is sometimes served with roast beef.

If boned and rolled the beef should be laid flat side up in the roasting tin.

Roast Fillet of Beef

A whole plainly roasted fillet of beef is an elegant but expensive dish for a formal dinner party. Because of its long slender shape it takes only a short time to cook — a good choice if there is little time before dinner.

The fillet or undercut lies underneath the sirloin. Though the two together make a perfect roast, the fillet can be separated from the sirloin for roasting (or for cutting into fillet steaks). Allow 2–3 lb in one piece for 6 people. Tuck in the narrow end of the fillet to make it more evenly thick. Tie it. The meat has almost no fat of its own, it must be rolled in hot butter or brushed thickly with oil, peppered, then frizzled before it goes into the oven.

Brown it all over in a frying pan over a fierce heat. Then lay the meat in a fireproof pottery dish, put it in a really hot oven (425°F, 230°C, Mark 7) pre-heated for 15 minutes to be sure.

Finish cooking the beef fillet for 20–25 minutes turning it once. When done, cut off the string, season it with salt, more pepper if liked, put it on a hot platter and let it stand by the open oven for a few moments to set.

It is sometimes carved in the kitchen in very thick slices and put together again so it can be dished with a garnish. Slice it with a thin sharp knife without pressing on the meat to avoid losing the natural juices.

Mushrooms done gently in butter, or, in season, *cèpes* cooked in oil with garlic, are very good with it. Horseradish sauce or Mrs. Beeton's Benton Sauce (see page 114) might be served. It is sometimes served with Pantry Butter or Devil Butter (see pages 116 and 20), hot jacket potatoes and a plain tossed salad.

Alternatively a sauce may be made by deglazing the roasting tin by stirring in 3 tablespoons of whisky and keeping the resulting gravy. Meanwhile melt 2 oz of butter in a frying pan, add 1 tablespoon of Newport Pagnell, or of strong Continental, mustard, stirring. Add ¼ pint thick cream, let it bubble up once or twice, keep it hot. Having carved the meat in thick slices pour both dish and pan gravy into the sauce.

Cold underdone thickly sliced beef fillet makes an elegant picnic dish, particularly when it has been rolled in finely chopped garlic and a little allspice, after buttering and before cooking (as above). Champagne and a tossed green salad should be served with this.

Rumpsteak and Onions
You can grill rumpsteak or fry it, but you cannot economize on it. Cheap steak is tough and there is nothing one can do about it. No cook and no steak is better than the butcher, for it must be well hung; but the butcher loses money in hanging meat because it evaporates and loses weight. He has to charge more for it. The steak must be "marbled"; this is the white fat connecting tissue in the red part which some people might think makes it fatty or gristly, but it is in fact the sign of perfect flavour, it virtually disappears when the steak is cooked but the fat ensures natural basting.

One needs about 1 lb of very tender rumpsteak about 1½ inches thick, well hung and marbled with fat. Trim it if necessary, brush it over with oil, set it aside. Peel 5 or 6 onions and cut them in thin slices. Heat some dripping in a frying pan, add all the onions at once, covering them with a lid or old plate. Fry them gently for 5–6 minutes on a low heat, stirring occasionally. Take them off the heat, add salt, pepper and a pinch of sugar. Drain off any surplus fat, stir them up with a fork, go on cooking them for about 5 minutes until just tender. If they are wanted crisp do this part without the lid, if wanted soft and melting leave it on except at the very end.

Start the steak after the onions have begun cooking, grill it 6–7 minutes per side. Arrange it on the onions with knobs of butter on it. Serve it at once.

Pepper Steak

A classic pepper steak is always prepared with whole crushed black peppercorns and traditionally is served with brandy sauce. In enjoying the steak one also relishes the peppercorns, crunching them with the teeth.

For 4 entrecôte* steaks crush 2 tablespoons of whole black peppercorns with a rolling pin, a pepper mill makes them too fine so they sink into the steak. Wipe the steaks, trimming off fat and gristle. Coat them on both sides with the peppercorns pressing them on with your fingers. Heat 1 tablespoon of oil with 2 oz of butter in a frying pan. Fry the steaks over a fierce heat for 2 minutes to seal the juices into the meat. Turn them once. Reduce the heat and go on frying for 5 minutes for rare steaks, 8–10 minutes for medium rare. Lift them on to a hot dish.

Pour 2 tablespoons of brandy, or whisky into the pan juices, set fire to it. Then, off the heat and when the flames have died down, stir in ¼ pint of double cream, heat and pour it over the steaks.

It may also be prepared with fillet steak. For grilling this is cut from the middle of the fillet, 4 oz steaks over 1 inch thick.

Soft green Madagascar peppers – *les poivres verts* – are now sold packed in brine in small tins. They have more flavour but are less hot than black or white pepper. They should be drained and rinsed and then crushed slightly before they are plastered on both sides of the raw steak. Thick cut rumpsteaks are sometimes served with green peppercorns (and without the sauce). They should be thick enough to be blue inside and crisp outside when cooked.

* Entrecôte steak means literally "a piece from between the ribs". It is similar to a sirloin steak but comes from the wing rib. Tender but tasty, it can be beaten out deliciously thin and is usually thought of as "a ladies' steak", popular with chefs for Steak Diane and so on.

Galway Steak

The rumpsteak in Ireland may well be a huge round cut right across the top of the leg of beef and weighing about 3 lb. It will look something like a vast gammon rasher or an enormous version of the gigot steaks of lamb sold in both Scotland and some parts of Ireland. In Galway the steak is often served smothered in local oysters.

Put this huge supersteak, about 1 inch thick, on a hot roasting tin with a little hot butter. Brown it quickly on top of the stove. Then put it in a hot oven (400°F, 200°C, Mark 6) for about 15 minutes. Sprinkle it with pepper and salt. Transfer it to a hot serving platter, then cover the steak with freshly opened raw oysters. Season it again and put the steak back in the oven until the oysters are plump, they should not be over cooked.

Pour the juices from the roasting tin over it and serve the whole thing as quickly as possible. It will be enough for four and should be carved diagonally across the grain into very thin slices. Drink stout or Black Velvet with it.

Mrs. Rundell, in common with other 18th century cooks, gives a recipe for Grilled Beefsteak and Oyster Sauce. The oysters were simmered, but not boiled, in thick well seasoned cream. A similar sauce was served with roast chicken, boiled and roast turkey and also with a cod's head and shoulders.

Carpetbag Steak

The Carpetbag Steak, popular in Victorian England, is a huge piece of rumpsteak stuffed with oysters, grilled, and served rather rare and enough for 4 to 5 people. It is still a hot favourite in Australia where the famous oysters from Bateman's Bay and Tom Ugly Point are plentiful. Men from the Outback, red in tooth and maw, are said to eat enormous steaks, ordinary "good tucker" being a tender juicy 12 oz steak from prime Australian cattle. It is seldom seen in England now, though some pubs specialize in large rumpsteaks stuffed with fried chicken livers instead of oysters. These, they maintain, are preferred by most customers.

These supersteaks should be brought out of the refrigerator 1–3 hours before cooking to lose their numbness, if straight from the butcher they should not be put in the refrigerator at all if to be cooked the same day.

Take a middle cut rumpsteak $2\frac{1}{2}$ inches thick. Make a slit through the fat end about 4 inches long and as deep as possible, with a sharp pointed knife. Shell 18—24 oysters (depending on size). Mix them with freshly ground black pepper, a little salt and a dash of lemon juice. Stuff them into the pocket in the steak. Fasten it with a thin metal skewer woven through both sides of the slit. Oil the grill rack. Lay the steak on it, spreading the meat thick with butter. Grill it for 10—12 minutes per side. If wanted well done, reduce the heat to moderate and grill it 5 minutes more per side, spreading more butter on it during cooking.

Before serving take out the skewer, serve the Carpetbag Steak cut in diagonal slices 1 inch thick, with a garnish of grilled tomatoes and watercress.

As these large pieces of meat go on cooking on the dish for a few moments after leaving the cooker, they should be carved and served as quickly as possible. If one of the party likes it less underdone than the others, leave that portion to the end.

Topside

Topside is a very popular English roasting cut which I seldom buy. It is to me the epitome of all those paper-thin slices of tasteless beef with packet gravy served up in nasty restaurants and canteens. It is often more expensive than sirloin, but is very lean and therefore dry and sometimes when it has not been hung properly it is very tough.

In Scotland topside is usually braised, it makes delicious casseroles and is very good when pot roasted and served with horseradish sauce, whole roasted Spanish onions and Potato Flounces or Scots Stovies (see pages 189 and 190).

This is an old fashioned method of cooking which combines frying and stewing, it makes a wonderful party dish, it looks and smells delicious and will wait quietly in the oven until all are ready.

Leave the meat in one piece. Brown it all over in lard or dripping with some peeled sliced onions. Then put it in an ovenproof casserole with a well fitting lid. Add salt, pepper and only $1\frac{1}{2}$ tablespoons of water, or ruby port.

Tie some foil over the top very firmly so it is as nearly air tight as possible, then put on the lid. Leave it in a fairly slow oven (325°F, 170°C, Mark 3) for about 4 hours. Unsalted silverside can also be cooked like this.

Boiled Beef and Carrots

Immortalized in the Victorian music hall song, *Boiled Beef and Carrots*, this Cockney dish was once a pub favourite, served hot with suet dumplings. It appeared cold next day, to be carved at the bar and eaten with pickles, Tewkesbury mustard and draught mild and bitter. Left-overs were then made into Bubble and Squeak.

Charles Elmé Francatelli, Chief-Cook-in-Ordinary to Queen Victoria, used to prepare an amazing version of it named Hunting Beef. He suggested putting a whole round of beef, about 30 lb, in lightly spiced pickle for three weeks then boiling it in home brewed ale. He apologized for the 'apparent extravagance of the recipe' pointing out that 'the broth could be given to the poor of the surrounding parishes'. The beef was often served cold for breakfast.

Silverside, very lean and with no bones, is mostly used for Boiled Beef and Carrots, though brisket which is cheaper and fatter is sometimes sold. Beef cuts that have been pickled in brine for boiling are of course an ugly grey when raw, the meat turns a mouth-watering pink during cooking.

Put the salt beef in a pan of fresh cold water with a peeled onion stuck with 2 cloves, a bayleaf, sprig of parsley and 12 peppercorns. Bring it to the boil, let it bubble gently. 1 lb of meat takes 1 hour to cook, 2–3 lb of meat take 2–3 hours of gentle boiling. During the last hour add some extra onions, peeled and roughly chopped and 4 oz of scraped carrots per person, *i.e.* to every 4–6 oz of meat.

Dumplings, if any, should be put in the pan to boil with the beef 30 minutes before it is cooked. Serve the beef piping hot garnished with chopped parsley, the carrots, onion, boiled potatoes, dumplings and some of its own broth for sauce. Wow-Wow Sauce (see page 139) may also be served. Hot pease pudding is sometimes served with boiled beef as well as the dumplings.

Beef is seldom salted so heavily nowadays as to need soaking before cooking, ask the butcher if this is so. If liked it may be soaked for 3 hours in cold water before being put in the pan.

Cold Pressed Beef

As a sea faring nation we were once famous for our pressed salted beef which often formed part of a ship's stores. Some of the recipes for it go back to the Middle Ages when, for lack of grazing, stock had to be killed off in autumn and salted down before the winter.

One simple modern method of preparing cold pressed beef is to buy salted brisket from the butcher. If very salt soak it for 3 hours in cold water. Put it in a pressure cooker with fresh cold water to come no more than one third up the pan. Then cook it for 10 minutes per lb at 15 lb pressure. Drain. Then press the meat until cold between two plates with a weight on top. This is very good cold with pickles and salad.

It is also used for the delicious hot pink meat sold in Jewish salt meat bars, sliced on to freshly made coarse brown bread (no butter, of course). One eats it with pickled gherkins and a glass of lemon tea.

The stock, if not excessively salt, will form the basis of very good broth for soup.

The salted beef may alternatively be cooked as for Boiled Beef and Carrots, then pressed between two plates as before.

Spiced Beef

This delicious dish was popular in Victorian England but has long been forgotten, like so much else, except in Ireland where everybody eats it at Christmas with the cold ham and turkey.

To spice 3 lb of beef silverside, or topside, mix 2 tablespoons of brown sugar, a pinch of freshly ground black pepper, a pinch of thyme and one of crushed bayleaves, with half a teaspoon each of freshly ground nutmeg, cloves and allspice, add a little finely chopped onion, 8 oz of coarse salt, 1 tablespoon of saltpetre (it is this that makes the meat pink when cooked). Rub the beef well with this mixture and leave it for 2 days before pouring 1 tablespoon of black treacle over it. Rub this sticky mixture into the meat for a week.

Then, having tied the meat firmly with string, cover it with warm water, bring it to the boil, then let it simmer bubbling gently for 3 hours. It is usually eaten cold.

This is very good, justly popular, and may well be related to those ancient recipes for beef preserved in treacle which were still fashionable in Regency England. In 1852 Admiral Belcher managed to persuade the Admiralty to have a quantity of beef pickled in treacle for his Arctic Expedition. This was a great success and, he said on his return, had remained in excellent condition. The beef was put in a large pot completely covered in treacle to shut out the air, then with muslin and a lid and sealed down for several months. It was washed before cooking.

Beef in Brown Ale, with Cheese Dumplings
Brown three peeled, sliced onions gently in lard or dripping, when golden add $1\frac{1}{2}$ lb of stewing steak, whole or cut in pieces. Brown it lightly and add 1 oz of flour, 1 teaspoon of brown sugar, some salt and pepper. Then stir in 1 pint of brown ale. Tip it into a stew jar and cover closely, or cook it in a casserole with a well-fitting lid. Bake it in a very moderate oven (325°F, 170°C, Mark 3) for $2\frac{3}{4}$–3 hours. Top it with Cheese Dumplings.

For the Dumplings: Mix 4 oz of self-raising flour, $1\frac{1}{2}$ oz of shredded or grated suet, $1\frac{1}{2}$ oz of grated cheese and a little salt and pepper. Stir in enough water to make a soft dough. Divide it at once into 8 dumplings, put them on top of the stew. Cover the casserole and cook for another 15–20 minutes. Suet pastry should be cooked as soon as it is made, otherwise it will be heavy.

For cooking in a stew jar see Old Fashioned Pot Pie (opposite).

Liverpool Scouse
This rib-sticking docklands dish has given its name to the local dialect, the Liverpool sound (as sung and spoken by the Beatles). *Scouseland* is naval and dockyard slang for Liverpool, Liverpudlians are known as *scousers* and *skowse* is naval slang for a Liverpool-born rating. According to Partridge's *Dictionary of Slang and Unconventional English*, *scouse* has some connection with *lobscouse*, a sailor's name for meat and vegetable hash.

Lobscouser was 19th century naval slang too for a sailor. Has it a Scandinavian origin? *Skipperlabskovs* is the Danish name of a popular sailors' stew of beef and vegetables.

Melt 2 oz of dripping in a pan or flameproof casserole. Add 1 lb of peeled, sliced onions, 1 lb of scraped, sliced carrots, a sliced (swede) turnip. Cook the vegetables gently, covered, so they melt rather than brown and absorb the fat. Stir occasionally. Add 2 lb of oxcheek or other stewing steak and brown it lightly. Add salt, pepper and water to cover. In north-west England 2–3 oz of dressed cowheel are often added to a stew to give "body" and make the gravy more gelatinous, sometimes a split pig's foot is substituted. Simmer very gently with a lid on until the meat is tender, or if liked in a fairly moderate oven (325°F, 170°C, Mark 3) for $2\frac{1}{2}$–3 hours. Towards the end add some peeled, quartered potatoes which will cook in the beef stock and help to thicken it. Exact quantities are unimportant, the proportions depend mostly on what is available and the skill of the cook. Pickled red cabbage is often eaten with scouse.

Old Fashioned Pot Pie
This is not a classic pie. The meat or game is jugged (or cooked in a covered stew jar which stands in a pan of water on top of the stove) and it is topped with suet crust pastry. It dates from a period before domestic ovens were universal. Fruit pies and the much loved sea pie of East Anglia are sometimes made like this too.

Put 8 oz of stewing steak and a pigeon cut in four into a stew pot, jar or jug. Add salt, 6 peppercorns, a sliced onion, carrot, stick of celery chopped, and water almost to cover. Roll out enough freshly made suet pastry to cover the top like a "lid". Place this over the meat and vegetables. Then cover the top of the stew jar with foil, pleated in the middle to allow room for the pastry to rise, and tied on firmly. Place it in a pan on an up-turned saucer with boiling water to come half way up. Let it cook, covered, gently bubbling for about 3 hours. The water should always boil and should be replenished with boiling water.

In Northumberland a "pot pie" is, however, what is known elsewhere as a steak and kidney pudding. Pot pie suppers are

71

popular in Newcastle clubs. A Leek Pudding is traditional too in the North East being a suet roll filled with chopped meat and leeks.

Bean Pot

Mixed beans are sold in Saint Helier, Jersey, for the traditional Channel Islands Bean Pot, three or four different kinds in varying sizes and colours. The recipe is prepared slightly differently in Guernsey from the one popular in Jersey.

Soak 12 oz of mixed beans in cold water overnight, then drain them. Put them in a large stone jar or pot, with a large peeled sliced onion, a piece of garlic peeled and chopped, two pig's feet split, a piece of shin beef and a bacon hock. Add $\frac{3}{4}$ pint of water, cover closely with foil and a lid, bake in a slow oven (300°F, 150°C, Mark 2) for 4–5 hours or in a moderate oven (350°F, 180°C, Mark 4) for 2–2$\frac{1}{2}$ hours.

Some cooks add chopped parsley and chopped carrot and lay peeled sliced potatoes on top of the beans 45 minutes before they are done. The lid is left off until cooking is finished. Before serving, brown a peeled, finely sliced, onion in dripping, stir in 1 tablespoon of flour, brown this too and stir it into the bean pot. This is an excellent winter dish.

Thick Oxtail with Pickled Walnuts

Plain boiled potatoes go well with this dish. It looks well sprinkled with chopped parsley – or with chopped coriander greens in the ancient manner – and a glass of red wine or stout greatly improves the gravy. If liked, two or three pickled walnuts may be laid on top of the stew in a silver entrée dish as a garnish. A tablespoon of walnut juice should be stirred into the gravy. Suet dumplings or forcemeat balls are generally put round the edge of the dish. See also the note on Oxtail Soup (page 54).

Brown some chopped onions and carrots in lard or dripping with a whole oxtail cut in pieces and, if possible, with 6 oz of sliced ox kidney to enrich the flavour. Sprinkle with flour and brown this lightly. Add $\frac{1}{2}$ pint of stout or ruby port and enough water to cover the meat, together with salt, pepper, and a good pinch of allspice. Cover the pot with foil and a lid. Leave it in a very slow oven (300°F, 150°C, Mark 2) for about 6 hours until the flesh is almost dropping off the bones, brown and tender. When cold it will all set in a stiff jelly, it is then easy to lift off the fat with a spoon. Re-heat everything else, adding the pickled walnuts and walnut pickle juice. Some cooks add a few whole shelled cooked chestnuts instead of walnuts. The dumplings or forcemeat balls must be freshly cooked, not re-heated.

In the pressure cooker: The meat and vegetables should first be browned, floured and seasoned as before. Add the liquor, cover and cook at 15 lb pressure for 45 minutes. Drain off the surplus fat and re-heat the rest with the desired garnish before serving.

Ox Tongue

An ox tongue, or neat's tongue as it was once called, is usually very good value with virtually no waste. It weighs from 3 lb to 4 lb and when cooked is enough for 8 to 10 people, and is usually relatively cheap. Smoked tongues are perhaps the most delicious but take longest to cook and are the most expensive. Before cooking they should be soaked in cold water overnight.

Ox tongues can also be had pickled (salted) or fresh. A pickled ox tongue, which is the type that goes pink when cooked, should be soaked in cold water for a couple of hours before cooking if very salt. It is as well to ask the butcher if this is necessary. A fresh tongue, which is unsalted and unsmoked, need not of course be soaked. Though it tastes good it will be grey instead of pink when cooked.

Put the tongue in a pan of cold water which bring to the boil, adding 12 peppercorns, 2 bayleaves and some soup vegetables — such as carrot, turnip, celery and onion, as available. Leave the skin on the onion as it gives the stock a good colour, and this can be used after for making soup. Let the tongue simmer bubbling gently on a low heat, either on top of the stove or in a moderate oven (350°F, 180°C, Mark 4). It will take about 3 hours to become tender and is cooked when the tip is soft. Prod it with a fork. When it is done pull off the outer skin and trim off the gristle at the root.

73

To serve the tongue hot: It may be sliced, hot, smothered in parsley sauce and flanked by boiled carrots and onions and large mealy potatoes cooked in the Lancashire fashion. In the North of England hot red currant jelly is also served with hot boiled tongue (or with hot boiled gammon or bacon). Boil ¼ pint of water in a pan adding 1 tablespoon of sugar, 3 tablespoons of red currant jelly. Stir until it melts, add a glass of cooking sherry.

Freshly grated horseradish stirred into hot thick cream is also very good with it. Hot boiled beetroot served in butter and some mounds of leaf spinach may be served round it as a garnish, making a good colour contrast.

To serve the tongue cold: Line a loose bottomed cake tin with foil. Peel and trim the tongue of gristle at the root. Put it in the lined cake tin. It should fit fairly well rolled up with a little of the meat trimmed from the thick part set in the middle to make it the right size. Add a little of the strained stock. Then put a plate and a heavy weight on top to press it into shape. A jug of cold water makes a handy weight for it. Let the tongue become cold and set and then, by pressing the loose bottom of the cake tin, one can slide it out easily. For a picnic the cold tongue is most conveniently transported in the cake tin and decanted on the site.

Liver
Calves' liver is the most delicate in flavour and also the tenderest, but it is extremely expensive. Lambs' liver though not quite so tender makes an excellent substitute and is considerably cheaper. Pigs' liver though tender is strong in flavour, used for many country dishes and is also popular for making pâté. Ox liver is tough but cheap and very good when properly cooked.

Liver and Bacon
Either calves' or lambs' liver is used for this much-loved dish. It should be well trimmed but cut about ½ inch thick then rolled in seasoned flour and fried in bacon fat.

Allow as many long rashers of bacon as there are slices of liver. Fry these first, then remove and keep them hot. Then fry the liver in the bacon fat. Remove it and stir a little water into the pan, heating and stirring to make a gravy which is poured over the liver and bacon.

Mrs. Beeton in her *Book of Household Management*, 1861, also garnishes it with slices of cut lemon or with forcemeat balls.

Calves' Liver, Château Latour

This is how Lord Cowdray's cook prepares it at Château Latour, Pauillac, in the Haut Médoc. It almost melts in the mouth.

The calves' liver must be sliced almost paper thin and have had all the stringy bits, tubes and so on, taken out. It is cut about an ⅛ inch thick, making about 16 small slices to the pound.

The secret in cooking it, she says, is to put the plain sliced liver in a *cool* pan with melted butter and to fry it very very gently, never letting the pan get really hot. Fierce cooking makes a hard outside crust and is a method more appropriate for searing steaks. I myself only add salt and pepper after the liver is cooked as the salt tends to toughen it.

This simple but perfectly delicious thing is served on a gratin of potato purée, browned in the oven. With it we drank an almost legendary first growth claret, Château Latour 1949, with which it goes perfectly.

Baked Stuffed Liver

A country dish which is very good served with hot baked jacket potatoes and red currant or medlar jelly. Buttered kale is delicious with it.

Ask the butcher to cut about 1 lb of ox liver in a single piece, without tubes and stringy bits. Get him to make a cut in the middle almost through to the other side. Make a stuffing by mixing a finely chopped onion and a chopped bacon rasher with a beaten egg and soft white crumbs moistened with hot water and squeezed out. Having stuffed the liver with this, tie it together with string. Cover it with streaky bacon rashers. Bake in a moderate oven (350°F, 180°C, Mark 4) until the liver is tender, in about an hour.

Baked Liver and Onions

Peel and slice two large onions and two or three large potatoes.

Slice 8 oz of pigs' liver. Put a layer of onion in a well-greased fireproof dish, then the liver and more onions, and cover them with potato slices. Add seasoning to taste. Cover with stock, dot with dripping. Bake in a moderate oven (350°F, 180°C, Mark 4) for 2 hours.

Liver and Bacon Pudding
An old fashioned pudding of excellent flavour
Dice $1\frac{1}{2}$–2 lb of ox liver and put it in a large pudding basin with two peeled, sliced onions and 2 oz of diced streaky bacon, or bacon pieces, in layers. Sprinkle it with pepper and a very little salt.

Make some gravy from stock or a cube, pouring it in to come about two thirds of the way up the meat. It should by no means fill the basin. Then put a rim of suet crust pastry round the top of the basin with a "lid" of suet crust pastry on top. The basin is not lined with pastry for this recipe, so as to leave more room for the meat and gravy. Tie on two thicknesses of kitchen foil, pleated in the middle to leave room for the pudding to rise. Stand the basin in a pan with boiling water to come half way up. Let it boil gently, seething and bubbling away quietly for three hours, filling up the pan with *boiling* water as the water boils away. If the pudding ceases to boil it usually becomes doughy and heavy.

It should not be turned out of the basin to serve but have a folded napkin pinned round it in the proper manner. Stand the basin on a dinner plate and just cut a slice of the crust, so the hot scented steam can gush out of it.

Serve it with more hot brown gravy in a jug, a dish of mashed buttery swedes and some Rowan Jelly or Pickled Walnuts. A good winter dish.

Steak and Kidney Pie
Opinions vary about the details. Some say the meat should be stewed before it is covered with pastry, others maintain with equal fervour that it should not. An impassioned correspondence on steak and kidney pie was continued for several weeks in *The Times'* letters column some years ago, with numerous distinguished protagonists on either side.

If oysters are added to the pie, the meat should undoubtedly be stewed first without pastry. They can then be put in the pie dish with the tender meat and the oyster liquor just before the pastry is laid on top, longer cooking can make them tough. Some North Country cooks say that, just as a good meat stew tastes even better the day after it was cooked when the meat and gravy are re-heated, so does the steak and kidney pie, while the pastry, on the other hand is at its best when cooked just long enough and no longer. Others put on the pastry crust from the start to seal in the dark meaty flavours. This faction included Miss Eliza Acton and Mrs. Elizabeth Raffald (who used rump-steak) and many other distinguished cooks. Some make it with shortcrust pastry, others prefer flaky pastry or rough puff pastry, all are good. Mrs. Raffald's 'Paste for dish pies' was made with a pound of fine flour, half a pound of butter, the yolks of two eggs beaten, and 'as much water as will make it a stiff paste'. In medieval times a pastry or pie case was known as a "coffin" or "coffyn", a firm container for something precious.

Some 6–8 oz of flour makes enough pastry for the average 6-portion pie made with $1\frac{1}{2}$–2 lb of stewing steak and an ox kidney. Sometimes 4–6 oz of lambs' kidney or pigs' kidney are used. Some cooks add a dash of Worcester sauce to a steak and kidney pie, others a little freshly mixed English mustard, or some freshly grated nutmeg.

Until Tudor times, when its popularity waned, a few fresh green coriander leaves were chopped and added to the pie with good effect.

If liked 4–6 oz of sliced mushrooms may be added to 2 lb of steak, preferably after it has been stewed. The kidney is then omitted.

Though the classic method is to roll the meat in flour, salt and pepper and then add water just to cover and then cook the meat, some cooks fry the meat first with sliced onions, rather ill advisedly we think.

Chuck (known in the North of England as chine) is the best type of stewing steak, widely used for pies and puddings and stews. It has plenty of flavour but is gristly and tough and must be cooked slowly. Do not attempt to fry or grill it even if the butcher says you could. Blade, sometimes sold as braising steak — is often diced with kidney for pies and puddings. Blade and chuck are sold together sometimes and known as shoulder in Scotland.

Steak and Kidney Pudding

Steak and Kidney Pudding, or in rhyming slang Kate and Sidney Pudding, was thought a rather vulgar plebeian dish, even so recently as the 1840s 'primarily for the lower classes, though popular with men'.

For this pudding the older method was to beat 2 lb of stewing steak with a wet rolling pin, then cut it in pieces. Nowadays it is mostly cut up by the butcher and accompanied by sliced ox kidney.

Line a well buttered pudding basin with suet crust pastry leaving a good margin of pastry hanging over the edges. Roll the steak and kidney in seasoned flour. Put a layer of it in the basin then a layer of sliced onion and more steak and kidney until the basin is almost full. Pour in water to come three quarters of the way up the meat. Then, having cut a piece of pastry the size of the basin lay it on top as a "lid". Wet the edges and fold over the margin of paste lining the basin and lay it on top. Press it down firmly so the gravy will not get out. Lay a buttered paper on top and tie two layers of foil, with a deep pleat down the middle, firmly over the basin.

Have ready a saucepan three parts full of boiling water, with an upturned saucer in the bottom, stand the basin on it, to prevent cracking. Boil it for at least 4 hours. Always add boiling water as it boils away. Keep a lid on the pan.

When cooked, remove foil and paper. Cut a piece of pastry the size of a shilling out of the middle of the pudding to let out the steam and prevent sogginess. Turn the pudding out onto a dish and sprinkle it with chopped parsley, or send it to table in the old fashioned way, still in the pudding basin with a folded napkin pinned round it. It may be served with a jug of extra gravy.

Welsh Stwns (see page 197) are delicious with it.

John Bull's Pudding

A Beefsteak or John Bull's Pudding is made in exactly the same way as a steak and kidney one. The kidneys are left out, though, and sliced onions and 3–4 oz of sliced mushrooms are substituted.

In Victorian England when oysters were cheap, half a dozen "family or sauce" oysters were included, together with the strained oyster liquor. In Victorian country houses a glass of port or sherry was often added as well – this spoils the flavour.

Tripe

In Victorian London tureens of curried tripe fierce enough to make your eyes water were very popular with those fashionable gentlemen who frequented Evans's Cider Cellars and other well-known supper rooms.

At Evans's they also specialized in huge sizzling kidneys and hot jacket potatoes. 'Shall I turn it out, Sir?' the waiter would ask as he seized the potato in its snow-white napkin, broke it in two and ejected the floury pyramid of it on your plate. There was a whistling comedian too and a fat gentleman called Harry Sidney who went in for topical satire set to music. You had to "remember the waiter" before you left and he usually offered you a pinch from his snuff box before you stepped out into the gas-lit streets.

In winter time at the Albion too, tripe was the staple food – though there was Welsh rabbit and grilled fowl. The Albion faced the stage door of Drury Lane, was famous for its good food as well as its entertainment and was run by the Cooper brothers – one kept the Rainbow in Fleet Street – who made a fortune by giving customers "the best of everything". Ladies were not encouraged but could sit in a room on the first floor if "in the profession". It was "all kidneys and 'armony" too at the Cave, a famous haunt of actors, barristers and journalists.

The Early Closing Act of 1872 had a disastrous effect upon these old London supper houses and gradually the licensed taverns which had specialized in serving curried tripe in the early hours of the morning began to close. They are now almost totally forgotten but Mr J. F. Curley, Master Cook at Simpson's-in-the-Strand, London, tells me that 'Tripe, far from being unobtainable in London, has been on my "Bill of Fare" every day for the past 27 years, which covers my period of service, but I understand it has never been off Simpson's "Bill of Fare" since the place opened in 1828. It is, of course, served plainly cooked in a cream sauce with onions and creamed potatoes, not curried or *à la Lyonnaise*, or *Provençal*, unless on request. As for the stew described in the *Old Curiosity Shop*, this stew, far from disappearing over the years is very well known to me and appears on my "Bill of Fare" frequently in the winter months, but can be, and is, served subject to 24 hours' notice.'

This is how Dickens describes it in *The Old Curiosity Shop*. At the *Jolly Sandboys* he wrote 'a mighty fire was blazing on the hearth and roaring up the chimney, with a cheerful sound, which a large cauldron bubbling and simmering in the heat, lent its pleasant aid to swell.'

Mr. Codlin, one of the customers, sat smiling in the chimney eyeing the landlord as 'with a roguish look he held the cover in his hand and feeling that his doing so was needful to the welfare of the cookery, suffered the delightful steam to tickle the nostrils of his guest. The glow of the fire was on the landlord's bald head, and upon his twinkling eyes and upon his watering mouth, and upon his pimpled face, and upon his round fat figure. Mr. Codlin drew his sleeve across his lips and said in a murmuring voice "What is it?"

' "It's a stew of tripe" said the landlord smacking his lips, "and cow-heel" smacking them again "and bacon" smacking them once more "and steak" smacking them for the fourth time, "and peas, cauliflowers, new potatoes and sparrow grass, all working up together in one delicious gravy."

'Having come to the climax he smacked his lips a great many times and taking a long hearty sniff of the fragrance that was hovering about put on the cover again with the air of one whose toils on earth were over. "At what time will it be ready?" asked Mr. Codlin faintly. "It'll be done to a turn" said the landlord looking up at the clock – the very clock had a colour in its fat white face and looked the clock for Jolly Sandboys to consult – "it'll be done to a turn at twenty-two minutes before eleven."

' "Then" said Mr. Codlin "fetch me a pint of warm ale, and don't let nobody bring into the room even so much as a biscuit till the time arrives." '

Tripe and Onions

On farms on the Derbyshire–Cheshire border they used quite recently to cook something not unlike the Jolly Sandboys dish adding both pork sausages and cowheel and crisp grilled bacon to the tripe and onions.

You will need 1 lb of dressed tripe and a dressed cowheel, leave the tripe in one piece, wash both, put them in a pan with cold water to cover. Bring it slowly to the boil, boil for 15 minutes then drain off the water. Add two large peeled, neatly sliced, onions to the tripe and cowheel as well as a pint of milk. Let it simmer very very gently for an hour just bubbling. Then add $\frac{3}{4}$ lb of well seasoned coarse cut country pork sausages pricking them first to prevent them bursting. Simmer for 30 minutes. Meanwhile grill four or five rashers of smoked streaky bacon, crumble or chop them in bits, add them to the stew to give it bite. The sauce is usually very thick by this time, deliciously tacky from the cowheel and well flavoured from the sausages (those fine cut mild factory sausages from the grocer won't do at all). If you want it thicker and creamier still mix 1 dessertspoon of cornflour to a paste with about 3 tablespoons of milk and stir it into the sauce. Boil it up stirring to thicken. Serve mashed potatoes with it.

Roast Loin of Veal

The kidney end of a loin of English veal is one of the best cuts. It used to be served with a piece of boiled bacon and an egg sauce as well as its own gravy, and it is usually stuffed before roasting. Sometimes it is served with mushroom sauce or with a good brown gravy and red currant jelly.

Veal has very little fat and, if roasted, it should be well smeared with butter or dripping and basted frequently. It is best cooked with a moist stuffing. The caul* (or flead fat) used to be laid over it till nearly done.

Make a stuffing or forcemeat of 1 tablespoon of soft breadcrumbs, 2 oz of suet, 1 tablespoon of fresh chopped parsley, the grated rind of half a lemon, 1 slice of chopped cooked bacon, 1 small onion finely chopped, salt and pepper to your liking. Spread this over the veal with a knife, as evenly as possible, place three whole shelled hard boiled eggs down the middle. Then roll the meat round all this and tie it with string. Roast it in a very moderate oven (325°F, 170°C, Mark 3) for 40 minutes per lb. Baste it frequently, with butter or dripping.

Of the meal to which Mr. and Mrs. Micawber invited David Copperfield, at a small inn near Canterbury, Charles Dickens wrote, 'We had a beautiful little dinner, quite an elegant dish of fish; the kidney end of a loin of veal, roasted; fried sausage-meat; a partridge, and a pudding. There was wine, and there was strong ale; and after dinner Mrs. Micawber made us a bowl of hot punch with her own hands.'

* The caul, or kell, or flead fat, or fleare, or veiling, as it is called by butchers in different parts of the country, is the delicate white veil of fat from near the kidneys of an animal (in French *crépine*). When soaked in warm water it softens and can be pulled out like a piece of fine white lace. It is used in making faggots and to wrap lean legs of lamb for roasting in some parts of Britain.

A Veal and Ham Pie with Sweetbreads and Forcemeat Balls
A delicacy which has almost vanished, once made with the meat from English bobby calves. Nowadays veal is scarce and has largely been replaced by chicken or turkey meat.

Bone and chop 3 lb of stewing veal. Put the bones in a pan of cold salted water with a chopped onion, carrot, some mixed herbs and 12 peppercorns. Bring it to the boil and simmer to make jellying stock for the pie. In it also blanch 12 oz of calves' or lambs' sweetbreads.

Put a layer of the chopped veal in a large pie dish sprinkling it with pepper, freshly grated nutmeg and the grated rind of a lemon. Add a layer of the blanched, trimmed and sliced sweetbreads, then a layer of chopped boiled ham, sliced hard boiled egg and some Forcemeat Balls. Continue thus until the dish is full. Pour in ½ pint of the veal bone stock. Add a pie funnel. Cover the dish with puff pastry, making a slit over the funnel for the steam to escape. Decorate it with pastry leaves and pastry acorns. Brush it with egg. Bake it in a hot oven (400°F, 200°C,

Mark 6) until the pastry is risen and browned in about 15 – 20 minutes. Then reduce the heat to moderate (350°F, 180°C, Mark 4) and go on cooking for 1–1½ hours or longer if the pie is very large. Cover the pastry lightly with a piece of foil if it seems to be getting too brown. When cooked, pour ½ pint of rich jellying veal bone stock through the hole in the pastry, using a funnel. When the pie is cold it should set in a jelly.

Sweetbreads

Pale, tender and having a most delicate flavour, sweetbreads are inexpensive but as some people do not know how to cook them they are mostly sold to the catering trade. They are the thymus gland and the pancreas, known as the throat and heart sweetbreads. Calves', lambs' and sometimes ox sweetbreads are sold. Chefs know very well how to make the most expensive-looking little delicacies from them.

Allow 4–5 oz for each portion. Whatever the recipe, sweetbreads must first be soaked in cold salted water for 2–3 hours to keep them as white as possible. Change the water when it becomes tinged with pink. Then put them in a pan of cold salted water, bring this slowly to the boil, let them simmer for about 2 minutes. Lift them out, hold them under a trickle of cold water, trim off the skin and any dark bits with the point of a knife. Wrap them in a cloth. Cool them between two plates with a weight on top to flatten them.

Fried Sweetbreads When prepared as above they can be sliced. Then shake them in a paper bag containing a little flour, some salt and pepper. Fry them with bacon and mushrooms.

A Fricassée of Sweetbreads

Scald and slice the sweetbreads as above. Put them in a tossing pan (sauté pan) with a pint of veal gravy (stock), a spoonful of white wine, the same of mushroom catsup, a little beaten mace (a blade of mace). Stew them a quarter of an hour. Thicken your gravy with flour and butter a little before they are cooked enough (melt a tablespoon of butter in another pan, stir in a dessert-spoon of flour and gradually heating and stirring add a little of

83

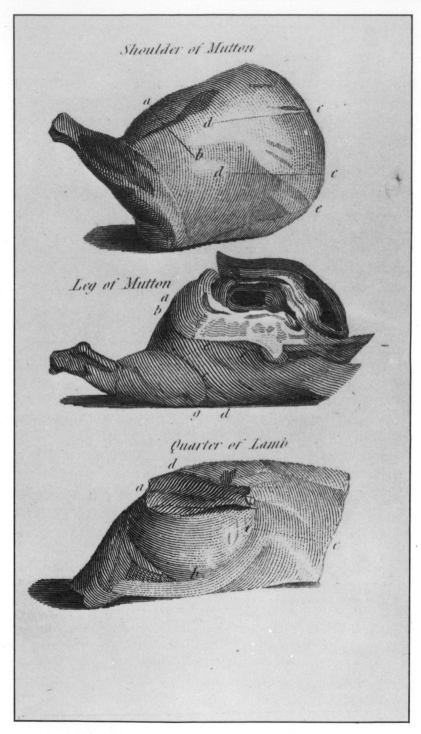

Shoulder of Mutton

Leg of Mutton

Quarter of Lamb

the stock from the sweetbreads, when smooth and thick stir it back in the pan with them).

When you are going to dish them up mix the yolk of an egg with a teacupful of thick cream, and a little grated nutmeg, put it into your tossing pan, and shake it well over the fire but do not let it boil. Lay your sweetbreads on your dish and pour your sauce over them: garnish with pickled red beet-root and kidney beans. From *The Experienced English Housekeeper* by Mrs. Elizabeth Raffald, 1769.

Lamb

A plain well roasted leg of lamb used to figure as the "cut off the joint with 2 veg." which appeared in the old eating houses before the apple pie and custard or jam roly-poly. It is an English classic which many families have been in the habit of eating about once a week for half a lifetime.

Young home killed lamb is at its most plentiful from July to October, at its most delicious in April and May. The best legs of lamb should look blue or bluish through the thin membrane, and the knuckle bone in the leg or shoulder of a young animal will be bluish in colour too. The flesh itself will probably be pale pink though some hill sheep have a deep colour even when young. The milk fed house lamb and the very young and tender Devon lamb which can very occasionally be bought in the early part of the year are a great delicacy. Much of this is exported and it has always been extremely expensive. Grass lamb, one which has seen a winter and been fed on grass, is what most people eat in Britain, it is called a yearling or yearling lamb when it has its upper incisor teeth. Older animals are more correctly known as hoggets, and could advantageously be used in mutton recipes when this is unobtainable.

New Zealand lamb is available during most of the year, but, since in the southern hemisphere the seasons are the opposite of those in Britain, it is at its most plentiful when ours is scarce and so a constant supply is maintained. The joints are smaller than those of English lamb not only because the New Zealand lambs are sold when slightly younger but also because they are a smaller breed. Both English and New Zealand lamb are of very good quality and do not vary as does beef, one seldom buys a poor quality cut.

The New Zealanders have been sending lamb since the old windjammer days of 1882, when the *Dunedin* sailed with its first cargo. All the passengers except two cancelled their passage as they were frightened that the crankshaft of the newly in-vented refrigeration machine would tear a hole in the ship's bottom. The captain had an anxious voyage too. On several occasions sparks from the steam engine powering the cooling plant set fire to the sails. Then in the tropics he found that the cool air was not circulating, so he crawled into the ship's hold to fix it, became frozen stiff, and nearly died before being rescued by the mate. He crawled in and hauled the captain out.

Nowadays they send us tons and tons of lamb, and it still makes a great difference to the housekeeping money.

Cuts of Lamb
In Scotland and Ireland the cuts of lamb and mutton are different from those in England and Wales.

A Fillet of Lamb, a joint popular in Southern Ireland, is cut right across the loin and includes the chump chops and part of both legs. It is a delicious roasting cut if from a young animal. It is often sold with the caul or flead fat, this is placed on top of the joint in roasting to baste the meat. Do not confuse it with "lamb fillet", the meat boned out of a whole neck of lamb into long fillets for grilling by some of the fancier London butchers.

Gigot steaks are popular both in Scotland and in Ireland. They are cut right across the top of the leg, or gigot, of lamb or mutton rather like a thick gammon rasher, and then grilled or fried. The left-over shank end of the leg is sold frequently with a piece of the breast for stews or for broth. In Co. Cork inexpensive stewing pieces of lamb or mutton are known as the "House-keeper's Cut".

The *Shoulder of Lamb* is boned and rolled and tied in a sausage shape before roasting in Scotland, as it is in France, and sometimes it is also stuffed with forcemeat before being rolled and tied. For this effect the shank bone and blade bone have to be removed, these are often sold separately for making soup.

Shetland lambs are a local delicacy. They are very small, about half the size of an English lamb. The whole carcase weighs 20–25 lb, while an English lamb may weigh 60 lb. They are very, very lean, almost like venison, and best roasted in the flead fat, they are only available during the lambing season which in the Shetlands is in late summer. At other times they may be had frozen by post in very limited quantities.

Red currant or rizer jelly is popular with lamb, mutton or venison in Scotland as is Rowan or Rodden Jelly, which is made from the berries of the mountain ash or rowan tree when tipped with frost. They are mixed with crab apples in the proportion of 2 lb of crab apples to 3 lb of rowan berries. Otherwise a standard jelly recipe is used. Rowan berries, which have a sour smoky taste, are also used to flavour stews and meat pies in Northumberland.

A Roast Leg of Lamb with Orange
It was fashionable in 18th century England to stuff a boned leg of lamb with the flesh of a boiled lobster, pounded and mixed with lemon peel, nutmeg, salt and pepper. Sometimes crab was used and, at the London Tavern, John Farley also served lobster sauce or crab sauce with it. Some cooks stuffed the leg with finely chopped oysters. Mrs. Glasse preferred cockles and shallots mixed. She also larded the leg with the cockles, spit roasted it, and served it with horseradish. In King Charles II's day, when oranges had first become fashionable and orangeries were built near the great country houses, a leg of lamb was often basted with bitter orange juice. The bitter marmalade oranges, or Seville oranges, which are in season and obtainable in January should be used. When unobtainable, the juice of sweet oranges mixed with the juice and grated rind of a lemon may be substituted, but Seville oranges freeze very well, whether whole or sliced. This recipe is for an oven roasted joint, though of course

in good King Charles's golden days it would have been spit roasted. See also **Seville Orange Sauce** (below) and Laver Sauce (page 124) once served with roast lamb in Wales.

Push three sprigs of rosemary into the leg of lamb here and there near the bone. Sprinkle it with a little salt, preferably sea salt. Roast it in a fairly hot oven (375°F, 190°C, Mark 5) for 10 minutes, pouring the juice of a bitter Seville orange over it. Then reduce the heat to moderate (350°F, 180°C, Mark 4) and roast it 20 minutes per lb — less if liked underdone. Baste it occasionally with the pan juices and after 30 minutes the juice of a second orange and 3 tablespoons of water.

Meanwhile cut the peel of one orange in strips, without the pith, as for marmalade. Boil these for about 20 minutes until soft. Put the meat on a hot platter and keep it warm. Pour the surplus fat off the juices in the pan. Mix 1 teaspoon of cornflour to a paste with water. Stir it into the pan juices and add the orange peel. Heat, stirring. Then pour the orange gravy over the joint.

Buttery sea kale, in season in the early part of the year, or salsify, so popular in the early 18th century, would be delicious with it. The potatoes must be roasted in a separate tin as they would spoil the gravy. A conventional orange and watercress salad might also be served.

Roast Leg of Lamb, or Mutton, Smothered with Onions

The recipe was one of Alexis Soyer's, and dates from the mid-19th century.

Roast the lamb 20 minutes per lb in a moderate oven (350°F, 180°C, Mark 4), and meanwhile peel and mince 2 lb of onions. Cook them very gently in 2 tablespoons of oil with a lid on the pan for about 10 minutes. Stir them occasionally so they become soft but not brown; then, gradually, stir in 1 tablespoon of flour and 1 pint of milk. Add salt, pepper and a little sugar. Heat simmering and stirring until the onions are very tender and the sauce is thick. Stir in the yolks of two eggs and remove the pan from the heat.

When the joint is cooked spread this, now very thick, onion sauce over the top in a good thick layer. Brush it with the beaten whites of the two eggs, then cover it with browned breadcrumbs. Put the joint into a hot oven (400°F, 200°C, Mark 6) for 10 minutes until there is a brown crust on top.

Serve it with a good brown gravy in which a peeled, chopped garlic clove has been simmered, but remove this before serving.

In Derbyshire a mint flavoured bilberry jelly is sometimes served with roast lamb.

A lump of butter mixed with chopped mint – or with lemon juice and Cayenne pepper, or all three – and then chilled, used to be laid under the joint in the meat dish, to mingle with the juices that came out of it in carving. It makes very good gravy.

"Colonial Goose"
This is an old Lancashire dish for which lamb, not poultry, was used. Now almost forgotten in England it is still popular in South Africa. The leg of lamb is stuffed, like a goose or duck, with sage and onion forcemeat, then roasted and served with apple sauce, roast potatoes, mashed turnips and green peas. The somewhat similar "Butcher's Goose" prepared with pork instead of poultry was an old Teesside Christmas dinner.

Take a small leg of lamb, which should have the bone removed but the knuckle left on. Stuff the pocket in it, where the bone once was, with sage and onion forcemeat as is commonly used for geese and ducks. Skewer or stitch up the meat when stuffed; then, with the aid of a skewer, shape the leg of lamb to form the neck and back of the "goose". Dust it over lightly with ground ginger. Roast it in a hot oven (400°F, 200°C, Mark 6) for 20 minutes per lb and 20 minutes over.

A Shoulder of Lamb, Stuffed and Roast, Sussex Fashion
Meat is cut differently in the North from the South of England, there are also West Country and Midlands cuts. Sussex butchers used to have a special way of boning a shoulder of lamb, which has a large bladebone through the middle, making it difficult to carve. In Scotland, as in France, this sweet and delicately flavoured joint is usually boned completely then rolled up with or without stuffing and tied before roasting. In Sussex they simply remove the bladebone, leaving in the shank bones. The

joint then has a better shape, yet is easy to carve, and is thought locally to cut better than boned and rolled meat which is carved across the grain. There is also a large pocket in the meat where the bladebone was which may be stuffed with mushrooms.

For the stuffing rinse 1 lb of button mushrooms and dry them in a tea towel. Slice and simmer them in a small saucepan in a mere $1\frac{1}{2}$ oz of butter, shaking them gently so they do not burn and sprinkling them with a little salt, grated nutmeg and Cayenne pepper. The butter will seem insufficient, but after a while black juice runs out of the mushrooms. When soft, stuff as many as possible into the pocket in the shoulder of lamb, fastening it with skewers. The remainder should be re-heated before serving and mixed with the roast potatoes. This stuffing is similar to one given by Eliza Acton in *Modern Cookery for Private Families*, 1845, for pheasant or for preparing potted mushrooms. She was born in Sussex on April 17th, 1799, at Battle, being the daughter of a Hastings brewer.

Roast the stuffed shoulder of lamb in a fairly hot oven (375°F, 190°C, Mark 5) for 10 minutes. Then reduce the heat to moderate (350°F, 180°C, Mark 4) and roast it for 25 minutes per lb or rather less if it is liked underdone. Baste it once or twice during roasting with two or three tablespoons of red wine. Before serving remove the skewers and garnish it with a bunch of watercress. Serve fresh mint sauce with it.

Sussex "Mock Duck"

The famous Southdown sheep have been grazed on the Sussex chalk downs since time immemorial. Nowadays, due to cross breeding, they are almost a thing of the past. They have a reputation for being a great delicacy. They used to have black feet and at one time butchers left the feet on legs and shoulders of Southdown lamb and mutton to show the superior breed. In some villages a shoulder of Southdown lamb boned as above was used for an old fashioned dish called "Mock Duck". The sides of the joint were tucked under, the shank bone fixed upright with a skewer, before roasting. When it came to table it looked very like a duck, head and all, sitting on a dish. 'But this is now mostly a dish for shepherds' they say locally.

A Saddle of Lamb, or Mutton

Roast saddle of Southdown lamb is still a speciality at Glynde-
bourne and it used to be served at City banquets. Sometimes it
was stuffed after roasting, for example, with *pâté de foie gras*, and
the slices of cold lamb were laid on top and glazed. Cold saddle of
lamb – or mutton – makes a succulent and splendid centrepiece
for a buffet and was the height of fashion in Victorian England.
Sometimes the little tail was trimmed with a paper frill.

This English classic, which is usually roasted, is of course,
especially delicious hot as it is always carved lengthways parallel
to the ribs and so tastes different from other cuts. Imagine the
pleasure of eating a thick loin chop served to you in the long
pink underdone slices which result from carving the meat
lengthways with the grain. A good claret, even a very distinguished first or second growth claret, would go well with a
roasted saddle of lamb.

It is a large prime joint weighing from $4\frac{1}{2}$–8 lb if lamb and
from 7–11 lb if mutton, it is usually skinned by the butcher of
the thin membrane before being dressed and the kidneys are
sometimes attached to the saddle to be roasted and served with
it, a slice of kidney being served with each portion.

The small sugar pod or mangetout peas available in early
spring are delicious with roast lamb, as are buttery new potatoes.
The Victorians liked to serve the saddle with a Brown Cucumber
Sauce or a White Cucumber Sauce (see page 120) as well as with
red currant jelly; Medlar Jelly is delicious with it too. A glass of
port or of red wine may be stirred into the pan gravy with good
effect. Some people also moisten the saddle with a little red wine
an hour before roasting it, and then they baste it with 2 tablespoons of water and some salt 5 minutes before serving.

To roast: The saddle should be roasted in a moderate oven
(350°F, 180°C, Mark 4) with plenty of good dripping on it.
Baste it well, and stand the meat in a roasting tin without a rack.
Lay a piece of paper or foil over the joint for the first half hour.
Allow 20 minutes per lb.

Some people like it roasted only 15 minutes per lb and really
underdone and pink inside, as they have lamb in France and as

it was eaten in England in the 18th century, but nowadays most British people object to this.

To carve: Steady the joint with a fork plunged in the centre of the back. Find the ridge on either side of the backbone, with the sharpest possible carving knife, cut down through the meat at this point holding the knife flat against the bone. Make two long cuts each side of and parallel to the backbone. Go on cutting wedge shaped slices.

If they are too long each may be divided in half. Since carving may take a little time, have the platters, the plates, the gravy and the sauces as hot as possible.

Welsh Lamb

Mountain lamb, the experts say, eats sweeter. The meat in Central Wales is like it used to be years ago, with a flavour one had forgotten, and almost melting in the mouth. In the 19th century high class family butchers made a speciality of this Welsh lamb and mutton. One still finds decorative tiles on the walls of old shops showing Welsh sheep, usually grazing on a background of blue pottery mountains, but Welsh lamb and mutton is now very difficult to find in the big cities. London butchers complain that it makes very small cutlets. The little lean agile Plinlimmon sheep with the white and speckled faces have a particularly delicate flavour, however, which is a pity to miss, and a well hung saddle of mutton from the Welsh hills is a joint for epicures, superb with hot red currant jelly in a sauceboat.

Until the closing of the railways many of the butchers in Central Wales made a speciality of sending lamb to London, and when David Lloyd George was Prime Minister he used to have a supply of Welsh lamb sent to him regularly at 10 Downing Street from the local butcher in Criccieth. Again, about 30 years ago, when there was still a railway in Llanidloes, Hamer's, the local butchers used to supply the Royal Family regularly with Welsh lamb and mutton. It is an old family business which the Hamers have had in Llanidloes for four generations. 'You put the meat on the train at 7 a.m.,' young Mr. Hamer once told me, 'and could guarantee delivery to a housewife anywhere in

London at eight o'clock the following morning. Every Monday there would be two hundred lambs or wethers and we had fifty men. Now we are down to four and that trade has gone.'

A Welsh Leg of Lamb, Roasted, in the Caul
Welsh lambs are small, lean and need basting. In Cheshire, Shropshire and perhaps other counties on the Welsh border, the legs of lamb are sold wrapped in flead fat – or caul – for roasting, as they are in Wales. These are the lacy sheets of very white fat which comes from near the kidney. It is called lamb's leaf, or flead, or flare fat, or veiling in other parts of the country and is obtainable from good butchers. This caul (pronounced "kell") is skewered round the joint which is then roasted in it, the caul brings out the flavour, makes the meat succulent and does away with the need for basting.

When wrapped in the caul, the leg of lamb may be roasted in a moderate oven (350°F, 180°C, Mark 4) for 25 minutes per lb if liked very well done, 20 minutes per lb if preferred slightly pink. Buttered leeks are traditional with it. It is delicious when served with the old White Cucumber Sauce (see page 120). In season in Wales Samphire Sauce (see page 133) used to be served with roast lamb and mutton as it still is served in Norfolk. Sometimes a little dish of rowan jelly, called *Saws Criafol* in Wales, appears with it.

A Welsh Shoulder of Lamb, Rolled, and Roasted in a Pastry Crust
From Mr. Heflin Williams, young chef at the Portmeirion Hotel, Penrhyndeudraeth
It must be a small shoulder of Welsh lamb, boned, rolled and tied in a sausage shape. Roast it in a moderate oven (350°F, 180°C, Mark 4) for 20 minutes per lb basting from time to time, then let it cool slightly before removing the string.

Meanwhile wash and pick over 8 oz of spinach. Place it in a pan with just the water which is clinging to it. Cook it over a fierce heat for only 5 minutes, turning it over until all is soft. Drain it, then rinse it in cold water, squeezing it to drain it well, add salt and pepper.

93

Roll out 8 oz of puff pastry about 12 inches square. Lay the spinach in the middle. Place the rolled and roasted shoulder on top. Wrap the meat and spinach completely in the puff pastry, bringing up the sides like a parcel and moistening the four corners to make them stick. Turn it over. Brush the top with beaten egg. Place it in a roasting tin in a fairly hot oven (375°F, 190°C, Mark 5) until the pastry is risen and golden in about 15 minutes. Excellent gravy can be made with the bones.

Welsh Marsh Lamb with Hot Laver Sauce

In South Wales one sometimes comes upon the local salt marsh lamb which has a flavour reminiscent of the better known Norman *pré salé*.* This used to be served, when roasted, with hot laver bread mixed with Seville orange juice and is perhaps an echo of a dish fashionable in London in the 17th century.

To make the sauce, as Mrs. Rundell wrote in *A New System of Domestic Cookery*, 1806: 'Set some of the laver "bread" in a dish with a lamp, with a bit of butter and a squeeze of a Seville orange, stir it till hot. It is eaten with roast meat and is a great cleanser of the blood. It is seldom liked at first but people become extremely fond of it by habit.'

Laver bread – which has little in common with ordinary bread – is made by first rinsing a special seaweed, *Porphyra lacinate*, called laver, first in sea water then in fresh water. It is then wrung dry and cooked in sea water for several hours, then drained. This delicacy – *Bara Lawr* or Laver Bread – is usually on sale in Swansea Market and was once eaten by gourmets in Bath.

* *Pré salé* is a term applied to lamb and mutton the best of which, French cooks say, are those that have grazed on salt marshes, or *préssalés*, for this gives a subtle flavour to the flesh. Usually those of Normandy near to Mont Saint Michel are the ones in mind, though the famous *agneaux de Pauillac*, much admired and very expensive, used to be those that fed on salt marshes in the village of Pauillac by the river Gironde, in the Médoc and near such famous vineyards as Mouton-Rothschild. The marshes were drained generations ago and have given way to a Shell oil refinery and the connection is largely forgotten.

Barnsley Chops
This is a Yorkshire dish, the meat is cut right across the saddle of lamb making a butterfly-shaped piece of meat which is really two loin chops joined together at the chine.

Barnsley chops are very similar to Alexis Soyer's once famous Patent Chops which, over a hundred years ago, were eaten in the best houses as a breakfast dish. They are still served in the United States where they are known as "English Chops".

They may be fried slowly and gently on either side in butter or dripping, very little is necessary, barely more than is enough to prevent the meat from sticking to the pan. When cooked, season them with salt and pepper. They may be served with a marrow sauce (see Aunt Alice's Marrow Dish, page 182).

Gigot Steaks
These are seen more often in Scotland or in Ireland than in England. The gigot steak is cut across the top of a leg of lamb and should have a small round bone left in the middle similar to the one found in thick gammon rashers. They are very good when served with Cauliflower Cheese, or with Highland Stovies. The old White Cucumber Sauce and some Potato Flounces are excellent with grilled gigot steaks (see pages 120 and 189).

To grill: Dip the gigot steaks lightly in oil. Heat the grill to maximum. Grill them 5—6 minutes per side if liked underdone. Season and garnish with Devil Butter (see page 20).

"Mixed Grill" – in the Oven
A Yorkshire family dish, once popular on farms where it was to be had ready and hot for high tea on one's return from market. It is a very practical dish for those with an oven with a time switch.

Grease a baking tin with good dripping or salted butter, and lay the following meat in it: 8 oz of lambs' liver cut in inch thick slices, 1 lb of coarse cut butcher's sausages, pricked with a fork, 4 lambs' kidneys skinned but left whole and with the fat removed, 4 lamb chops or cutlets, trimmed of surplus fat (the edges may also be nicked with scissors to stop them curling up in cooking).

Cover the meat with 1 lb of bacon rashers in two layers. Arrange the rashers to overlap and to cover the other pieces of meat completely. Bake it in a slow oven (300°F, 150°C, Mark 2) for about 2 hours. Jacket potatoes may be done at the same time.

When the meat is cooked pour the melted fat and dripping into a pot and store it in the refrigerator. It makes marvellous dripping toast, savoury pastry and is useful in general for cooking.

Lancashire Hot Pot (*Blackburn recipe*)

In 1845 Eliza Acton called it a 'Baked Irish Stew' and said it should be made in a 'brown upright Nottingham jar'. Could it have originated with the Liverpool Irish who had flocked to Lancashire during the Potato Famine in the early 19th century? Was it then a new dish? 'We have not considered it necessary to try this receipt, which was given to us by some friends who keep an excellent table', Miss Acton added, 'and who recommended it much. It is, of course, suited only to a *quite plain* family dinner.' Perhaps a Hot Pot does really have something in common with Irish Stew, the ingredients are similar but the proportions and method of cooking are different.

In my grandfather's house in Blackburn it sometimes had chopped lambs' kidneys, or black pudding, or diced bacon in it as well as the classic ingredients. Some cooks added oysters but this appears to have been an Edwardian fashion. It eats well with a good claret or burgundy and can be left for a long time in a slow oven. It used to remain to cook in the old coal fired kitchen ranges while the women were out at work in the mills. When cooked it can also be kept hot for a long time, wrapped in thick newspaper and blankets. Some Lancashire lassies took it to bed with them. (See also Liverpool Scouse, page 70.)

Take 2 lb of lamb cutlets. Best end cutlets are very good in Hot Pot, but the leaner, cheaper middle neck or scrag end are often used. Roll them in seasoned flour together with 1 lb of peeled sliced onions. Peel 2 lb, or slightly more, of potatoes and cut these in rounds as thick as an old penny. The Hot Pot is best cooked in the traditional straight sided brown glazed earthenware pot. Warm this, put in a spoonful of dripping, rolling it round to grease the inside. Put in the potatoes, meat and onions in layers, well seasoned with salt and pepper, the top layer being potatoes. Pack them closely and dot the top with dripping. Pour in a good $\frac{1}{2}$ pint of hot stock, enough to come almost level with the top of the potatoes. Quantities are important, it must not cover them. Put a lid on the pot and bake it in a moderate oven (350°F, 180°C, Mark 4) for 2 hours, removing the lid during the last 40 minutes to brown the potatoes on top. It can also be left longer in the oven or cooked for about 4 hours at a lower heat.

This is a good winter meal with a bottle of red wine and some Leigh Toaster or Stilton cheese to follow. Pickled red cabbage is eaten traditionally with Hot Pot in Lancashire.

Irish Stew

This should be made just with onions, mutton or lamb, potatoes, salt, pepper and water. Carrots are superfluous and spoil the delicate flavour, though in Ireland they are sometimes served with the stew as a separate vegetable.

In Edwardian England, Irish Stew laced with mushrooms and oysters was sometimes served at shooting parties and on similar occasions, and was considered to go well with a good claret. It is not necessarily any better than the classic dish.

Alfred Suzanne, one time chef at Woburn Abbey to a 19th century Duke of Bedford, often wrote somewhat off-handedly about our cooking but even he was enthusiastic about *Ragoût irlandais*, which 'makes a fine entrée which we French will like as a change.'

'Take a neck of mutton (lamb) and cut it into pieces as for a stew. Put the meat into a pot with 3 or 4 onions and 10 potatoes, all sliced thin. Season with salt and a generous amount of pepper, cover with cold water and cook 2 hours. When cooked the liquid will be thickened by the crumbled potatoes. Serve it as it is.

'To make a richer dish add some small potatoes half an hour before serving; these will stay whole while the other potatoes thicken the sauce. Sprinkle it with chopped parsley and pepper the sauce heavily before serving.'

Scrag end of venison makes a very good stew on these lines also.

Mutton

A boiled leg of mutton with caper sauce and mashed turnips is an old fashioned dish still popular in East Anglia, well worth reviving, but perhaps seen more often now in pubs than in private houses. It was a leg of mutton with caper sauce with which Sam Weller was regaled when he dined with the Bath footmen.

In Scotland they sometimes simmer a gigot (or leg) of mutton in milk. In Norfolk they used to boil it, most succulently in a suet crust which was removed before serving having fulfilled its purpose – to keep all the aroma and flavour in the meat.

Modern farming policies have now made mutton almost a thing of the past in Britain, for it is uneconomic to feed the animals to a mature age. Now rare in London and the South of England mutton is sometimes obtainable from country butchers and is in fact preferred to lamb in some districts, but unless well and properly hung it may be tough. Some butchers, perhaps because they cannot be bothered with these subtleties, say there is no demand for it nowadays. It can occasionally be had in Wales between October and Christmas, if ordered, and is still prized very rightly in Scotland.

It was once one of the glories of British cooking. Connoisseurs maintain that a roasted saddle of Scotch or Welsh mutton – with its rich gamey flavour and shortness of texture – is a great delicacy which may be served with the most subtle clarets.

'Mutton, roasted and basted with port is out of this world . . .', as Alice B. Toklas wrote about 30 years ago. Mrs. Hannah Glasse, whose *The Art of Cookery made Plain and Easy* was published in 1747, used to marinade a "hand of mutton" (or shoulder) in red wine. It was then spit roasted and basted with the marinade. In prime mutton, the fat should be hard, white and waxy, not in the least yellow, and the lean firm and close textured.

Smoked salted mutton hams are a speciality of Cumberland and Westmorland now almost forgotten, though they were prepared on farms during the present century. They are not unlike the smoked mutton hams so popular in Norway. There the hams are carved into thin almost transparent slices like the better known *viande séchée* of the Swiss Canton du Valais. It is very good when eaten with farmhouse bread and small glasses of ice cold "snaps" or of Akvavit. Mutton hams were prepared in Wales too a hundred years ago, earlier still there appears to have been Sheep Bacon which was sliced in rashers. 'It don't eat well boiled, but it eats finely broiled' Mrs. Glasse wrote in 1747 when commending it to sea captains.

A Boiled Leg of Mutton or Lamb, with Caper Sauce
Trim any excess fat off the leg and put it in a large pan almost covering it with cold water. A fish kettle or a jam pan are often useful for cooking these large pieces of meat. Bring the water to the boil gently, skim, and then let it simmer, just bubbling quietly, for 2 hours, or longer depending on the size and quality of the joint. After the first hour add 6 carrots cut in chunks, 6 medium onions peeled and sliced, 2 parsnips peeled and chopped and 3 small swede turnips similarly prepared. Add a little salt and pepper, let it cook for a further hour, or longer until tender.

If available, and if there is enough room in the pan, some beef or lamb bones may be added to cook with the meat. These will not only improve its flavour but make an excellent stock from the pot liquor.

The joint should be served with rich and creamy Caper Sauce (see page 116) and garnished with mashed buttered swede turnips, a dish popularly known in Scotland as Neep Purry. Sometimes turnips and potatoes which have been cooked separately are well drained, mashed, then mixed together, and heated with butter, salt and plenty of black pepper. This dish is known in Wales as Stwns and in the Orkneys as Clapshot. It eats well with roast par-boiled mutton.

A Gigot (or Leg) of Mutton Simmered in Milk (*Scotland*)
Put the leg of lamb or mutton in a large pan, pour 1 pint or more

of milk over it to come three quarters of the way up. Add a little salt and pepper and a pot posy or bunch of herbs tied together with cotton. Add 1 peeled sliced onion and 1 large peeled sliced carrot. Bring it to the boil and let it simmer for 2–3 hours with a lid on the pan, the exact time depending on the quality of the meat. This simmering must be done very gently as otherwise the milk burns and may also curdle. This curdling will not affect the flavour but may alter the appearance of the sauce. Add more milk during cooking if necessary.

When cooked remove the gigot from the pan and place it on a hot dish, or ashet, either whole or carved in slices. Make a thick Onion Sauce (see page 127) from the strained pan liquor and pour it over the meat, which may be served hot or cold. Two tablespoons of capers may be added to the sauce if liked.

A Leg of Mutton, Boiled in a Suet Crust

Wipe the leg of mutton or lamb with a clean cloth and sprinkle it with salt. Make about $1\frac{1}{2}$ lb of suet crust pastry, depending on the size of the joint and using half as much suet as self-raising flour. Roll it out when mixed on a floured board, place the leg of mutton on top, fold the pastry round it. Moisten and pinch the edges together so the pastry covers it like a parcel. Tie it firmly in a floured cloth to cover it completely and put it in a pan of very hot water. Let it simmer, bubbling gently, for about 4 hours, exact time depending on the size. When the meat is cooked, remove and discard the crust before serving. A 19th century Norfolk recipe. The pot liquor makes the basis of superb soup. Samphire Sauce (see page 133) is sometimes served with the meat.

Pork

Sunday lunch is a time for the best dinner service, old friends and relatives, hot apple dumplings or hand-made rice pudding served with treacle tart and thick yellow cream. It can be a most elegant way to entertain your friends, quite formal in that correct English way with just the right bulky tweeds and well clipped conversation.

Think of roast pork with the crackling and Mrs. Glasse's Bread and Wine Sauce (see page 115) round a large polished table. Three or four garden vegetables, home made bread.

Roast Bladebone of Pork

Pork cooked abroad is usually without any crackling at all. The rind and most of the fat is cut off to tie round leaner joints, but crackling is a British delicacy which I personally enjoy very much. And I wouldn't bother with any stuffing. A bladebone or an English sparerib of pork both from the front end of the animal makes a nice little joint, not too expensive. Though sparerib hasn't as much crackling as a bladebone, it roasts well and is very popular in the Midlands. Don't confuse it with the American cut of the same name, which is from a very different part of the pig and is just the pared down ends of cutlet bones used in Chinese cooking.

Of course the rind must be scored by the butcher before roasting or you will not be able to carve it when it is cooked. If well and deeply scored, the fat runs down and bastes the meat in cooking. Rub the scored crackling well with salt to make it crisp. Roast the joint 25 minutes per lb and 25 minutes over in a pre-heated, fairly hot oven (375°F, 190°C, Mark 5). If it weighs less than 3 lb allow 25 minutes per lb and 40 minutes over.

Put in the potatoes to roast during the last 40—50 minutes. I usually part boil them first then roll them in seasoned flour and put them in the meat dish. Baste them with the juices and fat; it makes them more crunchy.

Boiled Hand of Pickled Pork

A delicate old fashioned dish. The so-called hand or front leg of pork is lightly salted in brine by the butcher, and is often very good value. When hot it is usually eaten with Pease Pudding (see page 186) – a dish so popular in Northumberland and Durham it is usually described as "the national dish of the North East".

Some families have the joint cut in two and roast the top part and boil the hock and shank end. It can also be boiled when unsalted.

Put the joint in a pan with cold water to cover, bring it to the boil skimming off any rising scum. Let it simmer bubbling gently 15 minutes per lb and 20 minutes over. If it boils fast the knuckle end may fall to pieces before the middle of the leg is done. Add 8 oz of peeled sliced onions, 1 lb of peeled sliced turnips or parsnips, 12 peppercorns, mixed herbs. Turn the meat over at half time and serve it with the vegetables arranged round about it.

If there is no pease pudding the boiled pickled pork might be served with dried butter beans or haricot beans. They are excellent when cooked, drained, and eaten with plenty of butter, some chopped parsley, and, if liked, crushed garlic. Alternatively Pantry Butter (see page 116) might be added to them.

A sauce boat of the pork broth and one of thick onion sauce are often served separately. No potatoes are necessary.

Pease pudding, let down with the liquor in which the meat was cooked, and garnished with a little chopped pork, makes excellent soup.

Pig's Fry

This is very popular in East Anglia, a delicacy not nearly well enough known elsewhere. In big cities it is often difficult to buy all the bits and pieces for this excellent dish.

Traditionally it consists of pig's kidney, liver, heart, some pork belly and melt all cut up in small pieces. The proportions vary locally as do the cooking methods.

Put it all in a roasting tin with sliced onions, salt, pepper and a little pork dripping and bake it in a moderate oven (350°F,

180°C, Mark 4). When tender, pour off some of the fat. Add ¼
pint of stock and ¼ pint of milk, return to the oven. Thicken
it with 1 heaped dessertspoon of cornflour mixed to a paste in a
couple of spoonsful of milk.

Serve with mashed potato, cabbage and **Lincolnshire Sage
and Onions**: whole peeled onions boiled in salted water for about
35 minutes then drained and served with a lump of butter and
chopped sage on top.

Faggots

This is a popular country dish all over Britain, recipes vary in
different parts of the country. Some scholars say the dish goes
back to Roman times, though the use of caul or flead fat suggests
an even earlier date. Excellent faggots or the very similar haslet
and savoury ducks can often be obtained from country
butchers.

Chop 1 lb of pig's fry and some extra pig's liver in little chunks.
Put it in a pan with cold water to cover and 4 oz of peeled sliced
onions. Bring it gently to the boil and simmer till cooked. When
cool mince the meat and onions. Keep the pot liquor for gravy.
Add pepper, salt and chopped sage to the meat together with
enough white breadcrumbs to make a good — not too wet —
mixture. Stir well.

Take some flead or caul fat, this is the lacey fat from near the
kidneys sometimes called leaf or veiling in different parts of the
country. Put it in a bowl of warm water for several minutes and
then pull out pieces to wrap each faggot in. Form the mixture
into small cakes or neat balls with floured hands, covering each
with a piece of flead fat. Pack them closely in a greased baking
tin. Bake them in a moderate oven (350°F, 180°C, Mark 4) for
about 45 minutes.

They are very good cold but delicious hot with mashed potatoes and gravy. Make this from the pot liquor and a little cold tea,
thickened with a spoonful of flour fried till brown in a little
dripping.

Welsh Ffagods

Mince 1 lb of pigs' liver with 1 lb of peeled onions, 1 lb of peeled

103

and cored cooking apples and 1 lb of soft white breadcrumbs, adding 4 oz of beef suet. Season the mixture well with salt, pepper and chopped sage, mixing well. Form it into little balls and place in a greased baking tin with a little water. Place a piece of caul or flead fat on each. If unavailable use a small knob of butter.

Bake them in a moderate oven (350°F, 180°C, Mark 4).

Brawn

Brawn is one of those things with a downbeat image. Few people make it now, probably because commercial brawn is frequently so awful with unmentionable scraps of meat embedded in a uniform pink jelly. Yet a well made brawn can be just as good as the most exquisite coarse cut farmhouse pâté. It is excellent thinly sliced and served for "starters" with oil, lemon juice and chopped parsley on it. It was a mainstay of Edwardian country house breakfasts. Lancashire farmhouse brawn is made with half a pig's head, usually a bargain, even today.

Ask the butcher to prepare and saw a half head in chunks which will fit in a large saucepan. Add water to cover, a good pinch of nutmeg, 6 cloves, 2 bayleaves, 12 peppercorns and a strip of lemon peel. (No salt if it has been pickled by the butcher.) Bring it to the boil and simmer gently for 4 hours or until the meat slips easily off the bone. In Lancashire the pig's tongue and heart are cooked with it and chopped and mixed with the other meat. Chop some in chunks, throwing away any off beat or gristly bits. Mince the rest. Put it back in the strained stock with $\frac{1}{4}$ pint of vinegar. Boil it up and pour it into basins. When cold it sets in a jelly.

Bath Chaps

Usually sold egged, crumbed and cooked they are made from a smoked and salted pig's cheek and were a delicacy sold in Bath when it was a fashionable spa in the 18th century. In those days the Gloucester Old Spot or local long-jawed pig which grazed in the apple orchards was the one prepared like this. Some grocers also sell Suffolk Sweet Cured Chaps and Bradenham Chaps, uncooked. In Yorkshire and Lincolnshire cold roasted pork chaps (neither smoked nor salted) are offered for sale. A similar cut is called a "chawl" in Herefordshire.

Pork Cheese

This is very popular round Cambridge and in Norfolk. It is especially good sliced when set and served with Yorkshire Mustard Sauce (see page 138) as noted in Elizabethan England. It is usually made with a hock of salt pork, the lower half of the front leg lightly pickled in brine by the butcher and always sold with the pig's foot. Put a hock or knuckle of pork in a pan with pepper, herbs and salt if liked. Add just enough water to cover it. Bring it to the boil and simmer for 2 hours or until the meat is dropping off the bone. Cut up all the meat and fat and everything. Place it in basins and strain the liquor over it. Let it set.

Pork Pies

Pork pies are a speciality of the old hunting shires, Northampton-shire, Leicestershire and Rutland, where most pork butchers and many bakers sell excellent raised pork pies made on the premises. The Melton Mowbray pie so much liked by Victorian sportsmen contains anchovy as well as pork (as did numerous 18th century English meat dishes). This makes it bright pink inside while most pork pies are brownish or greyish. In Cheshire one sees rows of very pale highly seasoned, straight-sided pork pies in the butchers' shops. They have a hard ivory-coloured crust delicately browned at the top. In Lincolnshire they are very different; dark brown with more crumbly pastry. These are raised by hand and, instead of being straight-sided, slope in sharply at the top, are almost dome-shaped, with a very small lid about quarter the size of the base.

This kind of pie is always eaten cold and has been popular at football matches and in country markets for generations, prob-ably since Simple Simon's day. There is no pie dish, the meat is enclosed completely in hot water crust pastry. This is sometimes moulded round a large jam jar (afterwards removed), or some-times used to line a baking tin, but sometimes it is "raised by hand" or moulded, hot, into a pie shape rather as if one were shaping clay for pottery.

In the 18th century the pie fillings were often very elaborate; game, poultry, truffles, wine and various spices were used, as in the very similar French *pâté en croûte* which has survived till the present day. Regency cookery books contain so many elaborate raised pie fillings, many of them excellent, that they must have been very fashionable, appearing on the long table at the ball suppers and rout suppers which were a feature of the period.

It is mixed with warm liquid – quickly – and the pastry must still be warm so you can mould or "raise" it into a pie shape. If the pastry is *very* hot it will be soft floppy and might collapse. If the pastry is very cold it will be difficult to handle without breaking it.

Sift 1 lb of flour and a pinch of salt into a bowl. Make a hollow in the middle. Heat 5 oz of lard or butter and $\frac{1}{4}$ pint of water or milk in a pan. When boiling remove from the heat. Pour it into the flour, mix it up quickly (in a warm place). Knead it gently, let it stand in a warm place for about 30 minutes to recover. Now roll it out gently on a floured pastry board. Mould or raise it into a pie.

A Raised Pork Pie
Chop $1\frac{1}{2}$ lb of pork, season it with salt, pepper, $\frac{1}{2}$ teaspoon of English mustard powder and $\frac{1}{2}$ teaspoon of allspice.

Grease a loose-bottomed 7 inch cake tin and line it with about three quarters of the hot water crust pastry, quickly before the lard has time to set and make it brittle. Keep the rest warm under a cloth. Fill it with seasoned pork, alternate layers of fat and lean, pressing it down well. Add 2 tablespoons of water. Put on a pastry "lid", damping the edges and pinching them together to seal it. Make a hole in the middle. (Decorate the top, if liked, with pastry roses and leaves or tassels. Brush it with beaten egg yolk. Bake it in a moderate oven (350°F, 180°C, Mark 4) for $1\frac{1}{2}$–2 hours.

Make up $\frac{1}{4}$ pint of aspic jelly, or have ready some jellying stock, just melted but not hot, when the pie has been taken out of the oven and cooled pour it through the hole in the top, using a funnel. Allow the pie to get cold before taking it out of the tin.

Sausages

'You've only got to say sausages', as George Robey the comedian once remarked, 'and people laugh. It's the funniest word in the English language.' Country butchers usually make excellent coarse cut sausages on the premises, spicier and meatier than the manufactured ones, sometimes to secret recipes and customers often travel miles to get them.

Tastes vary from town to town and county to county. Lincolnshire sausages are usually flavoured with sage and onions, in Yorkshire they make a thick cut tomato flavoured pork sausage, but in the West Country sausages are often made from beef and pork mixed. Traditional Cumberland sausages are made, not in links, but in one long piece which may be coiled, nautically like a rope or festooned above the butcher's counter, while in Birmingham there is a near white sausage minced so fine that it is almost a paste; we do not traditionally produce those hard dry slicing sausages so popular on the Continent though nowadays even these are made here in small quantities. The white puddings, black puddings, and mealy puddings sold in pork butchers' shops up and down the country are often exquisite. The ordinary sausage should be pricked with a fork before cooking to prevent the skin from bursting, and is then mostly fried or baked in the oven.

The Dublin Coddle

The famous Dublin Coddle used to be popular for breakfast, lunch or supper in Ireland and it is said Dean Swift used to eat it in the deanery of St Patrick's Cathedral in Dublin 250 years ago.

Simply put some sausages, sliced onions, peeled potatoes, bacon rashers, bacon bones, pepper, salt and water or stock in a pot and simmer until it is cooked in about 40 minutes. Exact quantities depend on what is available.

Sausages in Milk

Sausages and onions simmered in milk with potatoes are popular in East Anglia, an excellent regional dish which does appear however, very occasionally in other parts of the country as "Friday Pie". The recipe does not appear in any cookery book

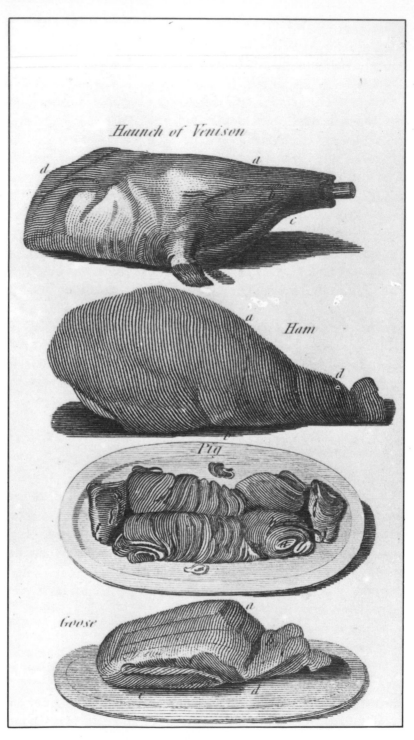

Haunch of Venison

Ham

Pig

Goose

ever seen by me though Eliza Acton did note in 1845 that: 'In Lincolnshire sausages are frequently boiled in the skins and served upon toast as a corner dish.' She did not explain however whether or not they were boiled in milk.

Put 2 lb of coarse cut country sausages in a pan, having first pricked them with a fork. Add two Spanish onions peeled and cut in large chunks, three or four large peeled and quartered potatoes. Add milk to cover. Bring it almost to the boil and let it all simmer very gently for about 40 minutes until the meat and vegetables are cooked. The sausages and onion will flavour the broth while the partially disintegrated potato will thicken it into a rich sauce. Too rapid cooking sometimes causes the milk to curdle slightly, it does not affect the flavour but if liked a little cornflour may be mixed to a smooth paste with a spoonful of milk, stirred into the sauce and heated in it briefly. This will thicken it and remove the curdling. Fine textured manufactured sausages are unsuitable for this lovely dish.

Ham and Gammon

The world famous York hams weigh 16–24 lb, are cured with dry salt and lightly smoked for eventual boiling, unlike some famous foreign hams which are sliced very thin and eaten raw, like smoked salmon. York ham has a rather long shape being cut off the flitch near the oyster bone and rounded off; prized in its home country at ham teas, perhaps with a little apple pie and cheese for "afters". Not all those labelled York ham, however, are the real thing.

The Suffolk sweet cured hams which once hung in every farmhouse in the county are pickled in beer and sugar and have a deep golden toasted looking skin, though nowadays they are not necessarily done locally. Fifty or sixty years ago most Suffolk villagers kept their own pigs and made a fine art of curing the bacon steeping it in old ale and smoking it over sawdust.

Most families then had a large earthenware pot glazed inside in which the pork was cured, first in salt then in the local sweet pickle. The fresh pork was dry salted (rubbed with salt and saltpetre) and left in the ham pot for a week, then wiped. They then rinsed out the pot and put the ham in a pickle, for instance 2 lb of dark brown sugar, 2 lb of black treacle and a quart of hot stout or porter which was poured over them. Once in the pot the ham was rubbed with stout and treacle and left there, weighted down with a stone, for about six weeks. It was then sent off to be dried in the "smoky house". This often belonged to the local joiner and undertaker who thus had a way of using up all his sawdust, wood shavings and oak chips. The sawdust was damped to make it smoke and the ham hung there about three weeks.

Bradenham hams have a coal-black skin and are dark red rather than pink inside, they weigh 14—16 lb and are cured in a similar way. Once a speciality of the Buckinghamshire village of Bradenham they are nowadays prepared elsewhere and are scarce and expensive.

Some ham cures contain mustard and red pepper. The delicate Cumberland hams are rubbed with brown sugar. Limerick hams are dry-salted and used to be smoked over peat and the wild juniper which grows locally.

A gammon is cut square at the top, unlike a ham, and is cheaper and coarser. Unlike a ham it is cured with the whole side of bacon, in brine, then cut from the carcase after brining. It weighs 12—14 lb but is often sold cut in little joints. In Scotland they sell it boned, rolled and tied, when it is called an Ayrshire gigot. Wiltshire ham is cured on the side of bacon and is really gammon, not ham. Small, mild and long-cut it is relatively cheap but does not keep so well as other ham.

The delicious little Belfast hams are still dry-salted, and smoked in the old way over peat, but they are, curiously enough, only sold now in the West of Scotland. They need to be soaked in cold water for two or three days before boiling.

Of course the flavour of a ham depended on how the pig was fed as well as how it was cured, whether in apple orchards or on acorns or the family pigs' swill. At one time hams used to be boiled in brewers' wort, a sweetish pleasant liquid which is really the malted beer before it has fermented. This is difficult to come by now, and having tried it for ham boiling I do not think it is really worth the effort.

To Boil a Ham

There are still various cures for ham and bacon traditional to different parts of Britain, though the availability of freezers has made them less popular than they were. People still talk lovingly in country pubs of the hams their father used to cure in brown ale and treacle, matured for three years before they were cut and so succulent 'when you put a knife in them you could smell the ham all over the house'. On farms a ham was often boiled in the kitchen copper, mostly with a bunch of hay in the bottom to stop it sticking to it. This gives it a faint fragrant flavour.

Since a well cured ham develops a bluish-green mould on the cut end, scrub off this "bloom" in water and detergent. Then dry it. Soak the ham for 24 hours in cold water — or longer if necessary. Ask the supplier who will tell you this.

Put it in a large pan or fish kettle with 1 quart of stout, 2 tablespoons of dark brown sugar. Add cold water to cover and a wisp of hay if possible. Bring it slowly to the boil. Then let it simmer gently for 25 minutes per lb or 20 minutes per lb for a very large ham. If boiled fiercely it will be stringy and tough.

A real ham is best eaten cold, leaving the roasts and fancy fruit toppings for the much cheaper gammon. It should be allowed to get cold in its own stock.

In the 19th century they often left part of the skin round the knuckle of the ham in a semi circular shape several inches deep. They then scalloped the edges of this or cut them in points, or in "Vandykes". This looks good on a black-skinned Bradenham ham and though now forgotten was once traditional. Sometimes the stripped off skin was cut in fanciful shapes, half moons, stars or a coronet and then fastened back on the white ham fat with the help of cloves.

Boiled Bacon

A collar or forehock, whether smoked or unsmoked, is easy to cook and serve — with onion sauce, or boiled leeks, pease pudding or dumplings. In the Fens hot boiled bacon with broad beans in parsley sauce, mashed potatoes and home made crusty bread is a traditional dish well liked that appears at many village feasts, sometimes with Norfolk Dumplings or "Twenty-minute Floaters" (see page 122). In Ireland it is mostly eaten with cabbage cooked deliciously in the bacon stock and with a side dish of potatoes boiled in their skins to peel and eat with butter.

Modern mild-cured bacon joints do not need to be soaked before cooking. Put a joint in cold water to cover, bring it to the boil, throw the water away. Cover it again with water, or half water and dry cider. Add an onion stuck with cloves, 12 pepper-corns, 2 bayleaves, a bunch of herbs. Bring it to the boil, boil it 10–15 minutes per pound and 20 minutes over.

In the pressure cooker bacon needs about a third of the normal time at 15 lb pressure and only about an inch of water. A few vegetables might be cooked with it but they will be very soft.

Roast Gammon with Crackling
Delicious with Hot Yorkshire Sauce and Season Pudding (see pages 138 and 130) and a bottle of old ale.

With a sharp knife cut a diamond pattern in the rind of a 4–5 lb piece of "green" (or unsmoked) corner gammon. If it has not been strung to keep it together, wrap it tightly in foil for the first 20 minutes in the oven.

Roast it in a moderate oven (350°F, 180°C, Mark 4) for 20 minutes per lb and 20 minutes over, basting it once or twice during cooking with old ale. When done the rind will be brown and crackling. Serve on a hot dish.

Chapter 4

Sauces, Forcemeats and Garnishes

Classic Apple Sauce
This is served of course with roast pork, duck or goose, especially when there is sage and onion stuffing.

Core three or four apples without peeling. Cut them in quarters and cover them with boiling water. Add a small piece of stick cinnamon and two cloves. Simmer until they are tender, then rub the fruit through a sieve.

Return it to the heat adding ½ cup of sugar and 1 dessertspoon of dry cider, or of sharp vinegar. Cook it, stirring, for 10 minutes and then add 1 teaspoon of butter.

Apple and Curry Sauce
Peel, core and chop 1 lb of apples, let them simmer in about ⅓ pint of British Curry Sauce (see page 121). Mash them into it when soft enough. Serve hot.

See also Mrs. Glasse's Bread and Wine Sauce (page 115).

Artichoke Sauce
When well made, then poured hot over lamb, mutton or poultry, the sauce adds greatly to the appearance of the dish. Swede turnips may be used for the sauce instead of artichokes, but they too must be peeled.

Peel enough Jerusalem artichokes to make about 1 lb when done. Drop them as they are peeled into a pan of milk to prevent discolouration. Boil them in it for 10–15 minutes, fishing them out as soon as they are soft. When overcooked they turn grey.

Mash them to a purée. Melt a knob of butter, stir in a dessertspoon of flour and gradually, heating and stirring, pour in about ¾ pint of the artichoke milk. Add the artichoke purée with salt and Cayenne pepper to your taste.

Cream may be added if liked.

Asparagus Sauce

A delicate Victorian asparagus and lemon sauce which is especially good with grilled lamb cutlets, or egged, crumbed and fried lamb chops. It is simpler to prepare than the famous Reform Club Sauce sometimes served with these, for that is a chef's sauce. If liked it can be made with the thin, wispy and inexpensive asparagus that growers call sprue grass.

Cut the tender part of 1 lb of asparagus in ½ inch lengths. Boil these in ¾ pint of stock. When tender remove and set them aside. Moisten a heaped teaspoon of cornflour or arrowroot, to make a smooth paste. Stir it into the asparagus stock. Beat up an egg with the juice of a lemon. Stir this into the warm stock adding the asparagus pieces. Heat without boiling.

Serve the sauce quickly, it soon becomes yellow.

Mrs. Beeton's Benton Sauce (1861)

For roast beef, hot or cold. 'With cold meat,' as she wrote, 'this is a very good substitute for pickles.'

Mix 1 tablespoon of very finely grated fresh horseradish with 1 teaspoon of freshly made English mustard, 1 teaspoon of sugar and 4 tablespoons of vinegar.

A Rich Victorian Bread Sauce

It is made with cream and stock, and traditionally served with roast chicken or turkey, grouse, or pheasant. Though these garnishes are bland in flavour the contrasting textures set off the flavours of well hung game, and a good claret, to perfection.

With game, freshly grated white crumbs fried crisp in butter are served too. Bill McLeod of Collins tells me he often adds a little garlic to his bread sauce, with good effect.

Soak 1 cup of white crumbs in ½ pint of stock. Add grated nutmeg, salt, pepper and when the breadcrumbs have soaked, let them simmer, stirring occasionally, until nearly all the liquid has gone. Then beat in 1 oz of butter and enough cream to make the sauce the right thickness.

Note: Cream is intended *not* milk, though tinned cream could be used in an emergency.

Mrs. Glasse's Bread and Wine Sauce (*For Roast pork*)

This is a forgotten English classic. It was once so popular, and deservedly so, that the recipe appears with variations in cookery books published 150 years later. It may, of course, pre-date Mrs. Glasse, but I found no reference to it before 1747.

'First take a large piece of bread without the crust. Boil it in 1 pint of water with a little sugar, a few currants, a blade of mace and peppercorns, drain off the water carefully. Beat up the bread to a thick sauce with a large lump of butter and a glass of red wine.'   From *The Art of Cookery Made Plain and Easy* by Mrs. Hannah Glasse, 1747.

English Butter Sauce

This old forgotten sauce is akin to the *Beurre Blanc* which is a speciality of the Loire district of France, often served there with pike. It is sometimes described, confusingly, as "Melted Butter" in old cookery books, and sometimes just as "Butter". It was so popular in the 18th and 19th centuries as often to be referred to as 'the one sauce of England', by visiting Frenchmen.

It was eaten with fish, with poultry, some meat and vegetables – much as hollandaise sauce is eaten today.

Make a *roux* (or *rue* as the old books say) by stirring 1½ dessertspoons of flour into 1½ dessertspoons of liquid butter, add ½ pint of boiling salted water all at once. Whip up the mixture rapidly with an egg whisk. Off the heat, stir in 1 tablespoon of thick hot cream.

Then strain the sauce through a muslin cloth, now gradually add 4 oz of softened butter, whisking all the time. The sauce should be smooth and the butter must not oil.

Whipped Butters

These are also very good with grilled meat or fish or hot jacket

115

potatoes. Simply whip the butter with a hot, wet spoon till light and fluffy.

Whipped Curry Butter is made by whipping 2 oz of butter to a cream and adding 1 teaspoon of curry powder, $\frac{1}{4}$ teaspoon of turmeric and 1 teaspoon of lemon juice.

Whipped Mustard Butter is similarly made by beating 2 oz of butter to a cream and adding 1 teaspoon of freshly made English mustard and 1 teaspoon of lemon juice.

Devil Butter See page 20.

Pantry Butter, also known as Maître d'Hôtel Butter, is used as a garnish on a wide variety of grills, steak as well as fish. It may be made at leisure, shaped into a roll, wrapped in foil and stored in the refrigerator. It is then simple to cut slices off as required.

Cream 2 oz of butter, add 1 teaspoon of chopped parsley and 2 teaspoons of lemon juice.

Caper Sauce

A rich and very smooth caper sauce can be made by stirring a large teaspoon of capers into $\frac{1}{2}$ pint English Butter Sauce (see page 115). It can also be made by adding the capers to an ordinary White Sauce (see page 138). It will however be much plainer than the above.

Caper Sauce is a classic with boiled lamb and mutton, and it is sometimes served with rabbit.

Cheese Sauce

Though these thick sauces may well be stirred and whipped up with a wooden spoon, the result is much smoother and better if one uses an old fashioned wire egg whisk.

Melt 2 tablespoons of butter. Stir in 2 tablespoons of flour and gradually, heating and stirring, whisk in a scant $\frac{3}{4}$ pint of hot milk. Add 3—4 oz of grated Cheddar or, better still, Lancashire cheese, a teaspoon of English mustard powder, a good pinch of ground nutmeg and a little salt and pepper.

If the sauce is intended for cauliflower, increase the amount of nutmeg.

Heat gently, stirring or whisking, until the sauce is smooth

Says Coachee to Cookey so charming you look,
Youve drove through my heart or I am mistook;
  My Horses are harnefsd let's go to the Church.
Nor leave your true lover to sigh in the lurch,
Says Cookey to Coachee, I'll down with the beef,
And hasten to give your fond heart its relief.

and thick. Off the heat, add another spoonful of butter. Do not overcook the sauce for the cheese will then become tough and stringy.

The Old Celery Sauce
This is a bland sauce, once popular with a Boiled Turkey (see page 162) and also with boiled pheasants and pigeons (these, in country houses up to the early part of the present century, were frequently served boiled). It is very good too with a braised loin of lamb.

Wash, string, and chop a large head of celery and cook it with a peeled and thinly chopped onion in stock to cover. Simmer with the lid on till tender. Drain off and keep the liquor.

Purée the onion and celery in the electric mixer (or if un-available by rubbing them through a sieve). Melt 1 tablespoon of butter, stir in 1 tablespoon of flour. Gradually add about ½ pint of the celery liquor, heating and stirring until the sauce is smooth and fairly thick. Stir in the vegetable purée (or press it through a sieve if there are any stringy bits). Heat, stirring. Taste for seasoning and add a little salt, pepper and nutmeg. Add cream if liked.

Hot Cider Sauce (*Forest of Dean*)
The sauce is still made on the Welsh border to serve with roast pork, goose 'and other meats', as they say locally. Farmhouse or scrumpy cider is used (bottled manufactured cider is too sweet for it) and when properly made the sauce has a dry, almost bitter flavour. It should not be missed. It is excellent, too, with a baked ham, though I have never seen it in any cookery book.

Melt 1 tablespoon of butter, stir in 1 tablespoon of flour, then, heating and stirring, gradually add ½ pint of draught farmhouse cider. Taste for seasoning, adding salt and pepper when the sauce is smooth and thick.

Cockle Sauce
This used to be made as a garnish for boiled cod, and for that Victorian favourite, a boiled cod's head and shoulders, but it was

also served with large grilled rumpsteaks. It is delicious with them. The cockles should be freshly cooked ones; those sold in vinegar or a salty pickle are unsuitable. Oysters may be substituted if available.

Mix ¼ pint of freshly cooked shelled cockles with 1 pint of White Sauce (see page 138) made with the strained cockle liquor instead of with milk.

Or, if preferred, mix ¼ pint of freshly cooked shelled cockles with Melted Butter Sauce (see Hot Crab Sauce below) adding a teaspoon of lemon juice, to your taste, and salt and pepper as required.

Hot Crab Sauce
It is similar to the lobster sauce served so frequently with poached turbot in the 19th century. It dates from the same period and is excellent with brill, turbot or salmon. This is a version of the sauce given by Eliza Acton in *Modern Cookery for Private Families*, 1845.

Make a **Melted Butter Sauce** by mixing 1 dessertspoon of flour, ½ teaspoon of salt gradually with ½ pint of cold water in a pan, with 4—6 oz of butter cut in bits, to make a sort of smooth batter. Shake the sauce strongly round almost without stopping, over heat, until the ingredients are perfectly mixed and on the point of boiling. (Nowadays some cooks prefer a piano wire balloon shaped whisk, or hand held electric whisk.)

Let the sauce stand for 2 or 3 minutes, add 1 teaspoon of freshly grated nutmeg and a pinch of Cayenne pepper. Then stir in 2 tablespoons of cream, if available.

Take a moderate sized cooked crab and, having divided the white flesh into small flakes, add this to the sauce having first incorporated some of the creamy part.

Note: **Shrimp Sauce:** This was similarly made and was once served, deliciously, with grilled rumpsteaks and elegantly fried fillet steaks as well as with the more aristocratic fish. It is well worth reviving.

'Shell quickly one pint of shrimps,' as Eliza Acton says, 'and mix them with half a pint of melted butter [as above], to which a few drops of essence of anchovies and a little mace and Cayenne have been added. As soon as the shrimps are heated through, dish and serve the sauce, which ought not to boil after they are put in. Many persons add a few spoonsful of rich cream to all shell-fish sauces.'

A Cream Sauce
An Edwardian sauce, flavoured faintly with tarragon to be served with hot boiled asparagus, grilled salmon or Dover sole.

Beat up three egg yolks lightly, then beat in 3 tablespoons of thick cream. Add a little salt and white pepper, and heat, stirring all the time, in the top of a double saucepan, until the sauce is thick enough to coat the back of a spoon. Do not cease stirring whilst heating it, nor let it boil, as it would then curdle. Stir in a little tarragon vinegar, to suit your taste, just before serving.

Brown Cucumber Sauce *(For roast lamb and mutton)*
Dice a peeled onion and a peeled cucumber, then roll them in seasoned flour. Fry them very, very gently in 1½ oz of butter, stirring occasionally, but putting a lid on the pan and taking about 15 minutes. The vegetables should melt into a purée, rather than brown. Then stir in about ½ pint of good stock and add a spoonful of mild vinegar just before serving.

White Cucumber Sauce
This is very good not only with gigot steaks and roast lamb but with salmon and sea trout, or with boiled bacon.

Peel and chop a cucumber in one inch lengths and boil these chunks for about 15 minutes in stock, just to cover. Press it through a sieve. Add the cooking stock and stir in the yolk of an egg beaten up with the juice of half a lemon. Heat the sauce, stirring, but do not let it boil, as the egg would scramble and curdle your sauce.

Cumberland Sauce
This sauce is especially good with cold venison
Melt 4 tablespoons of red currant jelly, add 6 tablespoons of port wine, ½ tablespoon of finely chopped shallot (previously plunged

momentarily in boiling water, then squeezed dry in a cloth), 1 tablespoon of grated orange rind and the same of lemon rind, add the juice of the orange and the juice of half a lemon.

Stir in 1 dessertspoon of dry powdered mustard, with ½ teaspoon of ground ginger and a dash of Cayenne pepper.

This is Escoffier's recipe, the sauce will keep for some time in a covered jar in the refrigerator.

British Curry Sauce
Melt 1 oz of butter in a saucepan. Add a peeled very finely chopped onion and cook gently stirring occasionally until it is soft and golden. Add a tablespoon of curry powder, stir and let it simmer for a couple of minutes. Then add a tablespoon of flour. Cook for a few minutes to brown it lightly. Then, heating gently and stirring, add about ¾ pint of water or stock. Bring it to the boil and simmer for 15–20 minutes stirring occasionally. Add salt.

Dumplings
Boiled meat or currant dumplings used to be cooked in cotton bags in large copper pans and then sold at a halfpenny each in the streets of London a hundred years ago, "Dumplin's, all 'ot" being a familiar street cry. The so-called **Sussex or Hard Dumplings** made with suet, are served with roast or boiled meat and often cooked in the broth with the latter. They are as good with a thick rib-sticking oxcheek stew as with jugged hare or boiled beef and carrots. Little dumplings are also good in soup, especially if chopped parsley, fried onion or crisp fried diced bacon are added to the suet pastry mixture before the little dumplings are rolled out.

Mix 3 oz of plain flour, 1 teaspoon of baking powder and a pinch of salt. Stir in 3 oz of soft white breadcrumbs and 3 oz of shredded suet but do not try to rub in the suet as when making ordinary pastry. Add enough water to mix it to a firm paste which leaves the bowl perfectly clean. Add a little chopped parsley if liked, or finely diced bacon, fried till crisp, or chopped fried onions. Then form it into small balls with floury hands, without delay. Drop these into a pan of boiling water or stock, or into the

121

pan in which the salt beef, etc., is boiling. Cover them with a lid and let them boil for 15 minutes undisturbed, if the lid is lifted at the beginning they will be heavy.

Norfolk Dumplings

These are very popular in East Anglia with pig's fry, jugged hare, and stewed steak. They are unusual in being made from bread dough, which may be made at home or bought, uncooked, from the baker.

Form the bread dough into dumplings and let them prove for 30–40 minutes. Then drop them into a pan of gently boiling salted water, and let them poach for 20 minutes. Turn them over after 10 minutes. When ready, they should be drained and served at once, or they become heavy.

In Norfolk and Suffolk these dumplings are popularly known as "Twenty-minute Floaters". Some eat them with butter or brown gravy.

Fried Forcemeat Balls

To serve as a garnish for roast veal and chicken and turkey, flanked by crisp bacon rolls and chipolata sausages
This is the classic lemon and parsley stuffing, or forcemeat, so often used as a stuffing for veal and poultry (as well as for force-meat balls) that it is sometimes known as **Veal Forcemeat.**

Mix 4 oz of soft white breadcrumbs with $1\frac{1}{2}$ oz of butter, the grated rind of half a lemon and 1 heaped dessertspoon of chopped parsley. Add salt and pepper and then stir in a lightly beaten egg to bind the mixture together. When well mixed form it into little balls and fry them in butter or poultry fat. Serve hot as a garnish round the hot roast bird.

This forcemeat may also be used to stuff the crop of the bird. See also Lemon and Parsley Forcemeat (page 124).

Sometimes suet dumplings are served instead of Forcemeat Balls with jugged hare.

The Old Gooseberry, or Rhubarb, Sauce

This was once served with a roast duck or a roast gosling, as well as with pork and with poached or fried mackerel. Rhubarb sauce was made in the same way and used for the same purpose, principally to serve in spring as soon as the apple crop was finished.

There is also a North Country store sauce which is made with gooseberries.

Wash 2 lb of gooseberries but do not trouble to remove the stalks and snouts. Just simmer them with a little beer and 8 oz of Demerara sugar – either in the oven or in the top of a double saucepan with hot water in the pan below – until they are soft enough to rub through a sieve. After sieving, gradually stir $1\frac{1}{2}$ tablespoons of butter into your gooseberry purée.

Sauce for Grilled Game (*Susan, Duchess of Somerset*)
'One tablespoon of mustard, one tablespoonful of salad oil, a little Harvey's sauce, cayenne pepper and salt to taste. Mix all together, and baste the game and grill it again. Then add the remains of the sauce with a little grease.'

Hanover Sauce
A delicious 18th-century sauce for poultry which may be served with a roast capon (or turkey) blistered with raspings.*

Poach the turkey liver or chicken liver for 3 or 4 minutes in $\frac{1}{2}$ pint of stock made from the giblets, or from water and a bouillon cube. Dice the thinly peeled rind of a lemon, mince or chop the liver as finely as possible.

Melt $1\frac{1}{2}$ tablespoons of butter in a pan, stir in 1 tablespoon of flour then, gradually, add the stock heating and stirring. Taste the sauce and season it with salt, pepper and grated nutmeg. Then add the chicken liver, or turkey liver, together with the lemon peel and the juice of the lemon.

* Raspings is the old name for breadcrumbs (stale and rasped, or grated, from a loaf). To blister with raspings is to baste, say a bird, with breadcrumbs and melted butter or fat shortly before it is served. It gives a crisp brown finish. "Frothing" with flour was a similar device. Blistering with raspings is a practice which seems to have died out in the first part of the 19th century, so the name too is forgotten.

123

Horseradish Sauce
This is served with a roast sirloin of beef, whether hot or cold, and with smoked mackerel, hot boiled ox tongue.

Freshly grated horseradish makes incomparably better sauce than the bottled kind, though to peel and grate it makes the eyes water. It is easy to grow and can often be found half wild on patches of waste land. If grated straight across the stalk it does not become stringy.

Mix 2 tablespoons of fresh grated horseradish with salt and pepper and ¼ pint thick stiffly whipped cream. Chill or ice it.

If liked, 2 tablespoons of freshly grated horseradish may be mixed with 1 tablespoon of chopped walnuts, add a piece of white bread soaked in milk and squeezed out, salt, pepper, a dash of lemon juice. Stir in ¼ pint of thick unwhipped cream. Chill.

The Irby Devil
'To be warmed up and used as a sauce for grilled chicken legs.' Make some bread sauce, and when it is cold stir in 1 tablespoon of made English mustard, 1 tablespoon of French mustard and a little butter. Add a teaspoonful each of black pepper, Harvey's sauce, Worcester sauce and anchovy sauce. Serve hot.

This is an old family recipe of Miss Irby of the Taplow and Hitcham Women's Institute, which was given in the 1933 edition of the *Buckinghamshire W.I. Cook Book*.

Welsh Laver Sauce
Laver Sauce is served with boiled salt duckling. Use an aluminium not an iron pan, and a silver fork or spoon, or a wooden spoon to stir it. Cook it gently, since the laver sticks when too fiercely heated.

Heat ½ pint of laver bread with the juice and grated rind of a Seville orange and a little butter, cover the pan and let it simmer over a low heat.

Lemon and Parsley Forcemeat
Mix 6 oz of soft white breadcrumbs with the grated rind of half a lemon, a pinch of freshly grated nutmeg, salt and pepper to

your taste, and 2 tablespoons of freshly chopped parsley. Add 4 oz shredded suet, 3 oz finely diced lean bacon and 2 beaten eggs, these are to bind the forcemeat. Mix well.

If a very fine forcemeat is wanted it could be puréed in the electric mixer.

This forcemeat is very good when rolled into balls the size of a walnut, rolled in flour and then fried in butter. They make a delicious garnish for roast turkey or chicken or for a rabbit stew. The forcemeat balls could alternatively be baked in a moderate oven (350°F, 180°C, Mark 4) for about an hour. They freeze well when uncooked. Open freeze, then pack in bags.

Mayonnaise
Cream an egg yolk in a pudding basin with a pinch of salt and pepper, using a wooden spoon. Pour ½ pint of oil into a jug and add it drop by drop at first, beating all the time, as the Mayonnaise goes pale and begins to thicken it can be added more rapidly. At first a very thin trickle but fairly rapidly towards the end until all the oil is absorbed.

The ingredients of Mayonnaise should all be at room temperature including the basin, do not refrigerate any of them, ever. Ground nut oil makes differently flavoured Mayonnaise from olive oil, some cooks use a mixture of both.

Add lemon juice when the sauce thickens, to sharpen the taste and thin it if necessary. If the Mayonnaise curdles (usually because the oil was added too fast) put an egg yolk in another basin and gradually beat the curdled mixture into it. It will right itself.

Curry Mayonnaise
Stir 2 teaspoons of curry powder very gradually into a classic Mayonnaise, tasting it as you do so for the strength of curry flavour required, it should be a mild sauce with just a faint prickle.

Gin Mayonnaise
A little shot of gin stirred into Mayonnaise at the end is very good and makes the Mayonnaise very light.

Melba Sauce

This classic sauce is much easier to make now than it was in Escoffier's day. It is excellent with ice cream and very many cold puddings, with Burnt Cream for instance.

Put 8 oz of fresh raspberries, or of frozen raspberries (frozen without sugar) into the blender part of the electric mixer. Add 4 to 5 tablespoons of caster sugar, or of sifted icing sugar. Blend for 5 to 10 seconds until it is quite liquid. Then rub the sauce through a nylon sieve to get rid of any tiny pieces of pip that remain. The sauce becomes quite thick, and if left it may set in a jelly. If liked, it could then be diluted with 1 tablespoon of cold water.

Mint Sauce

Best made by chopping a little bunch of fresh mint leaves lightly sprinkled with sugar. Add vinegar diluted with a little water, sugar, salt and pepper to your taste.

Inspector Tweedie's Mushroom Sauce

Inspector Tweedie is an R.S.P.C.A. inspector whom I once encountered in a country cattle market. His mushrooms stewed in butter and milk form a black and flavoursome dish half way between a sauce and a vegetable, and are delicious. Very good with a dinner of boiled bacon, leeks and boiled celery.

Put 8 oz of mushrooms in a pan with $\frac{1}{2}$ pint of milk and 1 tablespoon of butter. Add pepper, salt and a good pinch of curry powder. Now let them simmer for about half an hour, suddenly all the milk disappears and goes black from the luscious juices running out of the mushrooms. One must watch them and stir them continually for they soon burn.

Mustard

English mustard is hotter and fiercer than the Continental kind. and although ready mixed English mustard is now sold, traditionally mustard comes in the familiar yellow powder in a familiar yellow tin. It is then mixed to a paste with cold water or with thick cream before it is eaten.

In Shakespeare's day most English mustard was grown round

Tewkesbury in Gloucestershire, the seeds being ground coarsely with a pestle and mortar or, according to some authorities, between old second hand cannon balls. The texture may well have been similar to that of the now fashionable French *moutarde de Meaux* which is sold in large earthenware jars containing uncrushed or partly crushed mustard seeds embedded in a more conventional mustard paste.

'His wits,' Falstaff said of a contemporary, 'are as thick as Tewkesbury mustard.' The Tewkesbury mustard made today has horseradish in it.

At the beginning of the 18th century a Mrs. Clements of Durham found a way of making 'better looking and finer ground' mustard powder than had been done before. She set up in business in Durham in 1710 and rapidly became famous. Her mustard was very popular with King George I (the Georgie Porgie pudding and pie of the nursery rhyme) and Durham was famous as a mustard centre for over a hundred years. Then, at the beginning of the 19th century, a young miller named Jonathan Coleman began experimenting with mustard seeds in Norfolk, was successful and the bulk of English mustard has been made there ever since.

English mustard, mixed with cream or water, is a classic with underdone roast beef or York ham, it is stirred into the cheese for a Welsh rabbit and usually found in buttered bloaters. Cold underdone beef sandwiched in brown bread and butter with freshly mixed English mustard spread on it is an experience not to be missed.

For Mustard Sauce: Make an ordinary white sauce but whisk in some dry mustard powder at the same time as the flour and before adding the stock or milk, in quantities to your liking.

Onion Sauce
This is a classic British sauce which is served with a boiled or roast leg of mutton. It is especially delicious with the latter. In the 18th century it was popular with a boiled rabbit and it is still correctly served with the traditional Welsh Salted Duck.

Mince or grate 2 lb of peeled onions. Then stew them gently

over a low heat in 3 oz of butter with a lid on the pan so they
"melt" rather than brown, stir them from time to time. Remove
the leg of mutton or the rabbit from the stock in which it was
cooked. Boil this to reduce to about ¾ pint. Stir this into the
onion purée, adding salt and pepper to your taste. Lastly stir in
some hot thick cream. Do not, however, use the stock from the
salted duck to make your sauce, it will be too salty. If nothing
else is available water and a bouillon cube must be used as a
substitute.

Orange Glaze for Baked Gammon
Mix 6 oz of brown sugar or a cup of honey with the juice and
grated rind of an orange and the grated rind of half a lemon.
When the gammon is almost cooked, remove it from the oven,
and skin it. Spread the mixture on the fat, put it back in the oven
(without any foil or other covering) for another 30−45 minutes,
until it acquires a crisp crust.

Cumberland Sauce (see page 120), or crab apple jelly are
served with hot or cold gammon. See also Hot Yorkshire Sauce
(page 138).

Oyster Stuffing, or Forcemeat *(For a boiled or a roast turkey)*
Grate enough bread very fine to make 1 cup of crumbs, being
careful that no large lumps remain. Put it in a basin with 1½ oz
of butter cut in small pieces. Add a teaspoon of mixed herbs − or
more if they are green and freshly chopped − salt and pepper to
your taste and a good pinch of grated nutmeg. Mix well.

Open 18 oysters, remove the pearls, chop them coarsely, add
them to the other ingredients, together with two beaten eggs.
Work the mixture together in your hands until it is really
smoothly mixed.

Stuff the turkey, but not too full, and stitch up or skewer the
openings, before covering. If there should be too much forcemeat roll it into balls, fry them just before serving and use them as
a garnish.

Fried Parsley *(A garnish for fish)*
Wash and pat the sprigs of parsley dry in a tea towel. Fry them

in hot oil or lard. The leaves become crisp but the stalks do not. If left too long in the hot oil or fat they will be brown and then taste burnt.

Bag Puddings

Boiled bag puddings and roly-polys used to be served hot with gravy before the meat in Kentish as well as Suffolk and Essex farmhouses in the earlier part of the present century. It took the edge off the appetite and in poor families was of course often served without any meat to follow. While the joint was roasting, this plain suet pudding was boiled in a floured cloth. Shortly before dinner it was cut in slices and laid in the dripping pan to brown briefly before the fire. Some were more elaborate.

Bag Pudding with Mushrooms

The name comes from the cloth or "bag" in which the puddings were boiled, nowadays they are usually steamed in a basin, not boiled in a cloth.

Butter a pudding basin, line it with suet pastry. Fill this with pieces of mushroom and small pieces of lean raw ham, adding pepper and a little stock or water. It should come two thirds up the basin. Put a pastry "lid" on top. Moisten and pinch the edges together to seal it. Cover the basin with two pieces of foil pleated in the middle so the pudding can rise. Tie it on firmly. Put the basin on an upturned saucer with boiling water to come half way up. Add a lid, boil for 2 hours or longer.

Durham Leek Pudding

Wash and chop 1 lb of leeks, keeping most of the green part, stir these into 8 oz of suet crust pastry and use this to three parts fill a buttered pudding basin. Cover it with two thicknesses of pleated foil, tied on. Put the pudding in a pan with boiling water as above.

It is turned out to serve with a good gravy.

Bacon Badgers

These were once popular in Bedfordshire and Buckinghamshire. They were made from suet pastry mixed with chopped bacon, chopped herbs and sliced onions and usually shaped into a long roly-poly and boiled in a floured cloth rather than a basin. They should be eaten as a garnish and, in some families, as a main dish.

Savoury Pudding (*Yorkshire*)

This is baked, cut in squares and served hot with a good thick gravy with roasts, especially with a roast goose.

Boil 2 large English onions in salted water for about 15 minutes, skin and chop them coarsely. Mix them with 8 oz of nice fine oatmeal, add some salt, pepper, a pinch of mixed herbs and ½ teaspoon of powdered sage. Then, having soaked 8 oz of stale bread in hot water for 30 minutes, drain and squeeze it fairly dry, beating out any lumps with a fork. Add this to the mixture, mix well. Finally at the last, add 2 beaten eggs.

Melt some dripping in a Yorkshire pudding tin so that it forms a thin layer on the bottom, add the Savoury Pudding mixture and spread it evenly. Bake it for about an hour in a moderate oven (350°F, 180°C, Mark 4).

Cut the pudding in squares and serve it hot (and hot) with a good gravy.

Season Pudding (*Yorkshire*)

When Yorkshire pudding is served with roast pork or roast lamb instead of beef, herbs are sometimes added to the batter. Sage and onions are popular but when, for example, the Season Pudding is to be served with roast chicken it may well be flavoured with thyme and parsley instead. Some season puddings have suet and breadcrumbs added too. Like Yorkshire pudding, it used to be eaten first, piping hot before the joint, but is now more often served with it. In Yorkshire it is served with pigs' fry too.

All these dishes are very old and must have been popular before potatoes were known in Britain.

For 4 people, boil 2 large onions, drain and chop them and mix them with 1 teaspoon of chopped sage, a little pepper and salt. Put 6 oz of flour in a basin. Add 2 eggs and 1 pint of milk gradually, beating the mixture until it is free of lumps. Finally add the onions and seasonings. Heat some dripping in a baking tin, when smoking hot pour in the batter. Bake it in a moderate oven (350°F, 180°C, Mark 4) for 40 minutes.

Sage and Onion Sauce (*after Escoffier*)
A well made sage and onion stuffing, with a few spoonsful of stock, or of duck gravy, added to make it thinner, makes a pleasant sauce which may be served separately in a sauce boat. It is particularly useful to serve with roast pork, or roast duck for example, if not all the guests like the flavour of sage and onion stuffing.

Also used as forcemeat balls and served separately, cooked in a fireproof dish in the oven at the same time as the meat or poultry.

English Salad Sauce (*Eliza Acton, 1845*)
As Miss Acton writes:
'The first essential for a smooth, well-made English salad dressing is to have the yolks of the eggs used for it sufficiently hard to be reduced easily to a perfect paste. They should be boiled at least fifteen minutes, and should have become *quite* cold before they are taken from the shells . . . To a couple of yolks broken up and mashed to a paste with the back of a wooden spoon, add a small saltspoonful of salt, a large one of pounded sugar, a few grains of fine cayenne, and a teaspoonful of cold water; mix these well, and stir to them by degrees a quarter of a pint of sweet cream; throw in next, stirring the sauce briskly, a tablespoonful of strong chili vinegar, and add as much common or French vinegar as will acidulate the mixture agreeably. A tablespoonful of either will be sufficient for many tastes, but it is easy to increase the proportion when more is liked.'

Oxford Brawn Sauce
This is a fierce sauce, still popular in many English families, with salad as well as with brawn, though a little sharp for my own palate.

It is just 2 tablespoons of brown sugar, 3 tablespoons of

vinegar, 1 teaspoon of made English mustard, a third as much salt, some pepper and a pinch of ground cloves, 'mingled' as Eliza Acton wrote, 'with four tablespoonsful of very fine salad-oil.'

At home we mingled it in a screw-topped gingerbeer bottle in the pantry before using.

Farmhouse Salad Dressing
Crush two hard boiled egg yolks to a paste with a little pepper, salt and unmixed mustard powder. Then stir in a cup of thick cream, $\frac{1}{2}$ cup of sugar and $\frac{1}{2}$ cup of pale mild vinegar.

Salt
Salt has been collected after high tide in the marshes at Maldon, Essex, since Roman times. Clive Osborne and his father, sister and 10 local craftsmen run an old family firm there, extracting the salt by boiling up sea water, rather like stock for soup. The salt is of excellent flavour, better than the more famous French sea salt, *le gros sel*, which is often unappetizing, grey and has hard little granules which do not melt so nicely on the food as the Maldon crystals which are pyramid shaped. They look like snow flakes. 'It leaves no bitter after-taste in your mouth', as Clive Osborne says, 'like common salt, yet it is slightly stronger.' It is now being exported to several countries. It is mentioned twice in Mrs. Glasse's *The Art of Cookery Made Plain and Easy*, published in 1747.

Cheshire Salt
I was brought up among the salt mines and brine pumping firms of mid-Cheshire, there are huge underground brine deposits all round there and even the cheese is said to have a slightly salty tang to it from the flavour of the local pasturage. In my childhood so much salt used to be pumped up from under Northwich that at intervals the town used to subside and have to be propped up on stilts. Most of the houses were then built on wooden rafts so they could be chocked up, the space was then filled in underneath. Great lakes appeared suddenly round Northwich at intervals and I have always been haunted by the story of the

19th-century inn complete with horses and carriages which disappeared during the night into one of them.

At Ingham Thompson's in Northwich they pump the brine out of the ground into open salt pans and heat it till the salt crystallizes on the surface and falls to the bottom. It is then raked to the sides of the pan and put in wooden tubs to store. The Lion Salt Works near the Marston Canal Bridge has been working since 1842. The salt is like little white cake crumbs, a natural coarse salt of excellent flavour. As there are no chemical additives it will not, of course, pour, one needs an old fashioned salt cellar for it. The old fashioned block cooking salt once used so much for bean salting, bacon and ham curing is available too, this is what used to be called "kitchen salt".

Saltpetre – Potassium nitrate KNO_3

This is a slightly different thing. It is what is used when salting beef and hams and ox tongues to give them that attractive pink colour when cooked. Without it they will be grey.

There are many excellent traditional ham and bacon cures and, as a seafaring nation, we were once renowned for our salt and pressed beef, which once formed part of a ship's stores. There was spiced, pickled, collared, smoked, bucaned, potted and dried beef. Some of the recipes go back to the Middle Ages when, for lack of grazing, stock had to be killed off in autumn and salted down for winter.

Saltpetre is also used in making gun powder.

Samphire Sauce

Samphire looks like a rock plant and is easy to grow on dry rocky soil in the garden. It has many branched, thin but succulent leaves or stalks, rather like glasswort. It grows wild on the salt marshes near Snettisham, Norfolk, on Sark and some of the other Channel Islands and along the sandy coast of France near Boulogne, where it is much enjoyed in local restaurants. It is sometimes sold by fishmongers and greengrocers in summer in Norfolk, but is rare elsewhere.

Wash the sprigs of samphire, cut off the roots. Boil the samphire for 10 minutes in a pan of salted water. Then cut the pieces in short lengths and stir them in a creamy white sauce. Serve hot.

Samphire is also very good cooked, chopped, and stirred into a cupful of melted butter with lemon juice. Pleasant with fish.

Skirly (*Scotland*)

In Scotland roasted game is often served with skirly and a garnish of watercress. Fried bread spread with the chopped livers of the game bird (also fried in butter and seasoned) is usually placed on a hot ashet or dish with the birds on top. This tastes even more delicious if the fried bread is put under the birds before roasting, so that they drip into it. Rowan or Rodden Jelly is handed separately.

To make the Skirly: Melt 2 oz of dripping, add a peeled, sliced onion and fry it gently until golden brown. Sprinkle 4 oz of medium oatmeal in the pan. Fry it gently until crisp and golden, stirring occasionally so it does not stick. Add salt, pepper and 1 teaspoon of freshly-made English mustard.

This is eaten hot with game dishes, but when cold is used as a stuffing for roasting chickens and turkeys. The so-called Pan Haggis is a very similar dish.

Bacon and Mushroom Stuffing
Peel, dice and fry an onion in butter with 3 oz of diced streaky bacon, and 8 oz of chopped mushrooms. Fry them gently for about 5 minutes. Mix 4 oz of white breadcrumbs with 2 tablespoons of water, an egg, a little chopped parsley, thyme and tarragon, add the fried mixture, stirring well. Use this to stuff the crop of a roasting chicken, or small turkey, increasing the quantity of stuffing as required.

Chestnut Stuffing for a Roast Turkey
This brilliantly simple recipe comes from Mrs. Hannah Glasse's *The Art of Cookery Made Plain and Easy*, first published in 1747, but a classic which remained in print for about a hundred years, with many pirated plagiarized versions. It is the cookery book

135

which was used in Dr. Johnson's household in Gough Square.

Mrs. Glasse stuffed the body of the turkey simply and sumptuously with $1\frac{1}{2}$ lb of whole roasted and peeled chestnuts, about 8 oz of butter and a good sprinkling of salt and pepper.

Some cooks later added small whole (chipolata-type) sausages fried in butter as well. Both ways are delicious.

A Rich Forcemeat or Stuffing for a Cold Roast Turkey
If the bird is to be eaten cold, and is perhaps to grace a cold table, it is better to stuff it at the crop end with a rich forcemeat similar to a coarse-cut country pâté. This will be very good sliced cold with the turkey meat. The body of the bird could be stuffed similarly but with a different though well-flavoured forcemeat.

Irish Potato Stuffing
This is a stuffing for a duck or goose. The plainness of it is a perfect foil to the rather rich meat.

To one very large breakfast cup of mashed potato, add 1 tablespoon of finely chopped celery, 1 dessertspoon of finely chopped onion and salt and pepper to your taste. Stuff the bird with it in the body rather than the crop.

Boxty Pudding
This is really a sort of potato pancake, delicious hot with brown gravy, carrots, buttered cabbage and underdone roast beef — usually a piece of Top Rib, known in Ireland as the "Housekeeper's Cut". Boxty was also eaten with butter and brown sugar in Northern Ireland for Hallowe'en, but is seldom made now.

Wash, peel and grate some large potatoes, add half as much white flour and a little salt. For instance to a breakfast cup of grated potato add half a breakfast cup of flour and 1 teaspoon of salt. Then stir in enough milk to make a batter of fairly stiff dropping consistency. Let it stand for an hour.

Fry the mixture in a very hot frying pan in bacon dip or beef dripping like pancakes. When it sets and is brown on the bottom turn it with a fish slice and fry the other side. Serve them sizzling hot instead of Yorkshire pudding with the lovely underdone beef.

Yorkshire Pudding

There are several kinds of Yorkshire Pudding, and many ways of making it, almost every family in Lancashire and Yorkshire has its own recipe and each one is the best. It should be served freshly made directly from the oven and then it can be delicious. There are two main sorts, both traditional, the thick and the thin. They used to be served before the roast, with thick gravy, perhaps to take the edge off the appetite. Nowadays Yorkshire Pudding is usually served with the roast beef.

The typical Yorkshire Pudding is usually made with milk and water, this makes it light and crisp. In some parts of Yorkshire it is thought best always to use "blue" or skim milk, but the batter is not then allowed to stand for any *length* of time. Yorkshire Pudding can also be made with beestings (a cow's first milk after calving), without eggs at all.

Another essential is some very hot fat (and not too much of it) to cook the pudding in – also a good oven. In the days of spit roasting before the fire, the pudding batter was poured into the tin over the hot fat and then put under the joint roasting on the spit. The juices from the meat dripped down deliciously on to the pudding. According to Donald Boyd in *On Foot In Yorkshire*, 1932, the thick sort of Yorkshire Pudding is 'very deep at the edges, three or four inches maybe, and is sometimes turned out of the baking dish and served so it looks like a cake, its ridges deeply browned, its centre a firm moist yellow.'
'The thin sort' he writes 'is like in colour, but much more moist. The edges of both should be crisp.'

'The Thin Sort

Take 1 egg, 4 good heaped tablespoons of flour, a little salt and one ½ teaspoon of baking powder. Beat up the egg in a basin, then add a little milk, then beat in the flour with a spoon. There should be about 4 tablespoons of milk so that the mixture is rather thicker than cream.

Put some dripping into a flat tin and melt it in the oven. When it is melted pour in the batter and put the tin in the bottom of the oven. The oven must be hot. Bake rather quickly at first and shift it to the top of the oven to brown.'

'The Thick Sort

Use the same method and materials as for the other, but with less milk and about 5 tablespoons of flour. Put some dripping into a pie dish or a round baking dish. Let it melt, pour in the batter, then bake quickly until it begins to set. As soon as ever it begins to set, put it on the top shelf of the oven, standing on an iron ring if the shelf is not high enough, and let it puff until it browns.

It is better, some believe, to serve it in the dish, because it may drop if turned out. It should in either event be served with gravy as a dish by itself before the meat course.'

Yorkshire Mustard Sauce or Yorkshire Relish

A very old sauce, once served at inns and posting houses, it is eaten, traditionally, with cold ham in Yorkshire and is to be made at least a day before it is used.

Mix 2 parts of dry mustard powder with 8 parts of caster sugar. Then stir in enough vinegar to moisten it well.

Hot Yorkshire Sauce

This is for roast hare or venison, braised ham, roast gammon.

Cook 1 tablespoon of thinly shredded orange peel in $\frac{1}{2}$ pint of red wine for a few minutes. Strain it but keep the peel and return the wine to the pan. Add 2 tablespoons of red currant jelly, a pinch of Cayenne pepper and one of cinnamon. Add 2 table-spoons of *demi-glace*, or of the jellied juices in the bottom of the dripping pot, or if unavailable a rich brown gravy. Let it boil for a few minutes, then strain it. Add the juice of an orange and the previously boiled shredded peel. Serve piping hot.

This is a useful sauce for re-heating cold boiled ham or bacon.

White Sauce

Melt a tablespoon of butter in a small pan. Stir in 2 tablespoons of flour. Then little by little heating and stirring add about $\frac{3}{4}$ pint of milk. Add salt, pepper and a little freshly grated nutmeg. Heat, stirring, until the sauce is smooth and thick.

Sometimes the sauce is made with the appropriate chicken or fish stock instead of with milk. Really it should then be called

Béchamel sauce after Louis de Béchameil, Marquis de Nointel, Lord Steward of the Royal Household to Louis XIV who is said to have invented it, or had it called after him by a court chef.

Parsley Sauce
This is simply a White Sauce to which chopped parsley is added in quantity before serving. If liked, a little chopped lemon balm from the garden may be mixed with the parsley when that is scarce.

Irish Parsley Sauce
This is served with boiled fowl and boiled bacon. Scald a large bunch of parsley in ½ pint of boiling milk, mixed with ½ pint of the hot, strained chicken-and-bacon stock. Add a good pinch of nutmeg. Melt 2 tablespoons of butter, stir in 2 tablespoons of flour, and gradually add the strained parsley liquor, heating and stirring until the sauce is smooth and thick. Chop the scalded parsley very fine and stir it in. Taste for seasoning.

Egg Sauce
Add two or three chopped hard-boiled eggs to ½ pint of White Sauce just before serving.

It used to be popular with cod, haddock and whiting, is served in Scotland with Cabbie Claw, a flaked cod and mashed potato dish. It is also poured over a hot boiled fowl in Scotland.

Wild Duck Sauce (*Susan, Duchess of Somerset*)
'One glass of port wine, one spoonful of ketchup, one spoonful of caviar, one spoonful of lemon juice, one slice of lemon peel, one large shallot sliced, four grains of dark cayenne pepper, two blades of mace. Scald and strain and add it to the pure gravy of the bird.'

Wow-Wow Sauce
This is a recipe which seems to have appeared first in 1817 in *The Cook's Oracle* by Dr Kitchiner, the well known gourmet and conversationalist of the Regency period on whom the Rev. Dr Ffolliott the hero of Thomas Love Peacock's *Crotchet Castle*, is

said to have been modelled. The sauce used to be served with boiled beef and carrots, but is good too with boiled bacon or ham.

Melt 1 tablespoon of butter, stir in 1 tablespoon of flour then about ½ pint of the boiled beef broth (or bacon stock). Heat, stirring until the sauce is smooth and thick, then add 1 tablespoon of English mustard and simmer, stirring until the sauce is as thick as you wish. Add a dessertspoon of chopped parsley and 2–3 pickled walnuts cut in small chunks or dice. Pour it hot over the meat, or dish it in a sauceboat.

Chapter 5
Poultry and Game

A Michaelmas or Harvest Goose

For generations the young Michaelmas or Harvest goose, fattened on corn stubble and the gleanings left by the reapers, was eaten by patriotic Englishmen on September 29th, the Feast of St Michael and All Angels. It may even now be illegal not to do so for they were celebrating not only the bringing home of the harvest but our victory over the Spanish Armada in 1588. Queen Elizabeth I relished good food — 'Lampreys' said she, 'are one of my passions' — and she was already at table munching a piece of roast stubble goose, a dish of which she was particularly fond, when the news of the great English victory over the Spaniards was brought to her. To mark the occasion she decreed that roast goose should be eaten on that day every year thereafter. Now all this is forgotten and lately it has become difficult to buy a goose except at Christmas. Law abiding English people will revive this custom.

Young three or four month old goslings or "green" geese were enjoyed in early summer usually spit-roasted unstuffed and served with giblet gravy. As the apples were not ripe, hot gooseberry sauce was served instead. It is from this that the fruit gets its name. The geese were still very tender by Michaelmas but without much flesh on them and country people with large families used to stuff the goose with rabbit pieces as well as sage and onion. The dry rabbit meat absorbed the delicious taste of goose and onions. Small children and maiden aunts got these inside pieces leaving the goose for the men.

At harvest time young rabbits, fat from nibbling the ripe corn, were caught in great numbers as the part in the middle of the field was cut. They were often served up at harvest suppers. The delicious Buckinghamshire Harvest Rabbit popular at village suppers within living memory is related to this Tudor delicacy.

Some people could not afford roast goose either at Christmas or Michaelmas. There are old well loved recipes for "Poor Man's Goose" done with pork or mutton, and traditional to different parts of England, there was even "Mock Goose", very similar to faggots. "Butcher's Goose", stuffed pickled pork in a huff paste, is an old Durham and Northumberland dish popular within living memory and once eaten at Christmas. "Colonial Goose" — lamb or mutton served with roast potatoes, apple sauce and mashed turnips — was enjoyed in Lancashire. It has been popular in South Africa too for a couple of centuries.

For the goose, if frozen, remove the giblets, keep back the liver, put the other giblets in a pan with water to cover, salt, pepper and a chopped onion. Simmer for a good hour, strain and keep the stock for gravy.

Sprinkle the goose inside and out with salt filling the body with, say, Irish Potato Stuffing (see page 136), and skewer the opening together. Place the bird breast down on a rack in a large roasting tin. Roast in a hot oven (400°F, 200°C, Mark 6) for 45 minutes then drain off and keep the fat. Reduce the heat to moderately slow (325°F, 170°C, Mark 3), roast the bird till tender when pierced with a fork and the juices running out are no longer pink but golden, in about an hour. Drain off the fat once more and keep it. Turn the goose breast-side up to brown in about 30 minutes.

A teaspoon of made English mustard, ½ teaspoon of salt, a pinch of Cayenne pepper mixed smooth in a glass of port or brown sherry may be poured into the goose through a hole cut in the apron just before serving, as Mr John Farlay of the London Tavern used to do in the 18th century.

Put the goose on a hot dish and keep it warm at the mouth of the oven for about 15 minutes to "set" before carving. Meanwhile skim the remaining fat off the juices in the tin. Mix 2 teaspoons of cornflour with a little cold water, add it to the juices in the pan, gradually stir in a pint of giblet stock, heating, stirring and scraping up the gubbins off the bottom. Serve it in a jug with the goose.

Traditionally the roast goose is served with a Rich Victorian Bread Sauce as well as the gravy, plain boiled potatoes or Yorkshire Season Pudding. Quince jelly and Hot Cider Sauce (see pages 278 and 118) are also appropriate with it. Up to a hundred years ago it was almost invariably served with creamed potatoes, and as Dickens wrote in *A Christmas Carol*, 'The youngest Cratchits in particular were . . . in sage and onion to the eyebrows.'

A Roast Capon Blistered with Raspings

A most delicious and unusual dish, the bird is stuffed with the old Lemon and Parsley Forcemeat and served with the 18th century Hanover Sauce (see pages 124 and 123). The recipe is also suitable for a small turkey.

Stuff the crop with Lemon and Parsley Forcemeat, the body of the bird with a large bunch of thyme, a tablespoon of butter or poultry dripping and a little pepper and salt. Then butter the bird thickly all over with a teacup of poultry dripping or warm soft butter. It may be smeared on with fingertips or with the help of a thin flexible knife. Ordinary dripping is unsuitable as it will spoil the delicate flavour of the dish.

Sprinkle the bird with salt and pepper and roast it in a moderate oven (350°F, 180°C, Mark 4) for 15–20 minutes per lb with a piece of foil laid lightly over the breast. Baste it from time to time with the pan juices and add a teacup of hot water to them after about 45 minutes.

Meanwhile grate enough stale white bread to make a breakfast cup of crumbs. Then mix them with 2 tablespoons of grated Cheddar or Lancashire cheese. About 15 minutes before the bird is ready take it from the oven and let it cool for a few minutes. Then spoon the fat and dripping from the roasting tin over it again and again.

Then coat it all over the upper surface with the breadcrumbs and cheese, patting them on the buttery thighs with the fingers.

143

Very gently spoon on a little more fat then more crumbs. Put the bird back into a hot oven (425°F, 220°C, Mark 7) to brown. Serve it with Hanover Sauce. If roast potatoes are to be served they should be cooked separately.

Hard breadcrumbs were formerly called raspings because the bread was dried in the oven, then rasped into crumbs on a metal grater.

Chicken Baked in Milk
A very old English dish, the recipe varies in different parts of the country, some families add celery, some do not, and the amount of onion varies. The flavour is of course different from that of the many famous French recipes in which white wine is used, but it is equally subtle. The dish is especially popular in East Anglia where they also cook rabbits and saddle of hare in milk, as well as sausages.

In Scotland a leg or gigot of mutton or lamb is sometimes simmered in milk, when tender, some of the liquor is used to make an onion or caper sauce for it. No one interested in the traditional dishes of these islands should fail to try it.

Sprinkle the chicken inside with pepper and salt. Put a peeled onion stuck with a clove inside it, then put it breast down in a deep casserole or fireproof dish. Pour in enough milk to come half way up, the exact quantity depends on the size of the bird and the casserole. Add salt, 12 peppercorns, half a coffee spoon of freshly grated nutmeg or a blade of mace, a bayleaf and a little chopped celery. Put on the lid. Let it simmer for about $2\frac{1}{2}$ hours in a slow oven (300°F, 150°C, Mark 2) the exact time depending on the age of the bird.

When done put the chicken on a hot dish and joint it if liked. Strain the milky cooking stock, melt 1 tablespoon of butter, stir in 1 tablespoon of flour, then gradually heating and stirring add the strained milky stock to make a rich sauce. Heat stirring until smooth and thick. Put the chicken back in the casserole with the sauce. Any left over makes delicious white soup, which may be served with toasted salted almonds. This is a dish which can be made in advance and re-heated. A well chilled, dry but fruity. white wine would be excellent to drink with it.

Old Fashioned Chicken Pudding

This is a recipe which may well go back to the Middle Ages, it was once a popular way of cooking tough old fowls, it is still useful for cooking the chicken portions sold separately nowadays, or for an oven-ready chicken.

Cut 4 chicken portions in delicate pieces without the bones. Have a small bag containing flour, salt and pepper, shake them in it, together with 1 tablespoon of chopped parsley, 4 oz of sliced mushrooms, 1 peeled sliced onion and 4 oz of chopped bacon.

Butter a 2 pint pudding basin. Roll out 8 oz of suet pastry, and use most of it to line the basin. Keep back a smaller portion to make the "lid".

Put the chicken pieces, etc. in the pastry lined basin. Add stock or water till half full. Put on a "lid" of pastry pinching the edges together.

Cover the basin with two layers of buttered pleated foil and tie this on. Stand the basin on an upturned saucer in a large pan with boiling water to come half way up the basin. Bring the water back to the boil, put a lid on the pan and continue boiling gently for 3 hours. Top up with boiling water as that in the pan boils away.

Cock-a-Leekie

This recipe for what is really a Scottish national dish, is given here, not among the soups, as the boiled fowl is served as a main dish.

Truss a fowl for boiling, put it in a pan with 4 pints of water, some salt, 1 clove, 12 peppercorns. Simmer for 2 hours. Remove the fowl and serve it with parsley sauce or with a rich egg sauce and a garnish of crisp bacon rolls or poached eggs.

If possible leave the broth till cold, skim off or lift off the fat. Cut up four nice leeks washing them well. Simmer them in the broth together with 2 oz of rice till tender. Cut up the remains of the fowl and add these chicken pieces to the broth a few minutes before serving.

A compôte of stewed prunes is sometimes served with it.

Note: In Sir Walter Scott's *The Fortunes of Nigel* King James VI

of Scotland and I of England says in the last line: 'Come my lords and lieges let us all to dinner for the cock-a-leekie is a'cooking'. It is, of course, a dish which has been popular in Scotland since the 16th century.

How Towdie is a traditional Scottish dish of boiled fowl with an oatmeal stuffing (see Skirly, page 134). It is usually garnished with eggs poached in the chicken broth. Boil it as for Cock-a-Leekie.

A Thick Egg Sauce is usually poured over a boiled fowl in Scotland with very hard boiled egg yolks grated over the top of the bird. Chopped chives are sometimes stirred into the sauce too and when it is wanted very rich raw egg yolks beaten up with ¼ pint of thick cream are stirred into it just before serving. Buttered barley or oatmeal replace the bacon and cabbage served with a boiled fowl in Ireland.

Irish Boiled Fowl, Bacon and Cabbage
In Ireland boiled fowl is cooked and served with a piece of boiled bacon to "stretch it". It used to be eaten on Sundays when there were visitors and appeared smothered in parsley sauce. The cabbage is boiled with it during the last 30 minutes. Boiled jacket potatoes are eaten and peeled from side plates hot with butter.

Simmer the bird in water to cover with herbs and vegetables as usual. If the piece of bacon is very salty soak it in cold water overnight first.
Note: The Irish version of Parsley Sauce (see page 139) is the very palest green with bright emerald parsley.

The dish is perhaps a relic of Victorian times when it was fashionable to serve a ham or boiled ox tongue or a piece of pickled pork flanked by a pair of hot boiled fowls to ensure that everyone had enough. Oyster Sauce similar to the one served on beefsteak (see page 66) was a popular garnish for boiled fowls in the 18th century.

The broth is sometimes served just with the meats and vegetables to follow.

Buttered Barley *(For boiled fowl)*
Pour 1 teacup of pearl barley into a pan of cold salted water. Bring this gently to the boil and cook simmering, and stirring occasionally, until the water has evaporated. Add a large knob of butter, stirring it in and serve the buttery barley, when tender, with the hot boiled chicken.

Oatmeal Dumplings *(For boiled Fowl)*
Toast 8 oz of oatmeal in the oven. Then mix it with 8 oz of shredded suet, some salt and pepper and a peeled, chopped onion.

No liquid is added, simply tie up the mixture firmly in a cloth, leaving room for it to swell in cooking. Then simply boil it gently for 1½ hours in the broth with the fowl, keeping the dumpling well covered. Turn it out to serve with the fowl. They are sometimes eaten as a meal in themselves — flavoured with the chicken broth.

147

A Jellied Hen

Put a boiling hen, old rooster, or a younger roasting chicken in a pan together with its giblets and two pig's feet cut in half. Add water to cover, salt, 12 peppercorns, the usual herbs and stock vegetables as available. Bring to the boil and then simmer until tender and the meat is dropping off the bones in 2 to 3 hours according to the age and toughness of the bird. If liked, it may be cooked in dry cider and water, half and half mixed.

Line the bottom of a wetted mould or large pudding basin with sliced hard boiled eggs. Add the chopped chicken and trotter meat. Pour on the still liquid jelly and leave it to set.

With this method the basin must be almost filled with chicken meat as it tends to sink to the bottom. When it has set turn it out to serve garnished with watercress.

To Line a Mould or Basin with Clear Jelly: Rinse it out first with cold water, then fill it with aspic jelly, or clear jellying stock to the top. Put it in the refrigerator. When the layer of jelly round the sides of the mould is set, pour out the rest from the middle very gently indeed. The mould is now ready for you to put in a layer of sliced lemon and hard boiled eggs. Spoon on more of the still liquid jelly and let it set. Then add the pieces of cooked chicken and trotter meat, more jelly. Chill and turn out to serve. It may be sliced for starters, and eaten with Oxford Brawn Sauce (see page 131), or served with a salad.

A Parsley Pie (Chicken)

Some of the early chicken pies were very elaborate, both Mrs. Charlotte Mason in *The Lady's Assistant*, 1773, and Mrs. Elizabeth Raffald in *The Experienced English Housekeeper*, 1769, give recipes for elegant pies containing sweetbreads, morels and truffles as well as chicken. Parsley Pie was a fashionable dish in Bath at the same period and is still made in the West Country. The sauce inside it is a delicate creamy green.

Wash a colander full of parsley picking out any weeds or grit, if there is not quite enough add a few spinach leaves or some leaves of lemon balm, if available. Scald the parsley etc. in a pan with a little boiling milk, then chop the parsley etc. and put it in a large pie dish with a chicken cut in convenient pieces.

Add a cupful of stock, made preferably with the giblets or the crushed chicken carcase. Add salt, pepper, a pie funnel. Roll out some short crust pastry, cover the pie with this and decorate the top with a pastry lattice. Brush with milk.

Bake the pie in a very hot oven (450°F, 230°C, Mark 8) until the pastry is risen, then reduce the heat to moderate (350°F, 180°C, Mark 4) and bake it for a total of $1-1\frac{1}{2}$ hours. Put a piece of foil over the pastry if it is becoming brown.

When the pie is cooked, pour $\frac{1}{4}$ pint of thick cream into it through the hole in the pie funnel. Shake the pie, gently and carefully, to mix the cream with the gravy already inside. Delicious.

Kentish Fowl Rice Pudding

An old country dish which used to be cooked slowly in an Aga or Raeburn cooker, or the old black-leaded kitchen range when the wife was away at Maidstone or Ashford Markets.

Simply put an old hen in a casserole. Add a cupful of rice, a pint of milk, plenty of salt and pepper, some grated nutmeg, four peeled sliced onions, some mixed herbs — it should be highly seasoned. Then cover it tightly. If the lid fits badly use foil as well. Put it in a very slow oven (250°F, 120°C, Mark $\frac{1}{2}$) and leave it all day. At lunchtime get someone to see if it needs more milk to keep the rice soft. It will need another pint unless it was done very gently indeed. By evening all will be ready. The fowl will be beautifully tender. The skin brown like an ordinary roaster and not at all dried up unless the oven was too hot. Dish the old thing, the rice round her, all creamy and crusty and garnished with chopped parsley and sliced hard boiled egg.

Mrs. Rundell's Duck with Cucumbers (1806)

Mrs. Rundell was a Shropshire lass from Ludlow who married a partner in a firm of fashionable jewellers on Ludgate Hill, London. They made a very good thing of supplying snuff boxes to foreign ministers at George IV's Coronation, for the then enormous sum of £8,205. Her book, *A New System of Domestic Cookery*, was famous. Five to ten thousand copies were published yearly, it became one of John Murray's most valuable properties and in

1812 when he bought the lease of a house in Albermarle Street part of the surety was the copyright of Mrs. Rundell's cookery book. She wrote most of it in Swansea as a series of hints and recipes for her married daughters.

This is a most unusual and delicious dish which is easy to cook, perfect for a small dinner party of four people.

Peel three large cucumbers, cut them in chunks and remove the seeds. Let them marinate for 3 to 4 hours with two large peeled sliced onions in wine vinegar to cover. The cucumber shrinks a great deal in cooking so that what may seem an extravagant quantity really is necessary.

Dust or dredge the duck with seasoned flour. Brown it gently on top of the stove in a heavy flameproof casserole or stew pot, turning it so all sides become brown and crisp. When the duck is half cooked, pour off the surplus fat into another pan. Add half a pint of giblet or other stock to the duck with $\frac{1}{4}$ pint of red wine, some salt, pepper, two sliced carrots and a peeled, sliced onion. Cover the duck and let it simmer until tender in about one and a half hours.

Meanwhile drain the cucumber and onions, pat them dry in a tea towel and fry them gently in the fat from the duck on a low heat with a lid on the pan, they should take nearly as long to cook as the duck itself. Add them to the duck stock just before serving, having again poured off any surplus fat. If liked thicken the stock by mixing a teaspoon of cornflour or arrowroot to a smooth paste in a dessertspoon of cold water, then add this to the stock and heat stirring until smooth and thick, then add the cucumber and onions.

The duck may be carved conventionally, or simply cut in four with poultry scissors.

Welsh Salted Duckling – Hwyader Halit Ferwedig

A very old Welsh farmhouse dish with a flavour reminiscent of the more famous *confit de canard* which is a speciality of the Périgord. A similar dish but in a more elaborate version is still popular too in the Scandinavian countries.

In Wales the salt duckling is boiled and served with a hot onion sauce, and sometimes with horseradish sauce as well, or with a hot laver and orange sauce. New potatoes and French beans in butter are delicious with it. It may also be eaten cold with salad.

Take one duck and lay it in a large pie dish in a cool larder, or refrigerator. Rub it all over with salt twice a day for 3 days, turning it over each time. Then rinse the salt off the duck, let it soak for a few minutes in fresh cold water.

Put it in a deep pan with hot water almost to cover, add 12 peppercorns and some sage leaves. (Some cooks tie the duck in a floured cloth to keep it together.) When the water boils reduce the heat and let the bird simmer, skimming off the scum as it rises, then gently bubbling until it is tender in about two hours, or longer depending on the age of the duck. Bear in mind that the slower it boils the plumper and more delicious it will be.

When cooked cut the duck in four portions in the kitchen with poultry or dressmaking scissors, serve it with hot laver sauce or onion sauce.

A duck has heavier bones and less flesh than a chicken, so one must allow larger portions. A 3 lb duck is only enough for two large portions. No duck is big enough for more than four portions.

Wild Duck, Widgeon or Pintail

If you wish to eat as well as your grandfather did go to a good game dealer and buy some wild duck. The taste is unexpected and simply delicious, one forgets that food can have so much flavour. Most butchers do not bother to sell them. The duck is to be eaten with hot boiled celery garnished with watercress and should have a little sherry stirred into the pan juices to make the gravy. One bird is enough for two persons.

All one does is to put a whole peeled tangerine or clementine or satsuma, and a knob of butter, inside the bird. Tie some bacon or barding fat over it and roast it in a fairly hot oven (375°F, 190°C, Mark 5) for about 30 minutes. If the duck is very high and too gamey, rub the insides with cut lemon and sprinkle them with a little ground ginger before roasting. Then stuff the duck with chopped apples and onions, these absorb much of the gameyness and are to be thrown away before the bird is served.

In autumn a plainly roasted wild duck – without any stuffing – may be cut lengthways down the breast and back bone and garnished with fried cèpes (mushrooms, see page 183) – these might be fresh or frozen. The latter need simply to be re-heated.

Grouse

Red Grouse are in season from August 12th to December 10th. This is a native bird unique to the British Isles, its nearest relative, in Norway, takes on white plumage in winter unlike the red grouse. The birds called grouse in the United States are a totally different species from *Lagopus scoticus*.

Grouse were not shot here for sport until 1850–60 when breach loading shot guns became available. Ever since then Parliament has begun its summer recess, traditionally, in time for the grouse season on the "Glorious Twelfth". Nowadays many more grouse die from shortage of heather than are shot.

Young birds are usually roasted, the older ones are for pies, terrines and skinks or soups. Prices vary, a great deal of game now goes for exports and most of it is very expensive. Grouse are a little cheaper later in the season, bargains are sometimes found during the shooting season in big Yorkshire markets such as Leeds – and also in Scotland.

Roast Grouse

Only the young grouse are worth roasting. Do not wash the birds. Put 1–2 oz of butter mixed with salt, pepper and lemon juice in each. Wrap the birds in barding fat or bacon.

Simmer the grouse livers with 8 oz of chicken livers for 10 minutes in salted water. Purée them with a little salt, butter and Cayenne pepper. Spread the mixture on thick sippets of bread toasted on one side only. Lay the grouse on top. Roast in a very hot oven (425°F, 220°C, Mark 7) for 25–30 minutes, according to size. Baste occasionally.

They must not be overcooked and should be taken from the oven *à point*. Serve them with buttered crumbs; heat ½ oz of butter, fry a handful of fresh white breadcrumbs in it gently with a little salt and pepper until light brown.

Scots Stoved Grouse

Suitable for older birds, also for chickens

Divide the bird into 8 portions saving the carcase and giblets to make stock. Peel and slice 1½ lb of potatoes in rounds ¼ inch thick. Peel and slice 8 oz of onions. Fry the portions of grouse in butter, adding salt and pepper. Butter a large pie dish, put a layer of sliced potatoes in it, then one of the grouse, then of sliced onions.

Add salt, pepper and butter and continue until everything is used, the last layer must be potato. Add grouse stock (made by cooking the carcase and giblets with water and seasoning either in a saucepan or the pressure cooker – see page 45). The stock is to come level with the top layer of potato. Cover tightly with foil so the pie dish is sealed. Bake it 1½–2 hours in a slow oven (300°F, 150°C, Mark 2), adding more stock later if necessary.

Serve garnished with chopped parsley.

Port Wine Sauce is made by heating ¼ pint of good game stock with 1 tablespoon of red currant or Rowan Jelly and 2 tablespoons of port.

Bilberry jelly flavoured with mint is served with roast grouse in Derbyshire.

A Hare Pie

If served cold the pie looks handsome garnished with one of the old fashioned paper pie frills still sold by good stationers.

Cut the meat in small neat boneless pieces. Season these highly, rolling them in a mixture of salt, pepper, nutmeg, ground ginger and cinnamon. Put them in a "jug", or deep fire-proof dish, with nearly half their own weight in butter. No water is necessary. Cover the top closely with foil and stand the "jug" in a dish of hot water to come half way up. Then put the whole thing, carefully, in a moderate oven (350°F, 180°C, Mark 4) for about $1\frac{1}{2}$ hours.

Meanwhile line a large pie dish with good sausage meat. Heap the pieces of cooked hare on top, adding the gravy from the "jug". Also a glass of red wine or port and a few fried force-meat balls.

Cover the top with pastry. Brush it with egg or milk, bake it in a hot oven (400°F, 200°C, Mark 6) for about 30 minutes, if liked when it comes out of the oven, pour a little more warmed wine through the hole in the top, with the aid of a funnel.

Venison could be used instead of hare, if liked. When available the forequarter or stewing cuts are usually very cheap as most people go for the roasting joints.

Roast Stuffed Saddle, or "Bawn", of Hare

A country house recipe for about four people

This is served garnished with watercress, crisp bacon rolls and with a green gooseberry jelly sauce handed separately.

Cut the fore and hind legs off the hare together with the rib portion (these may be jugged or made into a pie).

The remaining part with the skin and flaps is the saddle and is ready for stuffing. Make a forcemeat or stuffing by mixing 2 oz of soft white breadcrumbs with some chopped parsley, thyme and marjoram. Add salt and pepper, 2 oz of grated or shredded suet and two eggs to bind it. Mix well. When the hare is stuffed fasten it with a game clip or skewer or stitch it up with coarse thread.

Cover it all over with bards of fat bacon, tie these on with coarse thread. Then cover it loosely in buttered foil, or greaseproof paper. Roast it in a hot oven (400°F, 200°C, Mark 6) for about an hour. Remove the foil from time to time and baste with beer or dripping. Mild ale, if available, is excellent. Remove the foil towards the end.

Forcemeat Balls are often served with roast hare, they can be made from the same forcemeat as the stuffing. Roll this into balls with floured hands, put them in a tin and bake them in a moderate oven (350°F, 180°C, Mark 4) for 30 minutes, or about 20 minutes in a hot one.

See Cumberland Sauce; Hot Yorkshire Sauce (see pages 120 and 138).

Partridge
They are in season from September 1st to February 1st. Young partridge are those shot in the winter of the year in which they were hatched. The native partridge is considered the best, and to have a finer flavour than the red-legged or French partridge which was introduced into England at the time of Charles II. Both are good. During the present century partridge stocks have declined, perhaps because of different farming methods. Most estates no longer shoot them.

Cold Partridge
Partridge to be eaten cold (according to the Warwickshire County Federation of the National Federation of Women's Institutes) should be boiled not roasted. Hot boiled pheasant, with celery sauce, was a popular country house dish until fifty or sixty years ago, better liked than roast pheasant, and in the 19th century pigeons were perhaps more frequently boiled than casseroled. Cold boiled grouse is pleasant, too, with lettuce, Cumberland Sauce and Pickled Walnuts (see pages 120 and 283).

Young partridge are roasted like grouse (see page 152).

Allow half a partridge per person. They are slightly larger than pigeons and have, of course, more flavour if well hung. 'Prepare the bird, then wrap it in slices of fat bacon and put it into a pan with enough boiling salted water just to cover. Simmer gently until tender, 30 to 40 minutes according to age and size. When cooked, leave it in the water until it is almost cold, then lift it from the pan and remove the bacon. When quite cold serve it with lettuce.'

Susan, Duchess of Somerset's **Rice Salad for Cold Game** would be pleasant with cold boiled grouse, partridge or pigeon: 'Half a pound of patna rice; boil for 20 minutes in some good veal or chicken stock. When cold, make a mayonnaise, add the rice, with some truffle and tongue cut in shreds.'

Gevrey-Chambertin or a good claret, or less expensively a Chianti Classico, might be drunk with the cold birds.

Partridge Pudding

This was a popular dish with English gypsies, being easy to cook in a pot on an open fire. It was once a speciality of the Ashdown Forest district in Sussex and was sometimes made with pigeons, rabbits 'or anything that had come in during the night'. Old casserole grouse also make an excellent pudding but any small game birds can be made into a pudding. Most puddings contained wild woodland mushrooms, once plentiful locally. One still finds cèpes there in quantity in autumn.

'The true flavour of the game', as Eliza Acton wrote in *Modern Cookery for Private Families*, 1845, 'is admirably preserved by this mode of cooking. When mushrooms are plentiful, put a layer of [them] cleaned as for pickling, alternately with a layer of partridge, in filling the pudding, which will then be most excellent eating . . . Puddings of veal, chickens, and young rabbits, may all be made by this receipt, or with the addition of oysters.'

Skin a brace of well hung partridges and cut them into joints. Line a well buttered deep pudding basin with suet pastry. Lay in the birds, highly seasoned with pepper and a very little Cayenne pepper but only lightly with salt, rolled in flour, add 4 oz of sliced mushrooms. Pour in water to come two thirds of the way up the pastry to make the gravy.

Close the pudding carefully with a "lid" of suet pastry, moistening the edges and pinching them together with your fingers to seal it. Pleat two pieces of buttered foil (to leave room for the pudding to rise). Tie them firmly over the top of the basin. Tie a cloth on if liked.

Stand the basin on a rack or upturned saucer in a pan of boiling water to come half way up. Boil 3 to $3\frac{1}{2}$ hours with a lid on the pan, being careful always to fill up with boiling water, as that in the pan evaporates.

Jugged Pigeons

Brown 4 pigeons in 4 oz of butter, turning them and cooking them gently, either in a heavy pan or a flameproof casserole, until they are brown all over. Wrap each in a bacon rasher. Cover the pan or casserole with foil and a tight fitting lid, and let them simmer very gently for 45 minutes. If the lid fits well they will stew in their own juice. If not, add no more than 2 tablespoons of water. When done, take them out and keep them hot. Stir 2 to 3 tablespoons of thick cream into the pan juices, add a dash of Worcester sauce, and a good tablespoon of red currant jelly (for 4 pigeons). Let it simmer, stirring, for about 5 minutes. This makes an excellent thick brown sauce to pour over the pigeons. Serve them with new potatoes and watercress.
Note: The same recipe can also be used very successfully for cooking lamb chops.

Mrs. Isabella Beeton's Original Epsom Grandstand Pie (Pigeon)

It must have been a family recipe for her step-father was Clerk of the Racecourse at Epsom and Isabella and her brothers and sisters were actually brought up in the grandstand. They were an enormous family, her mother and step-father having between them twenty-three children who during the race meetings were sent to relatives in Brighton.

Cut $1\frac{1}{2}$ lb of rumpsteak into pieces about 3 inches square and with it line the bottom of a large pie-dish seasoning it well with pepper and salt. Clean two or three pigeons, rub them with pepper and salt inside and out and put into the body of each rather more than $\frac{1}{2}$ oz of butter. Lay them on the steak with a slice of ham on each pigeon. If liked a seasoning of ground mace may be added. Add four hard-boiled egg yolks and half fill the dish with stock. Cover the pie with puff pastry, ornament it in any way that may be preferred. Clean three of the pigeon's feet and place them in a hole made in the crust at the top, this shows what kind of pie it is.

Glaze the crust – that is to say brush it over with the yolk of an egg – and bake it in a well heated oven (375°F, 190°C, Mark 5) for about 1¼ hours. Cover the pastry lightly with a sheet of foil or greaseproof paper at about half time if it seems to be getting too brown. The pie should be cooked for about another ¾ hour if the pigeons are very tough. For this reduce the heat to moderate (350°F, 180°C, Mark 4).

Nowadays one would almost certainly leave out the pigeon's feet and decorate the pie crust with pastry roses and rose leaves or pastry acorns and oak leaves. Mrs Beeton says the pie is enough for five or six people and in her day it cost 5/3d. It may be eaten hot or cold and looks particularly well on the cold buffet table.

Pheasant

Most good game dealers have pheasant hung for one, two or three weeks according to what the customers want. Unfortunately very many people imagine that game must be hung until it is extremely high and smelly. This is not so. Nowadays 80% of it is eaten after 10 days hanging, no longer than the normal time for hanging beef or lamb.

Roast Pheasant with Foie Gras

This is from a recipe in the *Cumberland Women's Institute Cookery Book*, 8th edition.

Sprinkle the bird with salt and pepper to your taste. Smear and coat it plentifully with butter, wrap it in a thin sheet of barding pork or fat bacon. Roast it for about 45 minutes in a moderate oven (350°F, 180°C, Mark 4). Remove the barding fat, place the bird on a hot dish, and arrange pieces of chilled *pâté de foie gras* over the hot dish.

Garnish with watercress and serve it at once with the pan juices partially freed of fat and strained into a jug or sauce boat. Serve also some plain boiled fluffy rice and bramble or bilberry jelly.

Jugged Pheasant with Grapes

Stuff the bird with a cupful of stemmed black or green grapes adding a little salt and pepper, and either skewer or stitch up the openings with coarse thread. Dust the pheasant with seasoned flour and then brown it slowly and gently all over in three tablespoons of melted butter, turn it so all sides are brown. Add a teacup of stock, cover the pan or casserole closely with foil and a lid, and simmer tightly covered for 45 minutes or until tender. Add 2 tablespoons of sherry or Madeira to the pan juices. Keep the pheasant hot while you boil the pan juices to reduce slightly, pour them over the bird. Garnish with grapes.

This is a recipe which is also suitable for guinea fowls. The small seedless Cyprus grapes sold in late summer make a good stuffing but are not on sale when pheasants are in season.

Old Pheasant and Mushroom Pudding

'A man's dish', very good with buttered parsnips, bramble or Rowan Jelly and a full bodied red wine. Curly kale with butter and lemon juice or hot Jerusalem artichokes done in milk would be delicious with it.

Cut all the meat off an old pheasant skinning and slicing it in neat collops. Pull the carcase apart with your hands and simmer it with the skin, bones, giblets, some salt and pepper, an onion and any mushroom trimmings.

Butter a 2-pint pudding basin thickly, line it with suet pastry keeping enough for the top. Put in the meat in layers, with 4 oz of peeled, trimmed and sliced mushrooms. Add about half a pint of the pheasant stock to come near the top of the pastry crust. Cover this with the rest of the suet pastry rolled out into a "lid", moisten the edges of the pastry and pinch them together. Tie on two thicknesses of buttered foil firmly so no water can get into the pudding, pleating the foil deeply in the centre to leave room for it to rise. Stand the basin on a rack or upturned saucer in a large pan with boiling water to come half way up. Put the lid on the pan. Let the water boil for $3-3\frac{1}{2}$ hours. When filling up with more water, as it boils away, be sure this is boiling or the pudding may be soggy.

It can be turned out to serve or come to table in the pudding basin with a folded napkin pinned round it. Stand the hot basin on a plate or dish.

Roast Pheasant Stuffed with Mushrooms (*delicious*)

Put 8 oz of mushrooms in a small pan with 1½oz of butter, a little salt, pepper, grated nutmeg. Cook it gently over a low heat stirring occasionally until black juices run out.

Sprinkle the pheasant with salt and pepper, stuff it with the mushrooms. Cover the breast with bacon or barding fat. Lay the pheasant on a thick slice of bread in the roasting tin. Roast in a hot oven (400°F, 200°C, Mark 6) for 45–60 minutes basting it frequently with butter and the pan juices. This may include the liquid which ran out of the mushrooms. The juices from the bird drip on to the bread in cooking and the flavour is excellent. Garnish it with watercress, stirring a little cooking sherry into the pan to thicken the gravy. Bread sauce, roast potatoes, medlar jelly may be served with the bird. 'Young celery alone', according to Eliza Acton 'sliced and dressed with a rich salad mixture is excellent: it is still in some families served thus always with roast pheasants.'

In Scotland a roast pheasant is often served with oatmeal Skirly (see page 134); Rowan or Rodden Jelly are handed also.

A Rabbit Pie with Forcemeat Balls

Joint and bone a nice rabbit. Put the bones in the pan with 12 peppercorns, some herbs, stock vegetables, a little salt and any trimmings from the rabbit. Add cold water to cover and bring this gradually to the boil, then simmer until reduced to about ½ pint.

Meanwhile put the rabbit meat in a pie dish with two quartered hard boiled eggs, some chopped bacon rashers and forcemeat balls. Add a pie funnel and the ½ pint of rabbit stock. Cover the dish with puff pastry and decorate this with pastry roses and rose leaves, which brush with milk.

Bake the pie first in a hot oven (400°F, 200°C, Mark 6) for about 10 minutes then reduce the heat to moderate (350°F, 180°C, Mark 4) until the pie is cooked in about 2 hours.

Cover the pastry with a piece of foil if getting too brown.

Baked Rabbit with Yorkshire Pudding

Cut up a rabbit, put it in an old brown stew pot with a large Spanish onion peeled and coarsely chopped. Add two or three thick slices of fat bacon cut in dice, some pepper, a little salt, and cold water just to cover. Cover the top closely with foil, then a lid and bake it in a moderate oven (350°F, 180°C, Mark 4) till tender, in about $1\frac{1}{2}$ hours depending on the age of the rabbit. It must not boil for the rabbit, when served, must be a nice pink colour. When done mix a little cornflour and milk to a smooth paste and add it to the rabbit stock. Cook it briefly in a pan, stirring until the milky gravy thickens, pour it back on the rabbit.

This is served from the pot accompanied by Yorkshire pudding and sprouts, or with hot jacket potatoes wrapped in a napkin, for warmth, if preferred.

Stuffed Baked Rabbit in Milk *(Also suitable for hare)*

Make some sage and onion stuffing, with it stuff the rabbit (or hare) and sew it in with coarse thread. Lay it in a casserole with a lid. Sprinkle it thickly with seasoned flour. Lay two rashers of bacon along the back. Add 4 oz of butter cut in slices. Pour in $\frac{1}{2}$ pint of good creamy milk. Put a lid on the casserole and bake in a fairly hot oven (375°F, 190°C, Mark 5) for 2 hours. Take off the lid for the last 15 minutes.

A Plain Stewed Rabbit with Dumplings

This is very good on a cold winter evening. The rabbit is garnished with carrots and turnips from the stew, and with little dumplings which have been cooked in its own stock.

Skin, joint and soak a couple of rabbits in cold salted water for 2 hours. Put them in a pan with 2 lb of salted pork belly cut in chunks, add fresh cold water to cover, bring it to the boil, skim off any rising scum. Add two large peeled, sliced onions, two or three sliced carrots and a piece of (swede) turnip cut in chunks. Add 12 peppercorns, 3 cloves, a blade of mace or good pinch of nutmeg. Simmer for about $1\frac{1}{2}$ hours or until tender.

Meanwhile make some suet pastry, form it into little dumplings with floured hands. Put them in the pan to boil 20 minutes before the rabbit is done. Serve with the rabbit. Norfolk Dumplings (see page 122) may be cooked with it if preferred. Serve with Quince or Medlar Jelly.

An inexpensive but full bodied earthy red wine such as Egri Bikaver, Bull's Blood from Hungary, goes well with it.

A Boiled Turkey

Choose if possible a small, plump hen turkey, but one of a size to fit into a very large saucepan. Stuff it in the crop if liked with Oyster Stuffing (see page 128) or with Lemon and Parsley Stuffing (see page 124) and stitch up the openings. Or leave it plain. Break the breast bone if liked to make the turkey look round and plump. Put it in a large pan and cover with warm water. Bring to the boil and simmer, bubbling gently for $1\frac{1}{2}-2\frac{1}{4}$ hours. Skim off the froth and rising scum during the first 15 minutes of cooking. Fast boiling will cause the skin of the bird to break and is to be avoided.

Serve it with the Old Celery Sauce or with Inspector Tweedie's Mushroom Sauce (see pages 118 and 126).

A Buttered Turkey

A fresh hand plucked turkey is delicious stuffed, roasted and Blistered with Raspings in the eighteenth century manner, like a capon and served with Hanover (liver and lemon) Sauce (see page 123).

Alternatively, to make a good festive dish for Easter, a small turkey could be stuffed in the crop with Victorian Oyster Forcemeat, then boiled or roast and dished up with Celery Sauce (see pages 128 and 118).

For a classic Christmas turkey the crop might be stuffed with Bacon and Mushroom Stuffing and the body with Mrs. Glasse's Chestnut Stuffing (see page 134). An entire chain of delicately browned pork sausages is sometimes laid across its breast, hot, just before it comes to table, when it is properly known as an "Alderman in Chains".

If it is to be slow roasted in foil, butter it first thickly all over with a good 8 oz of butter, thick over the breast and drumsticks. Stand the stuffed and buttered bird on a wide sheet of foil.

Sprinkle it with pepper and salt, a little fresh or dried tarragon if available. Pour 3 tablespoons of white wine into the parcel before wrapping the bird completely in foil. Roast it in a slow oven (325°F, 170°C, Mark 3) 20 minutes per lb and 20 minutes over for birds under 14 lb, 15 minutes per lb for larger birds.

Do not forget to include the weight of the stuffing when calculating the cooking time, and if it is an oven-ready bird be sure that it is completely thawed *inside* before cooking begins. Turn back the foil for the last 40 minutes to brown the breast. The turkey is cooked if you thrust a skewer into the thick bit of the drumstick and no juice runs out.

The traditional accompaniments for a roast turkey are a good giblet gravy and A Rich Victorian Bread Sauce (see page 114), but the almost forgotten Artichoke Sauce (see page 113) is, however delicious with it.

Devilled Turkey, or Pheasant

Cut the cold cooked bird in boneless slices. Heat these in a little stock, made preferably from turkey giblets (or the pheasant bones). Whip ½ pint of double cream till stiff. Stir in 1 tablespoon of Worcester sauce and 1 teaspoon of fresh mixed English mustard.

Put the turkey or pheasant in a pie dish when warm, pour the sauce over. Bake it in a hot oven (400°F, 200°C, Mark 6) for only about 5 minutes.

Venison in Beer

Most deer are as lean as an Olympic runner, and venison can be dry and tough if not properly cooked. This is a North Yorkshire recipe, and they mostly cook it locally with Theakston's beer brewed since 1827 at nearby Masham. Any good draught bitter or a brown ale would be suitable. It is a delicious winter dish to eat with mashed, buttered swede turnips, and perhaps some baked jacket potatoes. Theakston's Old Peculiar is very good to drink with it.

Melt 1 tablespoon of black treacle and 8 oz of Demerara sugar in 1 pint of beer in a suitable sized pan, heat gently, stirring until the sugar has dissolved. Put a well hung joint of venison, a shoulder or one of the cheaper cuts, in a flameproof casserole or heavy pan. Cover it with the liquid making more to the same proportions if necessary. Add salt and pepper. Put on a lid, bring it to the boil and let it simmer till tender in a moderate oven (350°F, 180°C, Mark 4) allowing 30 minutes to the pound and 30 minutes over.

Venison Roasted in a Suet Crust (*Scotland*)
The best roasting cuts are the leg, the haunch, the loin and the saddle. Venison being very lean is very dry and tough unless either wrapped in fat, or in foil, or in a huff paste, or a wrapping of brown paper − or perhaps larded. In the North of Scotland one of the old ways of cooking it was to wrap it in a suet crust, which was much better than the usual cheap huff paste, for it retained the juices and towards the end of the cooking time became richly brown from being basted with the butter in the tin, and it could be served and eaten with the meat. A huff paste is always thrown away after the joint is cooked, it used to be wrapped round the joint *on top of several layers of paper* which had been well greased or dipped in oil. Brown paper was then tied on over the huff taste, and the whole caboodle thrown out before eating the venison.

A solid bone-free piece from the haunch is the best cut for this recipe. Season with salt and pepper. Roll out enough ordinary suet crust pastry to enclose the meat completely, the pastry should be about ½ inch thick. It must enclose the meat completely. Seal up all the joins in the pastry by moistening them with water and pinching them together.

Melt 2 oz of butter in a roasting tin with a grid on which the joint can stand, to lift it off the bottom. Roast it in a moderately hot oven (375°F, 190°C, Mark 5) for about 30 minutes per lb on the grid. Baste the pastry with the butter occasionally and especially towards the end.

The meat is served with crab apple jelly or rowan jelly, buttered French beans or runner beans, roast or boiled or new potatoes, and with the deliciously savoury crust.

Cumberland Sauce and Oxford Brawn Sauce (see pages 120 and 131) are served with cold venison.

Chapter 6

The Kitchen Garden

There is nothing quite like the flavour of vegetables fresh pulled from the garden still with the warm, damp earth clinging to them, rinsed and cooked at once and then eaten with melted butter and a little lemon juice. Almost all vegetables need plenty of butter on them and the lemon juice brings out their flavour even more sharply than it does that of fish. Most of them are over-cooked and when fresh out of the garden are best still crisp and *al dente*, lightly boiled like home made *tagliatelle*. Soda should never be used in cooking them.

All summer vegetables should be eaten within a few hours of being cut, their flavour is never so fine later. They are best laid on a cool brick floor. Sweetcorn loses much of its flavour a few hours after picking, fresh peas should be shelled only a few minutes before they are to be cooked, if this is impossible wrap them in a damp tea towel after shelling them. Asparagus in particular loses flavour and is best cooked the day it is cut. If the vegetable has been bought in a shop or sent by post some of the freshness can be restored by standing it in a jug of cold water to within an inch of the top of the spears and then putting it in the refrigerator for a couple of hours.

Cucumbers and globe artichokes should be put into two inches of cold water. Parsley and watercress are best kept in little jugs.

When buying root vegetables if possible choose those with the earth still on them, potatoes especially. Washed potatoes in plastic bags lose much of their taste and texture, it will be noticed that after a short time therein they go green and sprout.

Globe Artichokes

Globe artichokes are easy-to-grow perennials and were once common in English gardens. There are various recipes for them in 17th century cookery books and in the kitchens of a hundred years ago globe artichokes were more commonly used than tomatoes, which were then thought rather "new fangled and unwholesome". Some Victorian cookery books suggest using globe artichokes, bottoms or hearts, as a cheap substitute for tomatoes. They were also used to flavour pies and stews. According to Thomas Culpeper they 'provoke lust'.

There are several types, from the huge round Breton artichoke to the small spiky Italian and Provençale ones which can be eaten raw.

To cook: Trim the stalks off the globe artichokes and, if liked, the spikey tips of the leaves or petals. Cook them in boiling salted water, preferably in an enamel pan to preserve the colour, for 30 to 40 minutes, or until they feel soft when a skewer is stuck into them. The exact time depends upon the size of the artichokes. Before being sent to the table they should be turned upside down and well drained.

They may be served with warm liquid butter, or cold with an oil and vinegar dressing and are eaten in the fingers, as is asparagus.

To Eat Globe Artichokes

Serve one globe artichoke per person. The leaves are pulled off one by one at table. Dip the broad fleshy part at the base into the hot melted butter (or other dressing). Nibble this, then discard the leaf and repeat until the centre with its tightly packed hair-like flower petals is reached. This is called the "choke" and is inedible. Pull or cut it away from the fleshy base and discard it.

This leaves the heart or bottom of the artichoke exposed. This is the best part. Eat it with more butter, etc., if necessary with a fork.

It is useful to have side plates or a dish for the spent leaves.

Hot Jerusalem Artichokes

Used in Belgium for making alcohol, they were introduced to

Europe after the Thirty Years War, they are not in any way related to Globe Artichokes. An easily grown vegetable, it is the tuberous potato-like root which is eaten.

The artichokes should be dropped into a pan of cold milk-and-water one by one as they are peeled, as the peeled vegetable darkens when exposed to the air. When all are ready, boil them gently in it. Add salt when they are half cooked, remove them from the pan immediately they are cooked. Overcooking makes them grey and soggy.

Use the milk-and-water to make a white sauce to serve on the artichokes. They may, however, simply be turned in melted butter and sprinkled with chopped parsley.

They may also be sliced, raw, and fried a crisp golden brown like chips and are then very good with pork chops.

Jerusalem Artichokes can also be cooked in the hot ashes of an open fire like chestnuts or jacket potatoes. Hold them in a napkin and rub off the skin with the fingers. Eat them hot with butter.

Jerusalem Artichoke Salad

When peeled and boiled in milk as above the artichokes may be drained and made into an autumn salad, garnished with peeled prawns or shrimps, or with halved hard boiled eggs and radishes.

When still warm from the pan turn them in a dressing of olive oil, lemon juice, salt and pepper and when cold arrange them on a wide shallow dish pouring off any surplus dressing and surrounding them with the chosen garnish.

Jerusalem Artichoke Soufflé

This is to be served straight from the oven with a jug of melted butter, or some mushroom sauce, or Hollandaise sauce. It makes a pleasing light luncheon dish.

Cook 1 lb of Jerusalem artichokes in milk as before, slice or chop them, and save the milk in which they were cooked.

Melt 2 tablespoons of butter, stir in 3 tablespoons of flour gradually, heating and stirring all the time. Add $\frac{1}{2}$ pint of the milk in which the vegetables were cooked, heating and stirring to make a smooth thick sauce. Stir in the yolks of three eggs, one after the other, then add the artichoke pieces, some salt, pepper, allspice.

Finally, just before the soufflé is to go into the oven, add the three egg whites so stiffly whisked the basin may be turned upside down without them falling out. Pour the mixture very gently into a well buttered $2\frac{1}{2}$ pint soufflé dish. Bake at once in a hot oven (400°F, 200°C, Mark 6) for about 25 minutes until the soufflé is well risen. It is perhaps at its most enjoyable when still moist in the middle.

Asparagus

There are various types of asparagus, white, purple, or green, thick and thin as well as the very thin English "sprue grass", usually relatively cheap and useful for sauces and soups. The pale Continental asparagus is shored up and blanched under the soil like celery and never becomes green as it does not see the light. That of Malines in Belgium and of Argenteuil in France (a fat purplish-pink asparagus) is especially famous.

Asparagus is of the same family as lily of the valley, it was known in ancient Rome and still grows wild in some parts of Europe, it used to be found near Kynance Cove in Cornwall a few years ago. Some of the asparagus sold in Sicily has thorns on it.

English growers usually begin cutting in May and continue until early July. The Vale of Evesham has been famous for its asparagus for generations. These are mostly small growers, families farming one or two acres, and when the crop is ready, aunts and grandfathers, come in to help. In Norfolk and Suffolk and Lincolnshire it is grown on a large scale on big farms. Some English asparagus is sold untrimmed and so has a long shank of hard and inedible white stalk. This type should of course be bought not by weight but by the bunch.

To Cook: Asparagus is best cooked upright in boiling salted water so that the tender tips may steam while the tougher, lower parts boil fiercely. Special asparagus steamers are sometimes sold for this, but are perhaps another example of the superfluous gadgets that proliferate in the kitchen equipment shops. A metal coffee pot or percolator will cook a small bunch of asparagus perfectly, holding the stalks upright; larger quantities can be boiled in a tallish pan, such as a pressure cooker without a lid.

Allow 6–9 heads per person. Put them in boiling salted water adding a lump of sugar. Boil them about 20 minutes.

One can also buy special asparagus dishes, silver asparagus serving tongs, and special circular silver implements for eating the Continental type of asparagus. A better idea would be more asparagus and less equipment.

THE FIRST ASPARAGUS OF THE SEASON.

Farmer (at Market Dinner). " Wull, Gen'elmen, I dunno wot be the c'rect way o' servin' these 'ere, but I gen'elly eats just the Ends of 'em myself ! "   [*Helps himself to the tops !*

To Serve: In England hot boiled asparagus is eaten in the fingers, usually with melted butter in which the pointed ends are dipped before one puts them in the mouth. For a polite or formal meal glass finger bowls containing warmed water and a slice of lemon, or a sprig of lemon balm from the garden, are served for rinsing the fingers.

Sauces for asparagus include English Butter Sauce (see page 115), Susan, Duchess of Somerset's Sauce (see page 123) and Mayonnaise (see page 125) for cold asparagus.

On the Continent however, asparagus is normally eaten with a knife and fork not in the fingers, and the sauces and garnishes for it are accordingly often more elaborate: grated cheese as well as melted butter, hollandaise sauce, melted butter and freshly poached piping hot eggs into which the heads of the asparagus are dipped.

Aubergines or Egg Plants
They should be sliced in rounds, unpeeled, sprinkled with salt and left for a couple of hours to "weep". Then wipe and rinse them clean. Dry in a tea towel, squeeze them between your hands to extract the black juice. Then dip the rounds in egg and fry them gently.

Basil
Sweet basil is an annual which is rather difficult to grow in Britain. It arrived here in the 16th century and in English cooking it is traditional in Turtle Soup as well as being one of the seasonings in the famous 17th century Fetter Lane sausages, and it was once used as a pot herb (*i.e. bouquet garni*) in soups and so on.

It has a delicious spicy scent, like warm summer greenhouses, and works miracles in tomato dishes, for it seems to taste more like tomatoes than tomatoes do themselves. Continental housewives, Italian ones especially, pride themselves on having a nice little pot of basil growing in the kitchen window for 'you can tell a good housewife', in the words of the old Italian saying, 'by her pot of basil.' The reader who is familiar with Keats' *Isabella* or Boccaccio's *Decameron* will remember the story of the girl who buried her murdered lover's head, secretly, in the large pot of basil she had growing in her bedroom window. This she tended and watered every day and was thus able to have him always by her. A more conventional use for this strongly scented herb is in a tomato salad.

It can be preserved in winter in the freezer. The herb is also sold dried by good grocers.

Basil Oil is made by putting some sprigs of fresh basil in a bottle of olive oil to flavour it.

For **Basil Sherry** (to sprinkle on turtle and other soup) steep the fresh leaves in cooking sherry for a fortnight. Then strain.

Bay Leaves
An edible member of the laurel family, though the laurel itself is poisonous. Bay leaves were used to make the wreaths worn to celebrate victory by the Greeks and Romans. English cooks used to add one or two bay leaves and a pinch of ground nutmeg to milk puddings. Some still do. The flavour is most delicate, well worth trying after a surfeit of vanilla, and is also pleasant in junket, egg custard, and burnt cream as well as in rice and sago puddings.

The bay leaf is one of the most widely used kitchen herbs. Bay leaves are put in the water when poaching fish or when cooking ox tongue, salt beef, or brawn, and should be added when boiling ham. They are used to flavour as well as to garnish potted meats and pâtés, are part of the bunch of mixed herbs added to soup, or casseroles, and they are invaluable for flavouring a white sauce.

Butchers once used them to give "that extra tang" to lard, they are added to the vinegar for many pickles, Greek women put them in cupboards to perfume the clean linen. Fresh green bay leaves also make an attractive garnish for frozen oranges and lemons, filled with water ice. They are pretty too with plain raw oranges if a traditional dessert service is used.

Borage
An annual which blooms with an intense Madonna-blue flower.

It sows itself easily, thrives in poor stony soil and is one of our native hardy plants, sometimes to be found growing in quantity on the chalk downs. A tall strong plant it is a great favourite with bee keepers. Easy to grow from seed.

It has a slight taste of cucumber and is used in drinks e.g. Pimms No 1 Cup and was popular in the 19th century in claret cup. Both the young leaves and flowers can be used in a green salad. It has been grown in England for centuries and was referred to by Chaucer. The chopped leaves may be added to mince — and to cucumber dishes.

Broad Beans

Broad beans in Parsley Sauce with hot boiled bacon and fresh pulled buttery new potatoes are a British classic, traditional about Whitsun in Kent and Sussex, and well liked in the Fens where they are served with the bacon at many village feasts. They are good too, with baked pickled pork belly and apple sauce.

They may be shelled, boiled in salted water until tender, then tossed in melted butter with a little chopped parsley, or served in a conventional Parsley Sauce (see page 139). No vegetable should be allowed to remain in the water after it is cooked, this ruins the taste.

At the beginning of the season broad beans are often tender enough for one to cook and eat the pods and everything without shelling them. They should be sliced in chunks then cooked in a pan of rapidly boiling salted water without a lid. They then have an almost earthy flavour, and should be well buttered.

Runner Beans with Buttered Onions

This is an easy dish to prepare in the intervals of cooking something else. The beans are delicious with roast chicken or simple dishes such as macaroni cheese.

String and slice 1 lb of runner beans coarsely, plunge them into a pan of boiling salted water, let them boil for 5 minutes, then drain them in a sieve. Put a large peeled chopped onion in a pan with a good big lump of butter and let it frizzle gently for a few minutes without browning. Add the well drained partly cooked runner beans, a little salt and pepper. Let it all simmer very gently with a lid on the pan for an hour on a low heat, stir occasionally.

Brussels Sprouts and Cheese

A good vegetable with roast pork, oven baked sausages or crisp fried herrings with mustard sauce, and buttery mashed potatoes.

Trim any faded leaves from the sprouts, rinse and then put them in a pan with only a little boiling salted water. Boil them for about 10 minutes, and meanwhile butter a fireproof dish, sprinkle it with grated cheese. Drain the cooked sprouts, heap them in the dish in a mound. Season them with pepper and a little ground nutmeg. Then cover the top and sides of the mound of sprouts with grated cheese and a few knobs of butter. Put the dish in a very hot oven (450°F, 230°C, Mark 8) for 7 or 8 minutes until the cheese is bubbling hot and toasted brown on top. Serve at once.

Brussels Sprouts with Chestnuts

To accompany a roast turkey (see also Chestnuts and Mushrooms p. 175). The bird should also be served with forcemeat balls, bacon rolls and sausages in addition to the sprouts and chestnuts.

Allow 8 oz of sprouts and 2 oz of butter per person. Wash and trim the sprouts. Boil them in a little salted water for about 10 minutes. Drain and toss them in the hot butter with an equal quantity of cooked and shelled chestnuts. Heat both vegetables and frizzle them slightly before serving.

Cabbage

Wash the cabbage and shred it finely just before it is to be cooked. Put it in a pan with a tightly fitting lid, adding 1 dessertspoon of butter, 2 tablespoons of water and ¼ teaspoon of salt, cook it rapidly. Drain, serve it hot and slightly crisp, with butter.

Cooked cabbage may be fried in dripping, and is very good with bacon and eggs.

For Colcannon and for Bubble and Squeak, see page 188 under Potatoes.

Stoved Carrots

Home grown vegetables have a different flavour from those bought in shops and one of the rewards after exhausting work in the kitchen garden is to be able to eat the very young vegetables, sometimes little more than trimmings, almost straight out of the earth. Fresh young carrots scrubbed and trimmed and cooked slowly in an earthenware dish in the oven are excellent.

Wash and trim them, slicing them if large enough in rounds. Put them in a fireproof dish, add water to come almost half an inch up the pot. Add a knob of butter, salt and pepper, chopped parsley and a teaspoon of sugar. Cover them with foil or a lettuce leaf and a lid. Cook them very slowly until the carrots are tender in a moderate oven (350°F, 180°C, Mark 4). This is also suitable for very young turnips or a mixture of both.

Cauliflower and Cheese

A favourite supper dish, this is also very good as a first course, or to eat with roast pork or grilled gigot steaks and Devil Butter (see page 20).

First boil the cauliflower, with a little nutmeg or mace as well as salt in the water to bring out the cauliflower flavour. As it will not be served whole it may be broken in large pieces, and the stalk part and some of the green cut in large chunks to cook it more quickly. It should be still slightly firm when taken out of the water or it will break up in the cheese sauce.

Put some pieces of cauliflower, stalk as well as flower, in a well buttered oven dish or pie dish. Pour $\frac{1}{2}$ pint of cheese sauce over it. Sprinkle breadcrumbs, grated cheese and dabs of butter on top. Bake it in a really hot oven (425°F, 220°C, Mark 7) for about 10 minutes till sauce and vegetable are both hot and the top is brown and bubbling. If liked the dish may be prepared in the morning and browned and heated in the oven at supper time.

Celery

The earthy garden celery is in prime condition at Christmas time. It is better to buy the local grown untidy looking kind, crisply fresh and with the earth still on it, rather than the neat washed limp heads of imported celery, packed in plastic bags. Not only is it pale green and flabby but there is no root on it – and the root is almost the best part, delectable raw with strong English cheese, oatcakes and unsalted butter.

The celery should be washed, scraped where necessary, divided into several pieces and placed on the table upright in a jug of cold water. With good salt to dip it in – Maldon sea salt, or Tidman's sea salt (from health food stores), or Northwich Cheshire salt – it goes perfectly with Stilton cheese.

See Celery Sauce for Boiled Turkey (page 118), Celery Salad for Pheasant (page 160).

Chestnuts and Mushrooms (*To serve with roast turkey*)
Whole cooked chestnuts are also served with game, especially venison. They may be added to an oxtail stew shortly before serving.

To prepare and cook chestnuts: Slit (say) 2 lb of raw fresh chestnuts round the centre. Put them in a frying pan and cook them dry over a moderate heat for about 25 minutes shaking the pan frequently. When they are cooked both the inner and the outer shells can be peeled off easily. This is easiest to do while the chestnuts are still warm. Peel a few at a time, wrapping the others in a tea towel for warmth until they are to be peeled.

Chestnuts may, alternatively, be slit and placed on a baking sheet in a hot oven (400°F, 200°C, Mark 6) until the shells and skins come off easily. They must be skinned while still hot. Some cooks prefer to slit the chestnuts then cook them in boiling water for about 10 minutes before peeling them as above. In peeling chestnuts it is important not to slit the actual nut as it breaks easily when cooked.

Whatever method used the skinned and shelled chestnuts must then be simmered in stock or water or milk until they are soft.

Dried Italian chestnuts are sold ready peeled and skinned. They should be soaked in warm water like dried beans until tender and can easily be cut with a knife. They can then be used as fresh peeled chestnuts with much less bother. They too should be simmered in stock. Whole peeled, skinned and *cooked* chestnuts in brine are sold in tins. They should be rinsed and drained, then re-heated in a little butter or stock.

For Chestnuts and Mushrooms: Chop the mushrooms if large and cook them gently in oil and butter mixed. Add the shelled, skinned and cooked chestnuts, turning and heating them with the mushrooms. Add a little salt and pepper at the end.

An equal volume of chestnuts and mushrooms make a pleasant dish, though the proportion may be varied. Whole button mushrooms of about the same size as chestnuts are especially good when cooked whole, as above, and heated with the cooked chestnuts as above.

Chives
These grow in tightly packed clumps and were once used with parsley to edge the beds in kitchen gardens. Much grown and much used in Ireland, they give a pleasant onion flavour, but are not so rich in sulphur as an onion and not so indigestible. It is known in some parts of the country as the "rush leek". A native herb and a perennial, it is very occasionally found wild, and is easy to grow in any garden soil. One can deep-freeze or keep them in a plastic bag in the refrigerator in winter.

In Ireland chopped chives are sometimes added to mashed potatoes. They may also be chopped and added to cottage cheese or cream cheese. They make a pleasant addition to a potato salad and can often be added chopped to dishes instead of parsley.

Coriander
This is what some people call Chinese parsley, it grows up to 2 feet high with white, pink or pale mauve flowers. The young leaves are used in Greece chopped in salads. They are very good chopped to sprinkle in chicken or turkey broth instead of chopped parsley, and in various fish dishes, and worth using experimentally.

The taste is as impossible to describe as that of thyme or celery but just as distinctive. These small flattish leaves were much used here in medieval times, but then forgotten. The plant is not difficult to grow and the leaves freeze well. One also finds bunches of fresh green coriander leaves in Indian, as well as Greek, grocery stores in Britain. They are used as a garnish and flavouring all over the Middle East and Far East and are one of the subtle flavours of real curry.

The seeds have a totally different flavour – small, round, scented and creamy white, they taste perhaps of tangerines or orange peel and are used in making vermouth. They are very pleasant with roast pork or roast lamb and should be pressed into the joint before roasting to flavour it. They are used whole in pickling spices and chutneys and two or three hundred years ago used to be added, whole, to steak, kidney and oyster pudding. The ground seeds were once used to flavour junket and milk pudding. Coriander is not to be missed.

Dandelions

To Dress Dandelions – As a Salad (*very wholesome*)
'This common weed of the fields and highways is an excellent vegetable, the young leaves forming an admirable adjunct to a salad . . . The slight bitterness of its flavour is to many persons very agreeable; and it is often served at well-appointed tables. It has also, we believe, the advantage of possessing valuable medicinal qualities. Take the roots before the blossom is at all advanced, if they can readily be found in that state; if not, pluck off and use the young leaves only . . . For a salad, take them very young and serve them entire, or break them quite small with the fingers; then wash and drain them. Dress them with oil and vinegar, or with any other sauce which may be preferred.'
From Eliza Acton's *Modern Cookery for Private Families*, 1845.

They are better known now in France than in England where they are cultivated as a salad crop, widely on sale in spring, and known as *pissenlits*, somewhat unjustifiably. The leaves of the young dandelions have an excellent flavour when blanched under stones or a brick for some days before picking. The following unusual dressing from Northern France, the Champagne district, is excellent on either dandelions, shaggy endives or Chinese beansprouts, or lamb's lettuce.

For the dressing: Fry 3 oz of diced streaky bacon slowly so most of the fat runs out. Season the salad with the juice of two lemons, pepper and salt. Then at the very moment of serving pour the hot fried bacon and the melted bacon fat over the salad. Toss it with the salad servers. It must be eaten at once before the bacon fat cools and sets, and is outstandingly good.

STATE O' TRADE.

Small Girl. " Please, Mrs. Greenstough, Mother says will you Give her a Lettuce ? "

Mrs. G. " Give ? ! Tell thee Mother Giv'um's dead, and Lendum's very bad. Nothink for Nothink 'ere, and Precious Little for Sixpence ! ! "

Fennel

There are two kinds of fennel. The tall slender herb with the feathery foliage grows wild in Britain. This is easy to grow in the garden and is used for Fennel Sauce and to season fish and also to lay under mackerel before grilling them. It was once widely used in English cooking as it still is abroad.

The other kind, Florence fennel so popular in Italy, is a fat white blanched vegetable which looks like celery. This is easy to grow too. The Italians eat it after the final course just as it is without any dressing, for its slight aniseed flavour cleans the mouth and makes a perfect ending to a meal.

To dress fennel as a salad: Cut it in slices, wash and dry them and serve with a dessertspoon of olive oil, a dash of lemon juice, salt to taste and freshly ground black pepper. It can also be braised like celery.

Kale

Curly kale, kail or "curly greens" is a hardy winter vegetable, easy to grow. It is a kind of cabbage with shaggy dark green leaves curled like ostrich feathers, much grown in Scotland.

Wash and strip the frilly bits off the centre stalks. Boil them about 10 minutes in salted water. Drain and eat them hot with plenty of butter and lemon juice and a good sprinkling of pepper. They may also be served with a hot cream sauce. Good with roast pork.

Sea Kale

A popular Victorian vegetable, the young shoots are "forced" like rhubarb and in old gardens were often covered by special sea kale pots made for this purpose. These are about 3 feet high, a foot across, and have a hole at the top with a flowerpot clay lid about the size of a breakfast saucer. Sea kale used to be grown commercially near Worthing but is now difficult to find in shops. It grows wild on rocky shores, near Dungeness for instance. When fully sprouted it has large frilled leaves and a sweet-scented white flower.

A delicious winter vegetable, the pale blanched shoots,

about 9 inches long with a small tightly curled knob of un-opened leaf at the top, need virtually no preparation for cooking. If there is a small foot of root attached, as in celery, then this may be peeled.

Cook the sea kale in boiling salted water for nearly 15 minutes. Serve it with melted butter and lemon juice. All the sauces suitable for asparagus are suitable for sea kale. It was sometimes served in a rich white sauce. The flavour is often compared with asparagus, perhaps because they are long sticks, but the flavour is really very different and they are ready much earlier in the year than asparagus.

Leeks
The leek is not so fully appreciated in the Southern part of England as it is in the North, and in Wales and Scotland. It is very hardy, untouched by the severest winter and especially popular in the North East, all the cottage gardens in Durham and Northumberland seem to have them. Some say that when stewed in gravy nothing can touch them for flavour and wholesomeness.

For Buttered (Durham) Leeks: Trim the leeks leaving on most of the green part. Wash them well, drain, then slice them finely and plunge them into boiling salted water. Remove them from the heat, leave them only 2 minutes then drain and plunge them into cold water to freshen them. Melt a little butter in a sauce-pan (allowing about $\frac{1}{2}$ oz per lb of leeks). Toss the pieces of sliced leeks in it till they are very shiny. Add some freshly ground black pepper, cook them gently for about 5 minutes, they should be soft but not mushy.

They are delicious with roast lamb or roast chicken. Thus cooked they also make the basis of a leek soufflé or leek pie. See also Durham Leek Pudding (page 129).

Lemon Balm
A sweet scented plant introduced by the Romans, it grows about 2 feet high, spreads like nettles. The finely chopped raw leaves smell delicately of lemons and are very good in salads or as a

garnish for fish. The leaves can also be chopped into forcemeat and stuffings. This is a mild flavoured herb and may be used in larger quantities than most. It is usually found in old gardens; the Victorians put a few sprigs in the finger bowls for dessert and used it for *tisanes*, and sometimes added a little to the pot when brewing Indian tea.

Known as *Melissa officinalis*. Melissa comes from the Greek word for "bee" — bees enjoy the small white flowers.

When making parsley sauce it can be made more piquant by the addition of 50 per cent lemon balm.

It should not be confused with "barm" which is of course the old word for yeast as in Barm Brack and the Barm Cakes and Barm Buns of Derbyshire and Cheshire.

Lovage
It used to be sold as a cordial in public houses in the 19th century. The herb was introduced by the Romans and widely grown here from the 14th century. The scented leaves have a flavour like celery, useful in summer when celery is unavailable. They may be chopped in salads and added chopped, before cooking, to soups — to leek and potato soup for instance. This is a neglected herb which is coming back into favour, an easily grown perennial.

Marrows
To be good they should be cut when small, about the size of a bathroom loofah. The classic Marrow in White Sauce is now un-fashionable and much disliked, because often badly cooked.

In fact if the marrow is picked when fairly small, chopped, de-seeded then lightly boiled and properly drained it is perfectly delicious with parsley sauce or cheese sauce.

In autumn marrows may be stored in a cool, dry place such as a shed or cellar and will remain fresh and firm for some months. The wide use of the vegetable marrow dates from the late 19th century. Earlier recipes use cucumbers — or "cowcumbers" — for much the same purpose.

Courgettes are a species of marrow, cut young when no bigger than small bananas, though they never grow very large. They are grown like marrows, and constant cutting ensures a heavy crop.

Slice them unpeeled in fingers. Put them in a heavy pan with a couple of tablespoons of butter or oil, a little chopped parsley, a finely chopped onion, salt and pepper. Let them simmer very gently in a pan with the lid on. No water is necessary, enough liquid comes out of them to prevent burning if they are cooked gently for about 30 minutes. When cooked in oil instead of butter they are equally good cold, I garnish them with lemon slices.

Ordinary marrows are quite good, cut in chunks without the seeds, and cooked like this too. I do not bother to peel them. If they need peeling they are tough and would be better used for Marrow and Ginger Jam (see page 274).

Aunt Alice's Marrow Dish
This is excellent not only with Barnsley chops and grilled lamb cutlets but with stewed and braised veal, 'boiled chicken or any other delicate meat', as the old cooks said.

Peel a half grown marrow and cut out the seeds. Slice 1 lb with 1 oz of peeled, chopped onion into 1 pint of stock. Let it simmer for about 1 hour, taste for seasoning, add salt and pepper if necessary. Purée the marrow in the mixer, re-heat it all and when boiling add about ¼ pint of double cream.

It looks delightful with small sippets of bread, fried in butter, arranged round the dish.

Mushrooms
The almost total disappearance of the horse does not seem to have affected the wild mushroom in the least, they seem to grow just as well in meadows where cows have been grazing, in autumn in some parts of the country you see them in the early morning sticking up, round and white, in the long grass – masses of them like rows of bald heads at the opera.

Large mushrooms are delicious left whole but with the stalks removed. Place a dab of butter on each with a little salt and pepper. Then put them in a tin of hot fat, pour some Yorkshire pudding batter over them and bake this as usual in the oven. It makes a good supper dish.

Cèpes

In autumn in the damper parts of the country on the edge of woods, pine woods especially, one can often gather quantities of *boletus edulis*; it is what is called *cèpes* in France, *porcini* in Italy and *steinpilzen* in Germany. There seems to be no proper English name for them although they are widespread throughout the British Isles. I have seen them growing, wild, in a hotel garden in Edinburgh in October, on the hillside near Derwentwater at the same period as well as on the far side – the lonely side – of Loch Broom in the far north of Scotland, and there are a great many of them in Kent and Sussex. They are those fat golden and white mushrooms one sees laid out to dry in autumn all over the Dordogne, the Ardèche and South West France on window sills, or strung up under the eaves beside the yellow corn cobs and scarlet peppers. The woods sometimes smell strongly of them. Before going out to pick wild mushrooms, however – of whatever variety – the first thing one needs is a good well illustrated mushroom book, for mistakes can be deadly.

I have no English recipe for this delicious fungus, I cook mine *à la bordelaise* as prepared for me by Madame Germaine Petit the Rothschilds' housekeeper at Château Lafite when I stayed there some years ago. Remove the stalks from ¾ lb of cèpes, wiping off any pine needles or dead leaves. Pour a teacup of olive oil into a shallow fireproof dish that can come to table. Lay in the mushrooms when it is good and hot, sprinkling them with salt and pepper. Turn them after 3 minutes and simmer till cooked. Chop 2 cloves of garlic and a dessertspoon of fresh parsley. Let this cook for a moment in the oil with the *cèpes*. Serve rapidly in the hot dish in which they were cooked.

They are very good as a dish on their own, or to accompany roast chicken, or fried entrecôte steaks. One needs hunks of crusty bread to mop up the delicious garlicky juices and, if possible, a bottle of first growth claret to go with it. At Château Lafite I have had them as a first course followed by Irish Stew and a bottle of their fabulous '59 vintage.

Cèpes à la bordelaise freeze well, though the flavour fades after a month or two. *Cèpes* are also sold dried, in packets by good grocers. These are very good added to soups and stews.

Onions
English onions are smaller, slightly greener and much stronger than the huge Spanish onions with the papery brown skins seen in greengrocers' shops. Spanish onions are the ones to bake whole or to serve whole, and boiled, with a sauce.

(See also Thespian Dumplings page 20, Onions with Liver page 75.)

Scallions is the Irish name for spring onions. They are called Scallions, or Holtsers, in some parts of the country.

Roast Onions
Whole roast onions are delicious with roast beef. Allow one large Spanish onion per person. Leave the skin on but cut the whiskers off. Put them in a roasting tin with no more than an inch of water. Bake them with the joint in the oven. They are done if they are soft when squeezed. To eat them, pull back the skin and eat the hot onion with salt, pepper and a pat of butter.

To Plait Onions or Home Grown Shallots or Garlic to Hang in the Kitchen
The vegetables should be picked and dried on trays. One needs three pieces of raffia knotted together at one end and about 2 feet long. Lay them on a table knotted end away from you. Now put a dry onion on each piece with their withered stalks towards you, plait them across and across, turn each piece of raffia in twice before putting three more onions on the raffia and plaiting them in. Go on weaving in the onions like this until you come almost to the end of the raffia. Tie the pieces firmly together then tie the ends in a loop with which to hang them up.

Fried Onion Rings
Peel the onions and slice them about ⅛ inch thick. Shake them out into separate rings which season with salt and dredge with

flour. Fry them in deep hot oil in a chip pan, drain and sprinkle them with salt before serving.

If liked they may be dipped in pancake or fritter batter instead of flour and then fried as usual.

Parsnips
'Fine words butter no parsnips'
They need butter. They are much neglected because so often badly cooked and are delicious when chopped and boiled in salted water, then mashed with butter. Cooked thus, they are the classic accompaniment to a roast sirloin of beef. Though they can also be peeled and chopped and roasted round it.

Parsnips can also be part-boiled, then finished in a frying pan with butter and a little brown sugar, they then have a unique sweet taste, surpassing that of sweet potatoes. Good with pork chops.

Much cultivated here up to the 18th century when it was ousted by the carrot, though the parsnip is more resistant to plant pests. Parsnips were once coated with sugar and cream.

Peas
Frozen peas are best cooked with one or two tablespoons of butter – no water – adding salt and pepper and a teaspoon of sugar when done.

Fresh peas should really be shelled only a few minutes before they are to be cooked. One pound usually yields about 6 oz when shelled and one should allow about 2 lb of unshelled peas for four people.

Put them in a pan with boiling salted water barely to cover them. Boil adding a little sugar and if liked a sprig of fresh mint. Drain when tender, garnish them with butter.

Mangetout Peas or Sugar Peas: An unusual kind of garden pea without the tough skin inside the pod. The pod presses against the seeds as they grow. One eats the whole small pod with the peas inside – boiled and served with butter. Mangetout peas from Spain and Morocco are available in early spring when many fresh vegetables are scarce, they are very good with roast lamb.

Pease Pudding

Pease pudding is very popular in Newcastle-upon-Tyne. Hot pease pudding and saveloys or faggots were a familiar sight in the windows of London eating houses and dining rooms until quite recently and are, perhaps, still to be seen in the hot pease pudding and saveloy shops of South London.

Pease pudding is one of our oldest English dishes, it pre-dated the potato by several centuries. It used to be sold in dishes in the streets of London. 'Pease pudding hot, pease pudding cold' is one of the very old London street cries.

For four: Rinse 8 oz of dried peas or split peas, soak them in 2 pints of water for an hour or more before cooking. This reduces the cooking time but is not essential. Put 2 pints of water or stock and an onion stuck with cloves in a pan with the peas tied loosely in an old floured tea cloth. It may be twice knotted like Dick Whittington's bundle of pantomime and hung from a wooden spoon handle. If this is laid across the pan the peas will be easy to lift. Boil gently till tender. Split peas take 30–45 minutes, dried peas 1½–2 hours. Lift out the peas, put them in the electric mixer or through a sieve. Beat 2 tablespoons of butter and an egg into the warm purée, taste for seasoning, put it in a greased basin covered with foil. Stand it in a pan with boiling water to come half way up, boil with the lid on for an hour. Turn out to serve with boiled beef, ox tongue, boiled salt pork, roast pork, hot roast gammon and crackling.

Boiled Potatoes

In Ireland and the North West of England where they were once the main food of the poor, potatoes are still well prepared and the simple art of boiling them to perfection is still practised, though more in people's homes than in restaurants. Continentally trained chefs when cooking what they optimistically call *pommes à l'anglaise,* far from trying to make them mealy and fluffy first peel the potatoes and boil them and finish by putting them in a warm oven to acquire a dry skin and the depressing appearance associated with canteen cooking.

As in Lancashire: 'Pare the potatoes, cover them with cold water and boil them slowly until they are quite tender, but watch them carefully, that they may not be overdone; drain off the water entirely, strew some salt over them, leave the saucepan uncovered by the side of the fire [*on a low heat*] and shake it forcibly every minute or two, until the whole of the potatoes appear dry and floury. Lancashire cooks dress the vegetable in this way to perfection, but it is far from an economical mode, as a large portion of the potato adheres to the saucepan; it has, however, many admirers.' From *Modern Cookery for Private Families* by Eliza Acton, 1845.

Potatoes are still cooked like this in Lancashire and it still ruins the saucepan in the end, but they taste superb.

In my childhood in Cheshire they were done a bit differently: The peeled potatoes were left for about 2 hours to soak in very salty cold water before cooking, then drained and put in a pan with cold water just to cover with a little Northwich rock salt added. Boil them till nearly done then stop the boiling by adding cold water, this makes them mealy. When almost cooked pour off all the water then *put a lid tightly on the pan* and cover it with a cloth. Let them finish cooking on a low heat. This ruins the saucepan too but as a method has as many fierce and no doubt bigoted partisans as the other one.

As in Ireland: 'Habitual potato eaters know well that this vegetable is never so good as when served in the skin the instant it is taken from the fire, dished in a hot napkin, or sent to the table without a cover over it. It should also be clean and dry that it may at pleasure be taken in the fingers and broken like bread, or held in the dinner napkin while the inside is scooped out with a fork, thus forming it into a sort of cup.'

The potatoes should be washed and scrubbed clean but not cut in any way even to take out the eyes. Then arrange them tightly fitting in a pan with just enough cold water to cover. When it boils add a teaspoon of salt per quart. Simmer till the potatoes are nearly done but boil them rapidly for the last 3 minutes. Prod them with a fork to see if they are ready. Drain them and leave them *uncovered* on a low heat until they are completely dry.

Bubble and Squeak *(False and True)*

I Nowadays this often is just cooked cabbage and cooked potato fried together till a crust forms underneath. It is then cut in chunks and served brown side up with grilled bacon.

II 'For *true* Bubble and Squeak,' according to Countess Morphy, 'boil, drain and squeeze a cabbage in a clean tea towel to extract the water, chop it finely.

'Brown some slices of cold boiled salt beef in butter, add the cabbage seasoning it with pepper and salt and frying it until lightly browned and mixing it with the meat. The cabbage should be heaped in the centre of an entrée dish with the slices of meat laid round it.'

Champs

Champs is the most marvellous Irish potato dish. When ready, it is a sort of creamy green fluff which is served in mounds in soup plates with a hollow on top of each, and a big lump of butter dropped into it. One eats from the outside, dipping the soft potato into the pool of melted butter.

This is really superb with crisp fried herrings or mackerel or a good juicy kipper on another plate, or just by itself.

Peel and boil 2 lb of potatoes in salted water till soft. Drain them well and dry them off by laying a folded tea towel on top. Then put the potatoes back on a low heat for some minutes. This makes the potatoes beautifully floury – though it does ruin the pan in the end.

Meanwhile trim and chop about 6 large spring onions, or more if they are wispy ones, (what the Irish call scallions) in short lengths including the green top. Pour boiling water over them, drain and set them to simmer in a little pan of milk, about $\frac{1}{4}$ pint. Mash the potatoes with salt and plenty of pepper adding the onion flavoured milk and beating them till light and fluffy. Add the onion pieces and a bit of butter. It must be very hot. Some people have ice-cold buttermilk with it.

Colcannon

This has chopped curly kale or finely chopped cabbage, mixed with chopped parsley added as well.

Boil and mash the potatoes as for Champs (see opposite) – with boiling onion flavoured milk – adding salt, pepper, butter, the chopped spring onions and also a tablespoon of chopped parsley. In some parts of Ireland 1½ cups of chopped boiled curly kale ("curly greens") or finely boiled green cabbage is tossed gently in a lot of melted butter and then folded into the potatoes too.

This is not the same as the English Bubble and Squeak (see opposite).

Cheshire Potato Pot
This dish is very good with sausages, or with gammon rashers done in the oven.

Peel and slice about 2 lb of potatoes in thin rounds. Put them in a fireproof dish with salt, pepper and a peeled sliced onion in layers. Add water to come more than half way up. Put dabs of dripping on top. Bake it either in a moderate oven (350°F, 180°C, Mark 4) for about an hour, or in a fairly slow oven (325°C, 170°C, Mark 3) for 1½ hours until the potatoes are cooked.

Chips
It is best to dry them in a tea towel before putting them in the pan, so as to get rid of excess starch as well as moisture, and stop them sticking together. They will also stick together if the chip pan is too small and too many are being cooked at once. (Use very firm yellow potatoes.) The fat should be hot but not excessively so. When they rise to the surface without bubbling increase the heat. They soon become brown and crisp.

Take them out, drain them on a cloth, sprinkle them with salt and eat them at once. Best fried in oil.

Potato Flounces
This is the old Irish name for a dish of thinly sliced potatoes cooked in a pie dish or crock in the oven, with butter, onions and milk. It is called Stovies in Scotland, and *Gratin Dauphinois* in France, and is currently very fashionable in country restaurants in France.

189

Delicious with stews and casserole dishes or a hot game pie, it will not be spoiled if it has to wait for some time in the oven when cooked and it can also be re-heated.

Peel 6 or 7 large potatoes, slicing them thinly, as for Hot Pot (see page 96) and leave them to soak in cold water for about an hour. Peel and slice two large onions in rings. Drain, then dry the potatoes in a cloth. Butter a very large pie dish. Lay the potatoes and onions in it neatly in layers, adding salt, pepper and a little butter here and there. Pour in enough milk to come almost to the top. Bake the Potato Flounces in a moderate oven (350°F, 180°C, Mark 4) until the potatoes are done and are browned on top in about 40 minutes.

Quick Method: Though the potatoes are best cooked slowly in the oven in milk, if time is lacking they may first be part-boiled in milk. Then when half cooked lay them in a well buttered ovenproof dish, with salt and pepper and dabs of butter between each layer, add a little grated cheese if liked instead of the onions. Pour in the milk in which the potatoes were cooked. Finish the dish in a hot oven (400°F, 200°C, Mark 6) for about 20 minutes to heat them through and brown the top.

Excellent with baked gammon rashers.

Scots Stovies

There are several kinds of Stovies, the word seems to be derived from the French *étuvée*. Some are cooked with chicken, or grouse, as well as potatoes and seem obviously related to a Lancashire Hot Pot. In the Isle of Skye, however, they simmer onions, potatoes and coarse cut sausages gently in milk to make stovies which are very like a dish popular in East Anglia. I also have a version cooked with cheese, and others prepared with dripping and left overs from the joint, but most usually Stovies are onions and potatoes done in milk but not browned on top, they are delicious with gigot steaks.

Scots Stovies with Cheese: Slice 6 large boiled potatoes in thin rounds. Put them in a buttered pie dish in layers with one large sliced onion and 2 oz of grated cheese. Sprinkle with pepper but very little salt. When the dish is full add ½ pint of milk, enough to come almost to the top of the potatoes. Bake them for 30 minutes in a moderate oven (350°F, 180°C, Mark 4).

Then sprinkle the top thickly with grated cheese which brown in the oven. To be eaten hot and hot.

New Potatoes

To be really good they should be freshly dug out of the garden, still damp with earth. The skin can then be rubbed off with one's thumb. They may be skinned by scrubbing them with a soft brush. If scraped and done so thoroughly that every scrap of brown is removed, the fragile inner yellow skin will be scraped off too together with most of the flavour.

They should be put into boiling salted water with a sprig of mint. Boil them about 15 minutes, till tender when tested with a fork. Drain. Cover the pot with a clean folded tea towel to absorb the steam, then put the potatoes back on a very low heat for a few minutes to dry. Toss them in butter, with chopped mint and parsley. If not dried out they will be soapy, though some prefer them this way.

Have you tried the very small new potatoes – hazelnut size – steamed in a wire strainer over a pan of boiling water. The skins may be left on and a sprig of mint could go in the strainer with them. The result is superb but they need plenty of butter when you eat them.

Northumbrian Pan Haggerty

This is a dish of potatoes frizzled with cheese and onions, they are served straight from the pan and make an excellent simple meal, perhaps with a tossed green salad, on side plates, or to follow.

Peel and slice 1 lb of potatoes in thin rounds, pat them dry in a cloth. Slice 8 oz of peeled onions finely. Heat 1 oz of butter in a frying pan. Spread the sliced potatoes over it, then the onions. Add salt and pepper and top the vegetables with about 4 oz of grated cheese. Put a lid on the pan and let the contents simmer and fry very very gently for about 40 minutes until the potatoes and onions are nearly cooked. Take off the lid and brown the top under the griller.

Roast Potatoes

Peel and cut the potatoes in half. Cook them in boiling salted water for a few minutes until just beginning to soften. Drain them well returning the dry pan of potatoes to the hot stove for a moment to be sure all the liquid has gone. Now roll them in a little flour with salt. Put them round the hot joint in the roasting tin in the oven for 30–40 minutes depending on the oven temperature required for the meat. Add extra dripping if necessary, turn them at about half time.

Potato Salad

Potatoes for a salad are especially good when baked in their skins in the hot ashes of an open fire, a turf fire gives a faint and subtle flavour to the finished dish. When the skins are dark and even slightly charred the potatoes should be peeled and chopped, hot, into a warm basin.

Alternatively they may be boiled in their skins, peeled when floury and chopped hot into the warm basin as before. Add salt, white pepper, chopped parsley and chopped onion, then some pale vinegar and oil. The hot potatoes absorb a great deal of this.

Sweet Potatoes

The proper cooking of potatoes is one of our great specialities. They were introduced from the Americas in Tudor times – perhaps by Drake, Raleigh, or Hawkins – and were eaten here while almost unknown on the Continent. At first sweet potatoes were more popular than ordinary ones, and they are apparently the kind Shakespeare meant when, in *The Merry Wives of Windsor*, Falstaff greets Mistress Ford by crying, 'Let the sky rain potatoes!'. They appeared on the royal table in 1619 apparently having been cooked in hot ashes. John Gerard refers to them in his *Herball* (1597) as the 'common potato', he grew them in his garden.

They are very good when scrubbed and baked in their jackets but take longer than ordinary potatoes, $1-1\frac{1}{2}$ hours in a moderate oven (350°F, 180°C, Mark 4). To roast with the meat they should be part-boiled then peeled, halved or quartered, and browned in the tin with the joint.

Tatws Rhost
A delicious supper or light luncheon dish, almost a meal in itself.
Heat 1 tablespoon of bacon dripping or butter in a heavy frying
pan, add 8 oz of diced thickly sliced bacon. Cook this gently for
5 minutes then add two peeled sliced onions. Stir. Add 2 lb of
peeled sliced potatoes, salt and pepper. Pour in enough water to
just cover the potatoes. Put a lid on the pan and cook it over a
low heat for about 30 minutes until the potatoes are done and
the liquid is absorbed.

Welsh Onion Cake
This is similar to Northumbrian Pan Haggerty (see page191)
but is baked in a well buttered cake tin.
Peel and slice the potatoes in thin rounds. Put them in layers in
the cake tin with butter and finely chopped onion, more butter
and grated cheese. Add salt and pepper and repeat. When the
cake tin is full, finishing with potatoes, cover the tin with an old
plate or a tin pie plate. Bake for 1 hour in a moderate oven
(350°F, 180°C, Mark 4).
Sometimes the cheese is left out.

Pot Posies and Pot Herbs
In Scotland a bunch of herbs or *bouquet garni* for flavouring
soups, stews, sauces and so on, is, or was, known as a pot posy;
this is roughly the same as the older English "faggot of herbs".
It is not to be confused with the term "pot herbs" which is really
a mixture of sliced root vegetables sold for making soups and
broth in the North of England and Scotland. Pot herbs are
generally a mixture of an onion/carrot/parsnip/stick of celery/
piece of swede or turnip, a small leek, and are invaluable for
making broth if one does not wish to buy quantities of different
vegetables. Pot herbs would doubtless be on sale elsewhere if
there were enough demand.

Pumpkin
This is one of the many excellent vegetables which grow well in
English gardens but appear to have been forgotten, they were
common in Tudor times and were still widely grown on the

Gower Peninsula in Wales in the 19th century, where they were chopped and made into soup, or cooked in mutton stew with currants.

Easy to grow they remain fresh and firm for several months if stored in late autumn in a cool dry place such as a shed or cellar. They may be cooked in a very little salted water then mashed like a swede turnip. The slice of pumpkin should be peeled, have the seeds removed, then be simmered till soft in a very little salt water. Drain it well and mash it with butter and a spoonful of cream. Add pepper, salt and ground mace or nutmeg to your liking.

Part of the pumpkin may also be cut in slices with the seeds and peel removed. Then sprinkle the slices with pepper and salt, dredge them with flour and fry them gently with a lid on the pan until they are nicely browned in about 20 minutes.

Raw Vegetables
The Victorians, perhaps in fear of the cholera which raged in epidemic form in London and other big European cities several times in the 1850s and 1860s cooked their vegetables for a very long time until pale, denuded of vitamins and much of the taste. They thought lightly cooked vegetables "unwholesome" and seldom ate salads. We still tend to over-cook vegetables, when boiled they should be put in only a little salted water and taken out when still crisp, cabbage leaves especially.

In fact, many vegetables have more flavour and character when eaten raw. Apart from such obvious ones as spring onions, radishes, lettuce and chicory there are more well worth trying.

Raw Jerusalem artichokes have a flavour not unlike Brazil nuts; they should be washed and dried but, like apples, only be peeled as they are eaten, for they darken when exposed to the air.

Brussels sprouts are good, too, when eaten raw either alone or in a salad – crisp, crunchy and with a fresh rich flavour.

Carrots are of course at their best when raw. One can slice them in fingers put them in a basin with a few ice cubes, a little cold water and perhaps a few fingers of unpeeled cucumber.

They are delicious to nibble thus at the start of a meal perhaps with other raw vegetables. They can also be grated raw in mounds and served with an oil and lemon dressing as part of a mixed salad.

Celeriac, or turnip rooted celery, is excellent grated and served with the carrots in a similar dressing.

Sweet green peas, straight from the garden and straight from the pod, are very good, too, raw in salads. So are very young broad beans, simply to shell and eat from the pod, perhaps accompanied by other raw fresh vegetables. Put a dish of them on the table so people can shell and dip them in salt and munch them at the beginning of a meal. The Suffolk asparagus growers like to eat a few raw asparagus spears at the same time.

All these things are very good and look very pretty when laid on a platter on the table to eat for "starters".

Salads

John Evelyn, the diarist, in his *Acetaria a Discourse on Sallets* lists 73 herbs and plants as possible ingredients.

Of garlic, he says: 'We absolutely forbid its entrance into our Salleting by reasons of its intolerable rankness . . . To be sure, 'tis not for Ladies' Palats, nor those who court them, further than to permit a light touch on the Dish with a Clove thereof.'

Eliza Acton: 'The herbs and vegetables for a salad cannot be too freshly gathered; they should be carefully cleaned from insects and washed with scrupulous nicety; they are better when not prepared until near the time of sending them to table, and they should not be sauced until the instant before they are served . . .'

Salsify and Scorzonera

Two unusual root vegetables with a unique mouth-watering flavour. Do not peel off the skins until after they are cooked so as to keep the delicious taste, the skins will then come off more easily also. Let them simmer for about 30 minutes in salted water with lemon juice. Then when tender hold the root in one hand and strip off the skin either with the fingers or a little paring knife. It is simplest to let the vegetables cool slightly first. When peeled they may be re-heated in butter and lemon juice.

Samphire

A Norfolk delicacy, the plant is sometimes on sale in shops in Norwich, Kings Lynn and elsewhere in July. It grows wild on the salt marshes near Snettisham and perhaps in other parts of the country. It thrives on rough shingle, looks like a rock plant and can indeed be grown in the garden on dry rocky soil. It never appears in London and there does not seem to be a restaurant outside Norfolk enterprising enough to serve this delicacy.

When obtainable, it should be boiled for about 10 minutes in salted water, then eaten in the fingers with butter, hot and melted, poured over it. It is best to leave on the small white root to hold it by, and then to suck it like asparagus. It can also be pickled, and a few country pubs in Norfolk serve it as a samphire cream sauce with roast chicken or sea trout.

Tomatoes

The tomato is a relatively recent arrival in Britain, it was almost unknown here in the kitchen 100 years ago. *Vide* Mrs. Beeton's *Analysis of the Tomato*, 1861: 'The fruit of the love apple is the only part used as an esculent . . . The whole plant has a disagreeable odour and its juice, subjected to the action of the fire, emits a vapour so powerful as to cause vertigo and vomiting.'

Basil, a herb which can be bought dried and sometimes fresh, adds greatly to the flavour of most tomato dishes.

Truffles

White truffles similar to those which are so popular in northern Italy and which are sold at such high prices in the truffle markets of Piedmont, are found all over the south of England and perhaps occasionally further north. One needs a trained pig or trained dog to find them however for they only grow wild.

A couple of generations ago there were people in Wiltshire and the West Country who had the necessary trained animals for collecting this underground fungus. The practice seems to have died out.

The famous Bath truffle mentioned in 18th century cookery books was probably a black truffle similar to those collected in Périgord, France.

There are recipes which include truffles in English cookery books going back about three centuries, sometimes they are used in such quantities that one imagines they must have been cheap and plentiful.

Turnips

Swede turnips: These are the big yellow turnips, the word "swede" appears to be used mainly in the South of England, elsewhere people simply call them turnips.

They may be peeled, sliced and then boiled in a little salted water. Then mashed quite plainly with salt and pepper. Or drained then mashed with bacon fat seasoned with plenty of pepper and served heaped in a mound, filled with brown gravy in the middle. Good with a roast.

They have a sweet yet peppery taste, are seldom expensive and used to be a great household standby among country people but are now thought rather old fashioned.

They used sometimes to be mixed with the potatoes and mashed with them. The dish is called Clapshot in the Orkneys.

To cook: Peel, slice and boil a (swede) turnip, drain it and put it back in the pan on the stove to dry out the turnip pieces before mashing them to a fine pulp. Add a large tablespoon of butter and add a cup of dry mashed potato, with plenty of pepper. Re-heat and serve.

On Welsh farms – where the dish is known as *stwns* – the potatoes are often mashed with buttermilk (now sold by most urban milkmen) before being added to the turnips. This is very nice with baked stuffed liver. In Welsh, beans and potatoes mashed together are called *stwns ffa*, peas and potatoes mashed together *stwns pys*.

Boiled (Swede) Turnips with Cream
Peel and chop 1 lb of yellow (swede) turnip, boil it, drain and squeeze out the water. Mash, then add pepper, 2–3 tablespoons of cream and a knob of butter. Re-heat.

White turnips: In the late spring the early juicy turnips are delectable eaten when they are no bigger than a knucklebone, they should be trimmed and boiled then simply served with melted butter.

White turnips can also be stewed in butter and dished in the centre of some nicely grilled lamb chops. Capers are added when they are served with boiled mutton.

Wash, dry and then dice them. Melt 1 oz of butter for each 8 oz of turnips. Pack them into a fireproof dish or pan, as flat as can be, and stew them very gently indeed in the butter, with foil and a lid on for 45 minutes to 1 hour in a slow oven (300°F, 150°C, Mark 2). When half done add salt and pepper and, if liked, a few capers.

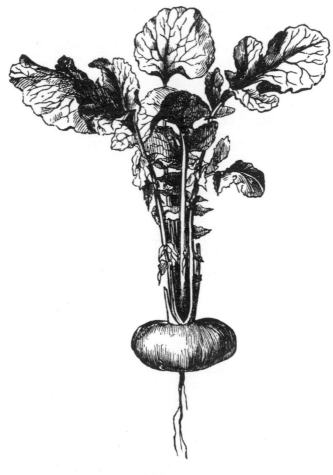

Chapter 7

Fish

Cod

Line caught cod, fresh out of the sea when its skin is green and glistening, is a great delicacy and might be a revelation to those accustomed to frozen fillets. That caught off Scarborough in late autumn and winter is said to be the finest in Britain; the fish migrate inshore at that time so that beach fishing methods can be used.

It may be poached gently in salted water and served with just a jug of plain melted butter — or the once popular Victorian Cockle Sauce (see page 118). Plain boiled cod and floury boiled potatoes, with hot frothing butter, are traditionally eaten in Denmark on New Year's Day. It must be no more than one or two hours out of the sea.

Poached Fresh Cod

Put 3 lb of best cod, cut in $1\frac{1}{2}$ inch steaks, in ice-cold running water for about an hour before it is to be cooked. Just before the meal sprinkle it thickly with salt and leave it 15 minutes. Have a pan of freshly boiled salted water, allowing $1\frac{1}{2}$ oz of salt per quart of water. Add 2 tablespoons of vinegar to the panful of salt water. Lower the fish into it in a tea towel. Bring fish and water gently to the boil, once more skimming off any rising scum. Turn off the heat. Let the pan of cod stand on the stove, with a tightly closed lid, for about 10 minutes.

Serve the well drained cod steaks on a folded napkin, with a dish of floury boiled potatoes and a sauce made by melting 5 oz of butter and stirring in a finely chopped hard boiled egg. Iced lager and plenty of English mustard.

Poached Fresh Cod in the Hebridean Manner
In the Hebrides the absolutely fresh caught cod is poached in salted water, skinned and boned, then put in a hot dish and sprinkled with salt and pepper. 8 oz of butter is laid on top of the fish. When it melts the whole lot is flaked together. The cod is then eaten with freshly boiled potatoes, hot and mashed with a little butter, pepper and some milk. Buttermilk is often drunk with it.

A Boiled Cod's Head and Shoulders
Once a delicacy better liked than the rest of the fish, it is still served in some deep sea fishing ports. Some of the older generation of fishmongers are also partial to fresh cod's liver which is poached and made into a sort of pâté. It is said to have a subtle flavour but is now almost impossible to obtain as the fish are gutted on the quayside and the livers sent either for fish meal, or to the cod liver oil factories. Cod's sounds, a fat jelly-like substance along the inside of the backbone, was another delicacy much relished in the 19th century but now forgotten. It tastes best served with hot Cockle Sauce or Oyster Sauce (see page 118).

Crabs
Partan is the Scots name for a crab. Until very recently in Scotland as in Northumberland only the claws of the beast were normally eaten, the rest being rejected as in some way inedible.

Underneath the crab is a small flap or apron. That of the hen crab is wider than that of the cock crab.

Crabs in Cream
Melt 2 tablespoons of butter, in it stir and brown lightly about 1 lb of crab meat. Heat 1½ tablespoons of butter elsewhere and fry 4 oz of slit skinned almonds in it till golden brown. Add salt, pepper, the hot crab meat, ¼ pint of thick cream, 1 tablespoon of chopped parsley. Heat to boiling point then reduce the heat and simmer for about 2 minutes. Serve in the hot shells.

Hot Buttered Crabs
Remove both the white and brown meat from the shells and

claws. Put it in a pan with a knob of butter, two or three crushed
anchovy fillets, some soft white breadcrumbs, a good pinch of
grated nutmeg and ½ pint of sherry. Simmer, stirring, until most
of the liquid has gone. Add pepper and a beaten egg yolk, taste
for seasoning and add salt with caution (because of the anchovy
fillets). Heat, stirring, for a moment. Pile it into the shell, brown
it in the oven. To be eaten with hot toast. The recipe (re-worded)
came from *England's Newest Way with all Sorts of Cooking*, 1710.

Lancashire Devilled Crabs

Melt 1 tablespoon of butter, stir in 2 tablespoons of flour, heat till
bubbling. Off the heat stir in ½ pint of cream and heat, stirring,
until the sauce thickens, adding 1 teaspoon of minced parsley,
4 hard boiled egg yolks pressed through a sieve, salt, pepper, 1
teaspoon of Worcester sauce and the meat of two large crabs.

Fill the two large crab shells with it. Top with buttered bread-crumbs. Bake in a moderately hot oven (375°F, 190°C, Mark 5) for about 10 minutes until the crumbs are lightly browned.

To be served hot and hot.

Potted Crab
Put 8 oz of white and brown crab meat in a pan with three raw egg yolks, 3 oz of butter, 2 tablespoons of cream and 1 table-spoon of brandy. Stir it over a low heat until it is well blended and thick. If very hot or not carefully stirred the eggs will scramble. Season it rather highly with salt, pepper and Cayenne pepper. Add 1 tablespoon of grated cheese. Pack it into little individual pots and chill. It is best made the day before it is to be eaten. Serve it with hot toast.

Dabs, Flukes and Flounders
These are small flatfish found all round the coast of Britain where the sea bed is sandy, often close inshore. Small locally caught ones are often sold cheaply in seaside fish shops, being very fresh they are delicious when dipped whole in seasoned flour, then fried in butter. They freeze well too.

Garfish
When poached, the bones go bright green. The fish is very good cold with Mayonnaise or horseradish sauce, and looks most dramatic on a cold table. It is something like a swordfish, being shaped like an eel with a long sharp pointed beak and rows of saw-like teeth.

It is considered a delicacy in some countries but seldom eaten in Britain though in warm fine summers it is plentiful inshore. It is sometimes sold, however, in spring and early summer in the more enlightened fish shops, being popular in Chinese restaurants. It can also be smoked and it adds both character and colour to fish soups.

Fresh Haddocks in Cream
A Scottish recipe suitable for small haddocks or whiting
The fish should be cleaned and skinned but left whole, then

dipped in seasoned flour. Warm 2 oz of butter in a large pan. Roll the fish in it, turning them over and over till well saturated, then add ½ pint of cream. Bring it to the boil and then simmer the whole thing over a low heat until the liquid is reduced and the fish are cooked. Stir in 1 teaspoon of freshly made English mustard. Dish the fish on a hot ashet (platter). Meanwhile reduce the sauce in the pan over a very fierce heat until it thickens, then 'scrape it out and put it over the fish in the hot dish, it gives a browny look and has the essence of the flavour.' From *The Cookery Book of Lady Clark of Tillypronie*, where it was served as a breakfast dish. The recipe is labelled *J. Emslie* 1893. She was one of the three Emslie sisters all of whom worked as cooks at Tillypronie. They are quoted frequently by Lady Clark. All came from Cromar in Aberdeenshire, and though, later, one of them 'filled a position of trust in England', another sister worked all her life at Tillypronie and 'died practically at her post faithful to the end.'

Roast Stuffed Haddock
Wash and gut one fresh haddock of about 1½ lb weight, removing the eyes and gills as well as the inside. Stuff it with Veal Forcemeat (see page 122). Sew it up, put the tail through the eye socket and fasten it with a skewer. Brush it over with milk. Lay it in a well greased fireproof dish. Sprinkle it with breadcrumbs and put a few knobs of dripping on top. Bake it in a moderate oven (350°F, 180°C, Mark 4) for 30 minutes, basting occasionally. Serve with Parsley Sauce (page 139).

Baked Hake with Mushrooms
This is a long, slim, grey-skinned fish with a fierce-looking face and cannibal habits. The taste is similar to cod and it is very popular in the North of England.

Sprinkle a whole gutted hake of about 1½ lb with a little salt and leave it about 30 minutes. Butter an oval fireproof dish, boil and mash 8 oz of potatoes. Break the stalks off 8 oz of button mushrooms. Chop and fry the stalks in 2 oz of butter, adding a pinch of nutmeg. Mix them with the well seasoned mashed potatoes. Stuff the well wiped fish with the mixture and lay it in the fireproof dish along with the mushroom caps on either side.

Melt 3 oz of butter, mix it with ½ pint of cream, the juice and grated rind of half a lemon. Pour it over the fish and mushrooms. Bake it in a hot oven (400°F, 200°C, Mark 6) for about 30 minutes basting frequently. Garnish with the other half of the lemon cut in chunks. This recipe is also suitable for pike.

Grilled Halibut *(Also suitable for turbot)*

Halibut is a huge flat fish (mostly sold in slices) which when fully grown can be 6–8 feet long and weigh 300 lb or more. They are caught, mostly in the Faroes and the North of Scotland, on long lines baited with small plaice.

Wash and dry 4 slices of halibut about 1½ inches thick. Sprinkle them with salt. Brush them on either side with melted butter. Grill 8–10 minutes either side under a moderate heat. Dish on a hot platter with lemon. Garnish with Pantry Butter or Mustard Butter (see page 116).

Fried Herrings with Mustard Sauce

The herring should be absolutely fresh, its eyes bright and full, the gills a clear bright red, the scales gleaming and the flesh firm. As the herring becomes stale the eyes grow redder and redder and slightly sunken and the flavour deteriorates so that it is barely worth eating.

Split, clean and bone the herring, dip it in coarse oatmeal or porridge oats mixed with salt and pepper so that it is evenly coated. Then fry it gently in hot bacon fat until brown and crisp on either side and completely cooked. It may then be served with Mustard Sauce (see page 127) and buttery mashed potatoes, or with dry mealy potatoes boiled as they are done in Lancashire (see page 186). This is a classic. Fresh brown trout may be similarly cooked and served.

Herrings and Tatties Boiled in Salt Water

In some places the herrings used to be cooked in sea water then dished on a napkin, with potatoes boiled in their skins that had been cooked with them. Accompany with some butter and hot (English) Mustard Sauce (see page 127).

Some cooks maintain that all sea fish — whether herring, cod or salmon — is best poached in sea water or very salt water. The fish itself does not become salty but keeps its flavour and remains moist, crisp and delicate. In some fishing ports sea water was used rather than home made brine. This is the old method. When potatoes are boiled in it the skins do not burst and the potatoes become deliciously floury. It is not the same of course with frozen fish.

Pickled Herrings
This used to be served for High Tea at the seaside with bread and butter, cherry cake, fish paste, pots of strong tea and enough else. It also makes a good beginning to a main meal like the more fashionable *maquereaux au vin blanc* of Northern French fishing ports.

Method 1. Cut off the heads, slit the fish all the way down from head to tail, run your thumb along the backbone to ease the flesh away from the bones, the whole cage of bone should come out in one. Hold the fish by the tail, scrape the skin towards the head to get rid of the scales. A kindly fishmonger might do all this for one.

Roll up the resultant herring fillets with a little salt and pepper inside, pack them in a pie dish. Make a pickle by boiling up ½ pint of beer, ¼ pint of vinegar, 1 sliced onion, 1 sliced carrot, a bayleaf, sprig of thyme, bunch of parsley, 6 cloves, 6 peppercorns, 1 teaspoon salt, 1 dessertspoon sugar. Simmer for 30 minutes. Pour over the rolled up herrings in the pie dish. Cover, bake in a moderate oven (350°F, 180°C, Mark 4) for 30 minutes. This is eaten cold after 24 hours.

Method 2. Put the whole cleaned, washed and scraped herrings head to tail in an earthenware pot, with thyme and bayleaf between each layer. Also cloves, rounds of onion, some salt and peppercorns — then more onion. Cover with pure distilled vinegar. Bring to the boil and after the first bubble it is done.

Lampreys and Lamperns
Both lampreys and the much smaller lampern are found in

British rivers, in the Severn for example as well as such Dorset streams as the Bere and the Piddle and perhaps in other parts of the British Isles, though seldom caught now except for scientific purposes.

A lamprey looks very like a huge eel as thick as an arm with sucker mouth, it is a seagoing creature that returns to a river to spawn, coming in with the salmon. Apparently it has no jaws, cartilage instead of a skeleton, a single nostril on top of the head, and is a sort of sea vampire which sucks at its victims' blood; perhaps salmon, shad or sturgeon.

A lampern is about 6 inches long, as thick as a pencil and is sold by some Gloucestershire fishmongers, mostly as bait for eel traps, though some eat them.

In Scandinavia both lampreys and lamperns are sold smoked and are regarded as a delicacy. They are much enjoyed in France too, unsmoked, but cooked in red wine and brandy, notably in the Périgord and in Bordeaux, and they are also a popular local dish in the Minho province of North Portugal.

Potted lampreys were a delicacy sold to the fashionable in 18th century Bath, and people used also to travel down to Worcester by stage coach especially to taste the lampreys to be had there in perfection.

To Stew Lamprey as at Worcester
Clean it, take out the cartilage. Season with pepper, mace, allspice, cloves – ground to a powder. Stew the lamprey in a covered pan with beef stock and sherry or cider to cover. When tender, take it out, keep it hot. Boil down the gravy (the stock) with two finely chopped (and de-salted, boned etc.) barrel anchovies. Add a *roux*. When smooth and thick strain it through a fine sieve, add the juice of a lemon, a teaspoon of English mustard. Serve with grated horseradish and sippets.

Evidently a well known 18th-century recipe, it also appears in various Victorian cookery books.

Lobsters in Whisky
Place two cooked lobsters on a board, back upwards. Split them in half portions down their entire length with a sharp knife.

Open out the two halves of the lobsters. Crack the claws. Discard the little bag near the head of the lobster, which contains some gravel. Keep the creamy green liver, which is a delicacy, also the red roe or coral found attached to the tail of the female lobster. It is often added to a sauce. Whitby fishermen sometimes remove the roe and eat it raw when it is black like caviar.

Heat all the lobster flesh slowly in about 2 tablespoons of butter per lobster, pour 1 tablespoon of warm whisky on it. Light it, add another tablespoon of whisky before the flames die down. Stir in ¼ pint of thick cream, heat it and put all the lobster meat back in the shells, previously brushed with butter and warmed in the oven. Put the filled lobster shells in a hot oven (400°F, 200°C, Mark 6) for about 8 minutes. Serves 4.

Crawfish (or *langoustes*) can be cooked in the same way. They are plentiful, for instance, off the coast of South Wales.

Mackerel Baked in Beer
This is an 18th century recipe, which is also suitable for herrings. Fish so prepared were sometimes called "soused fish", and the expression "soused", for a person who is drunk, may have a similar origin. They are equally good when eaten hot or cold.

Have the fish cleaned without opening them. Then wash, drain and season them with salt, ground cloves and powdered allspice. Lay them in a pie dish with some black peppercorns, a peeled sliced onion and some bayleaves. Add enough beer and vinegar to cover them (using two thirds light ale to one third malt vinegar). Bake them for an hour in a fairly hot oven (375°F, 190°C, Mark 5).

Grilled Mackerel
Split the fish down the back, clean, remove the big bones, head and so on. Season sprinkling it with salt and a very little Cayenne pepper. Brush it with oil or butter. Put it under the hot grill, turning to cook both sides. Allow 10 minutes on the inner side and 3—4 minutes on the skin side. The heat should not be too fierce.

Mackerel are especially good when plainly grilled, to serve

207

with cauliflower and cheese, or Highland stovies. They may be garnished with Mustard Butter (see page 116) or served with freshly made horseradish sauce.

Mackerel Grilled with Fennel

In England in the 18th century mackerel was commonly cooked with fennel, then the taste was forgotten. This dish is still fashionable in the South of France, where it is prepared sometimes with mackerel and sometimes with the *loup de mer* or sea bass. Restaurants along the *Côte d'Azur* charge high prices for this popular dish which most people would not think of trying at home.

Fennel grows wild in English lanes and is not difficult to cultivate. A tall feathery plant with flat yellow umbels of flowers, it can be found for instance by the roadside near Sandwich, Kent, in quantity in the West Country and South Wales. Toasting and scorching the plant gives the fish added flavour and it has a most attractive smell. Bunches of thyme or fresh bayleaves can also be used (see Trout, page 221) though obviously with a different effect. This dish is very suitable too for a barbecue or charcoal grill.

Clean the fish leaving the head on. Stuff the inside with coarsely chopped fennel, salt and pepper. Brush the fish with melted butter. Lay more fennel on the rack of the grill pan, with the stalks just chopped, if necessary, so they will fit. Lay the fish carefully upon it. Grill it, turning it when half done, to grill the other side.

Le loup grillé au fenouil is a speciality of *La Réserve* at Beaulieu-sur-Mer.

Cold Poached Mackerel

They have a texture rather like cold salmon or tuna and may be served with lettuce and English salad dressing.

Leave the heads on, clean the fish without splitting them or, if possible, clean them through the gills so they remain whole.

Bring a pan of hot salted water to a gentle boil. Reduce the heat, put in the mackerel and simmer 10–15 minutes if they are small 14–20 minutes if large. They should be poached gently, fast boiling ruins the flavour and they fall to pieces. Do not let them cool in the liquid, and skin before serving.

Grey Mullet
A silvery grey fish found inshore in tidal estuaries, small harbours and shallow creeks, it has a few small bones but the scales are thick and heavy. They are best removed before cooking. Hold the mullet by the tail and scrape it with a knife towards the head. It can be stuffed and baked.

Red Mullet
In King George II's day, red mullet were a speciality of Weymouth, in Dorset, but are now difficult to buy in England except where there is a large immigrant population. Frederick W. Davis, writing in 1856, says it is 'called the Sea Woodcock', perhaps because like a woodcock the guts are left inside in cooking it. 'Clean but leave the inside,' he goes on, 'fold in oiled paper and gently bake in a small dish. Make a sauce from the liquor that comes from the fish, with a piece of butter, a little flour, a little essence of anchovy and a glass of sherry. Give it a boil and serve in a boat, and the fish in paper cases.'   From Frederick W. Davis' *English Cookery Book*, 1856, which is mostly a crib from a much earlier and more famous work by Mrs. Rundell.

Nowadays the fish could be baked in oiled or buttered foil instead of paper. First scrape the scales off the mullet by holding its tail and scraping them towards the head with a sharp knife, leave the liver etc. inside the fish as these are considered a delicacy. Oil or butter a sheet of foil, or greaseproof paper, add salt and pepper. Wrap the mullet in it completely like a parcel. Bake the parcels of mullet in a moderate oven (350°F, 180°C, Mark 4) for about 20 minutes. Meanwhile melt 1 tablespoon of butter, stir in 1 tablespoon of flour, add a little anchovy essence and a large wine glass of sherry. Heat stirring. Then open the foil parcels and pour the liquor inside them into the pan. Bring it gently to the boil, stirring till you have a smooth thick, well flavoured sauce which should be served in a warm sauce boat, the fish in paper cases.

Plain boiled buttery white turnips are excellent with it.

Sweetings' Fish Pie

From Sweetings' restaurant in the City of London, a somewhat Edwardian establishment which specializes in oysters and Black Velvet (Guinness laced with champagne), fish cakes, steamed jam roll, grilled herrings with hot mustard sauce and ripe Stilton cheese. It is full of businessmen at lunchtime and was formerly patronized by Toulouse-Lautrec.

Poach 1 lb of cod or haddock fillet gently in hot salted water. Skin and flake it and put it in a medium pie dish with 2 oz of potted shrimps. Put the whole contents of another 2 oz carton of potted shrimps into a small pan and melt the delicately seasoned butter over a low heat. Add 1 tablespoon of flour and cook for a few moments. Stir in ¼ pint of milk, heat, stirring until smooth. Then beat up an egg yolk with another ¼ pint of milk and whisk it into the sauce without letting it boil. Add a squeeze of lemon juice, pour it over the fish. Now beat 4 oz of butter and about a third of a cup of hot milk into ½ lb of fresh hot potato purée. Add salt and pepper and whip it until it is all fluffy. Pile it over the fish in the pie dish and brown it in the oven.

Mrs. Mulligan's Fish Ordinary

Butter a pie dish. Mix some soft white breadcrumbs with salt and pepper. Tip a spoonful of them into the pie dish, tilting it backwards and forwards until the whole of the inside is coated. Put in a layer of coley fillets, then some pieces of butter and more seasoned crumbs, adding a little dry English mustard powder. Then cover the fish and crumbs with thin slices of cheese. Repeat until the dish is full, the top layer being cheese.

Bake it in a moderate oven (350°F, 180°C, Mark 4) for about 35 minutes until the fish is cooked and the cheese is browned on top. The pie dish may be covered with a sheet of foil or greaseproof paper if the cheese is browning too fast.

A Fish Pie with Mussels and a Puff Pastry Crust

Wash one quart of fresh mussels in cold running water, and in a basin of cold water changing it several times. Pull off the whiskers with which they cling to the rocks. Throw away any that are broken or remain open. Put the rest into a shallow pan with a dessertspoon of butter, a little pepper and, if liked, some finely chopped celery and onion. Cook them over a fierce heat for 4–5 minutes till all the mussels open. Cut ¾ lb cod fillets into inch cubes. Put them in a pie dish with a little pepper and grated nutmeg, add the strained liquor from the pan of mussels (it comes out of their shells). Cover it with foil and bake in a moderate oven (350°F, 180°C, Mark 4) for about 30 minutes. Melt 1 oz of butter, stir in 1 tablespoon of flour then gradually stir in the fish liquor from the pie dish and heat, stirring, until you have a thick smooth sauce. Pour it back into the pie dish adding the shelled mussels.

Cover the pie dish with puff pastry which brush with milk. Bake it in a very hot oven (450°F, 230°C, Mark 8) for about 15–20 minutes.

Baked Fish with Walnut Stuffing
Suitable for grey mullet, haddock or a whole gutted sea bream (redfish or sebastes). The sea bream looks like a huge perch with an ugly head, big mouth and pinkish scales. Not to be confused with fresh water bream or that from the Norfolk Broads, which is bony, brackish and not very good to eat. It comes from the cold waters off Greenland and, having a pink skin, is what the trawlermen call "soldiers", possibly after the old redcoats of Napoleonic England. There is little sale for it in Britain as customers don't know what it is. Now mostly made into fish fingers. It is popular in the United States and in France where it is baked with wine and mushrooms or used in *bouillabaisse*.

Sprinkle a whole gutted 3 lb fish with salt and let it stand for about 30 minutes, then wipe it well. Having soaked bread in milk and squeezed it out, mix it with a little salt, pepper, two raw egg yolks and 8 oz of coarsely ground walnuts and a good pinch of thyme. Whip the whites of two eggs so stiff the basin may be turned upside down without them falling out, add them to the mixture and stuff the fish with it. Fasten it with the toothpicks or skewers. Lay it in a buttery fireproof dish, spread 2 oz of butter on the fish. Bake it in a hot oven (400°F, 200°C, Mark 6) for about 30 minutes and serve it piping hot with cucumber salad.

Small Fish Puffs or Smoked Haddock Charlottes with Egg Sauce
Skin, bone and mash 1 lb of cooked smoked haddock. Add 2 oz
of soft white breadcrumbs, the juice and grated rind of a lemon,
1 tablespoon of melted butter, 1 teaspoon of mustard powder
and three well beaten eggs. Mix well and then spoon it into well
buttered teacups. Set these at once in a dish of hot water to come
within 1 inch of the tops of the cups. Cook in a hot oven (400°F,
200°C, Mark 6) for about 30 minutes.

Turn them out into a silver entrée dish to serve, and coat with
Egg Sauce (see page 139).

Fish Puddings
The old steamed fish pudding, and fish loaves, use less eggs than
a conventional soufflé and they will not collapse if kept waiting.
They are not often made now, though a very similar dish is still
popular in Central Europe as well as Northern Italy. It makes the
lightest most delicate mousse, an elegant beginning to a meal.
When done the pudding is usually turned out of its basin and
garnished with parsley and lemon, or prawns or poached eggs
and served with a hot sauce.

A Fish Pudding or Charlotte with Melted Butter
The use of soft white breadcrumbs with fish as a sort of thicken-
ing goes back to Mrs. Glasse's day at least.
Flake 8 oz of cooked salmon or fresh cod into a pan with 2 oz
of soft white breadcrumbs. Add salt and pepper to your taste, a
tablespoon of chopped parsley, a little grated nutmeg and the
grated rind of half a lemon, a teaspoon of butter. Add $\frac{1}{4}$ pint of
milk and let it cook over a very gentle heat for about 7 minutes,
stirring. Then add the yolks of two eggs and a tablespoon of
lemon juice. Stir them in. Whip the whites of the two eggs so
stiffly the basin may be turned upside down without them falling
out, fold them in, tip the mixture into a well buttered pudding
basin or Charlotte mould, which cover with foil pleated in the
middle and tied firmly on to the basin. Steam for $1\frac{1}{4}$ hours by
standing the basin on an upturned saucer in a pan of boiling
water to come half way up. Put a lid on the pan and fill up with
boiling water when necessary.

Turn it out to serve, or send it to table in the basin with a folded napkin pinned round it. A jug of melted butter (mixed with a handful of chopped parsley or some hard boiled egg) may be served with it.

Oswestry Salmon Pudding
Mix 8 oz of cold poached salmon, pulled apart and chopped finely with 4 oz of mashed potatoes. These should have been pressed through a sieve whilst hot and then mixed with 2 oz of unsalted butter, 2 tablespoons of fresh cream and two raw eggs, some pepper and salt.

When this is ready mix it with the fish adding a teaspoon of essence of shrimps (or of anchovy if more readily available).

Put it into a well buttered pudding basin or mould, cover with a paper and a lid, or with two thicknesses of kitchen foil pleated in the middle to allow the pudding to rise; this must be tied firmly on to the mould or basin. Stand the pudding mould, or basin, in a pan with boiling water to come half way up. Put a lid on the pan, let it boil unceasingly for 2 hours, filling up if necessary with boiling water.

This is re-written (though not changed) from the *Cookery Book of Lady Clark of Tillypronie*. The pudding was steamed then turned out to serve with a Shrimp, or Cockle, or Parsley Sauce (see pages 119, 118 and 139).

Lady Clark's Fish Pudding No 2
A baked pudding, this was made with smoked haddock and described as 'a luncheon make-out'. Smoked haddock was more salty in the 19th century than it is today, and had to be soaked in cold water before cooking, but this is seldom necessary now.

Put the smoked haddock in cold water, which bring to the boil and boil it for 10 minutes. Then drain it well. Have ready some potatoes boiled and mashed with plenty of warm melted butter, a dessertspoon of cream and one egg.

Having boiled the fish and pulled it in small pieces, mix it with the mashed potatoes and a little pepper, not salt. Then fill a well buttered pie dish with the mixture. Rough the top of the pudding with a fork, and brown it in a hot oven (400°F, 200°C,

Mark 6) for about 30 minutes. 'It should come up a nice brown', she wrote. Nowadays it would probably be described as a pie not a pudding.

Salmon

A whole salmon, salmon trout, or sea trout as fishmongers call them may conveniently be cooked in the oven in buttered foil. Place the whole cleaned fish on a large sheet of well-buttered foil, with salt, pepper, some slices of lemon and a few sprigs of fresh tarragon if available. It should be well oiled or buttered particularly about the head and tail which tend to stick. Enclose it completely in foil like a parcel, lay this in a meat tin in a moderate oven (350°F, 180°C, Mark 4). The cooking time depends more on the thickness of the fish than its total weight. A long, slim salmon trout will take about 40 minutes, a thick middle cut of salmon about an hour. It is essential to open the parcel and look right inside the fish. If it is dark red along the back bone it is not cooked. Cook for a further 15 minutes.

Serve with a jug of plainly melted butter. Salmon may also be grilled and served with Pantry Butter (see page 116) and

A Sefton of Salmon
A quickly made dish, excellent for the summer luncheon table. It may be made in individual pots, if liked, and can be hot or cold.

The word "Sefton" usually indicates that a dish originated with Louis Eustache Ude, ci-devant chef to Louis XVI. During the Revolution he escaped to England and worked for Lord Sefton, a noted gourmet. The dish may originally have been prepared for ball suppers, though not of course with tinned salmon. Fresh could be used if liked.

Flake the contents of a 7½ oz tin of salmon with a fork. Add salt, pepper and a little grated nutmeg. Beat up two eggs adding ½ pint of milk, mix well with the fish. Bake it in a moderate oven (350°F, 180°C, Mark 4) for about 30 minutes, standing the dish in a shallow tin, or dish, with a little warm water in it, to prevent the custard from boiling.

Shellfish
'She wheeled her wheelbarrow, through streets broad and narrow, crying cockles and mussels – alive, alive-o.' Sweet Mollie Malone has disappeared long ago from the streets of Dublin's fair city, and the taste for shellfish with her.

No oysters are fished now in Oystermouth, nor mussels in Musselburgh, though they were a generation ago. Oysters have been eaten in Britain since ancient times. Roman soldiers used to send Colchester and West Mersea oysters home to their families and English oyster shells have been found among the ruins of ancient Rome.

In the 18th and 19th centuries they were a staple food of the London poor, and very cheap. Dr. Johnson used to go out himself and buy them for Hodge his cat 'lest the servants having that trouble should take a dislike to the poor creature.' The old cookery books are full of recipes for using them in quantity. Now they are so expensive that most people have lost the taste for them, though some London oyster bars are still famous.

The taste for shellfish began to decline at the end of the 19th century, and there are many neglected or extinct or half forgotten oyster beds all round the coast of Britain which could no doubt be revived if there were a demand for them.

People must have grown frightened of shellfish during the Industrial Revolution. As cities grew bigger and more crowded pollution increased, the local sources of shellfish were fouled. They were also sent increasingly by carrier to the big cities from further and further afield, often just by horse and cart and they must frequently have been in very poor condition when they arrived.

Health regulations were slow to catch up with all this and Victorian magazines were full of cartoons showing people being poisoned by shellfish, so that gradually people became too frightened to eat them.

Oysters *A Note*

Our native oysters are protected too, like grouse, partridge or pheasants, during the breeding season and it is illegal to gather or offer them for sale during this season, which is from the beginning of May until the end of August. Portuguese re-laid oysters are not so protected, however, and may be eaten at any time. Thus, the well known stricture about 'not eating oysters unless there is an R in the month' is not for the protection of the public against inferior fish but to preserve the oyster during its breeding season. Oyster shells have annual ring markings and by counting these one can (in theory) tell the oyster's age. They are at their best when 3 to 5 years old.

Recipes including oysters: John Bull's Pudding (see page 78), Carpetbag Steak (see page 66), Galway Steak (see page 65), Oyster Stuffing for Poultry (see page 128).

Oysters

These may be served raw as an *hors d'oeuvre*.

Allow 6 to 12 oysters per person. Brush them clean and rinse them thoroughly under cold running water, and see that all the shells are closed or, if already open, that the shell shuts at once on being tapped. If not the oysters may be dead and are probably very stale.

To open oysters: Before serving they should be opened at the end with the straight pieces at the sides, preferably with the aid of an oyster knife (which has a hand guard like the hilt of a sword) though any firm broad bladed knife would do, except for the increased danger of cutting one's hands.

Put a thick cloth or table napkin over the palm of your hand, lay the oyster on the cloth with the deep shell downwards and the rounded end turned towards your wrist. Push the knife in between the upper and lower shell at one side, and cut the muscle inside the oyster. Then, having pushed in the blade on the knife, twist it with a half turn of the wrist. This will prise the shell open. Any shell splinters can be removed with a brush, such as a pastry brush.

Now put the opened oysters on a large dish of crushed ice. They should be embedded and wedged in the ice chunks so that the liquid stays in their shells. Serve them at once with tabasco, Cayenne pepper, lemon wedges and thin brown bread and butter.

Miss Acton's Oyster Patties (*entrée*)
This would make an excellent beginning to an elegant meal.

'Line some small patty-pans with fine puff paste rolled thin, and to preserve their form when baked, put a bit of bread in each. Lay on the covers, pinch and trim the edges, and send the patties to a brisk oven. [Bake in a hot oven 400°F, 200°C, Mark 6.]

'Plump and beard 2 to 3 doz small oysters (sauce oysters). Mix very smoothly 1 teaspoon of flour with 1 oz of butter, put into a clean saucepan, shake around over a gentle fire, and let simmer for 2 to 3 minutes. Throw in a little salt, pounded mace and Cayenne. Then add by slow degrees 2 or 3 spoonfuls of rich cream, give these a boil and pour in the strained liquor of the oysters. Next lay in the fish (oysters) and keep at the point of boiling for a couple of minutes. Raise the covers from the patties, take out the bread. Fill them with the oysters and their sauce, and replace the covers.

'We have found it an improvement to stew the beards of the fish with a strip or two of lemon peel in a little good veal stock for a quarter of an hour then to strain and add it to the sauce. The oysters unless very small should be once or twice divided.'
Note: Not quite verbatim, these quantities are for a great number of patties and could be reduced.

Cockles, Whelks and Winkles

Cockles vary in size and colour, perhaps in flavour, all round the coast of Britain. They reproduce at an extraordinary rate, as many as half a million per acre are found in large beds in sandy regions. Oil pollution has destroyed them in some places.

Most Londoners know the little ones from Leigh-on-Sea for which the men go out in boats to the Goodwin Sands. They are scalded in the famous sheds, packed in brine and then sold on small saucers, or in muslin bags for people to take away. A local bye-law dating from some time in the 19th century makes it an offence for the Leigh cockle men to sell them raw, though this does not apply in other parts of the country. Unfortunately cockles sold in brine or in vinegar have too strong a flavour to be suitable for cooking, though they can be very pleasant when sprinkled in a mixed salad. If well rinsed they may be stirred into a mild home made mayonnaise.

Cockles, whelks and mussels are also gathered in Morecambe Bay as well as in the Wash, and the sandy beaches off Torbay were once famous for the rednose, spring cockle, or "Paignton cockle", though it is now forgotten. The cockles gathered at Penclawdd in Glamorgan, South Wales, are famous too, as famous as the cockle women who in their thick shawls and good, striped Welsh flannel have gathered them for generations. They used to come in from the cockle beds on little donkeys, baskets over their arms and trays of cockles balanced on their heads. It is a peaceful if chilly occupation getting cockles out of the sand at low water, but the industry goes back to the days of the Ancient Britons. Queen Boadicea is thought to have been just as fond of them as the Welsh miners who, trousers rolled up at the knee, used to go paddling for them on summer holidays.

Both cockles and whelks have been caught along the Norfolk coast since Roman times and have been sent to London and eaten by the saucerful for centuries. At the Jolly Sailors, Brancaster Staithe, Norfolk, they specialize in roast chicken with hot cockle sauce, and also sell hot buttered Brancaster cockles with brown bread and butter. The local boatmen go out six or seven miles here for the whelk fishing, boiling their catch in big washhouse coppers in sheds on the edge of the marshes, and sending the whelks by motor lorry to Birmingham and London. The Norfolk fishermen like to eat them freshly boiled and hot. When recently and only lightly cooked whelks are delicious as part of a platter of seafood to begin a meal. The large common whelk grows to 4 inches long and feeds on oysters by waiting for their valves to open; it then slips the edge of its own shell quickly into the gap, so holding the valves of the oyster's shell apart while it eats the flesh of the delicious creature inside.

Winkles are very good cooked and cold in a platter of seafood. They also go well with drinks before a meal, are less fattening than crisps, and should be served with pins for getting them out of their shells. When speared on pins they may be dipped in a sharp sauce such as garlic mayonnaise.

Cockles with Bread and Butter
If the cockles are in shells wash them well in cold water, changing it several times and leave them for a time in a basin of cold salted water to disgorge any sand in their shells. Throw away any cockles that remain open. Roast the rest in a meat tin on top of the fire for about 5 minutes.

When they are open eat them sizzling hot with vinegar and brown bread and butter. In Lancashire they like them on hot buttered toast with pepper and pickles for High Tea. Fresh hot cockles may also be mixed with scrambled eggs. They can also be eaten raw like oysters, seasoned with lemon juice.

Welsh Cockle Cakes – Teison Gocos
Prepare the cockles as above, then remove the freshly cooked cockles from their shells. Drop them in thick fritter batter and fry them a spoonful at a time in hot fat or oil. Drain. Eat them hot.

Cockles and Bacon
After the cockles are open roll them in flour with a little pepper. Fry the bacon, then put them in the pan with the bacon fat until they are brown and crisp.

Cockles and Cream
Open the cockles as above, take them out of their shells and

keep them hot. Strain the liquid which came out of them into a small pan. Mix a heaped teaspoon of cornflour with a tablespoon of water until smooth. Stir it into the cockle liquor. Heat, stirring, until it thickens adding ¼ pint of thick cream. Pour it over the cockles and serve at once.

Queens

Queens, or closheens as they are called in Ireland, look and taste like a small scallop though of a different species. They are found in Devon, Cornwall, and parts of Scotland and are now fished in the West Country, largely for export, though some years ago the fishermen used them for bait. A huge bank of queens was discovered recently near Plymouth and is now being fished for export to France and the United States.

When absolutely fresh from the sea, queens are very good raw straight from their shells. Most mussel recipes are also suitable.

Queens in Cheese Sauce *(A Recipe from Girvan, Scotland)*

Poach about 12 queens in ½ pint of milk for 5 minutes. Strain but keep the liquor. Melt 2 oz of butter, stir in 2 oz of flour, ½ teaspoon of English mustard powder. Then, gradually heating and stirring, add the milky fish stock, heating and stirring for 5 minutes, adding 3 tablespoons of grated cheese. Beat two egg yolks with 3 tablespoons of thick cream. Add this to the sauce with the queens and a little pepper. Pour it into a fireproof dish, brown under the grill.

Smelts

A little fish with a greenish skin it is known as the "cucumber of the sea" as it both smells and tastes of cucumber. This delicate fish was once fashionable fried as a garnish for whole poached turbot at banquets. Those in the shops, rare nowadays, mostly come from Holland. A hundred years ago when whitebait were still found in the River Thames there were smelts too, and more recently in the River Medway but pollution has killed them. Perhaps after the ministrations of the newly formed River Boards have taken they may return.

Clean, rinse and dry the smelts. Shake them gently one by

one in a bag with seasoned flour until lightly coated. Deep fry them, a few at a time, in a pan of very hot oil until golden brown. They are to be eaten crisp and hot, on hot plates with quartered lemon. Thin brown bread and butter.

Grilled Dover Sole
This classic is perhaps the most perfect dish which comes out of an English kitchen. Dover sole is not found in American waters, nor in British waters north of the Wash. If sold further north it is almost certainly another kind of fish or a frozen one. When ordering it in a restaurant one can usefully ask if it is fresh or frozen.

Dover sole is different from lemon sole, Torbay sole, witch or megrim which are inferior. In Ireland and Scotland it is some-times known as "black sole".

Wash and dry one skinned 8–12 oz sole per person, brush them with oil or with melted butter, sprinkle with salt and pepper. Make the grill very hot, put the fish on the rack, grill slowly 7–10 minutes about 3 inches from the heat; turn once. It should be browned nicely on either side and have the marks of the grill. Serve it with hunks of lemon and, in spring when it is in season, with hot buttered sea kale.

Never turn the fish over to eat the flesh on the other side if you are either on board ship or with a sailor. It is, or was, people in the Royal Navy thought, unlucky in that the ship might turn turtle. Lift off the bones, put them on a side plate and eat the flesh underneath.

Trout
Wild brown and lake trout cooked soon after they are caught are not the same thing as the frozen rainbow trout in fish-mongers' shops. These are reared in farms and have less flavour.

Fresh caught trout are best simply cooked, dipped in seasoned flour and fried gently in bacon fat or hot frothing butter.

Turbot and Brill
This is a huge expensive flatfish which would require an old

fashioned turbot "kettle" to cook it whole. Nowadays large turbot go mostly to the catering trade, though sometimes they are sold sliced across in steaks.

Turbot used to be served at the vast 19th century City livery company banquets such as Wm. M. Thackeray describes in his *Book of Snobs*. The fish usually appeared, whole and boiled, and garnished with mounds of horseradish, crisp fried smelts and lobster sauce. The contrast between its white skin and the lobster coral laid over it in patterns, evidently with the help of some sort of stencil plate, was much admired. In the 1860s, however, it became the thing to serve the fish the other way up, with its dark skin uppermost, as this side was said to have more flavour. The lobster coral decorations disappeared.

Small turbot and brill, a smaller slightly cheaper but similar fish, are sometimes sold in seaside fish shops, fresh and locally caught. They can be delicious when poached gently in milk; those weighing up to about 3 lb will usually fit into an ordinary large pan.

Do not allow the fishmonger to trim off the fins as these are a delicacy. Make a slit along the backbone on the dark skinned side to prevent the turbot from curling up in cooking. Pour enough cold milk and water into a large pan to cover the fish. Add salt, white pepper, a bayleaf, some sliced onion, mixed herbs (parsley, thyme, tarragon) tied together with cotton. To make it easy to lift the cooked fish out of the pan in one piece, lay it on a plate, sling this in a tea towel or table napkin. Lower it into the pan. Then knot the ends of the cloth loosely over a wooden spoon, which lay across the top of the pan. When cooked, it is easy to lift the fish out whole on its plate.

Bring the milk-and-water gently to the boil. Simmer gently 15–20 minutes. Remove the turbot, lay it on a platter. Drain well. Garnish it with quartered lemon, bunches of parsley, new potatoes; a little paprika pepper sprinkled on the fish looks almost as pretty as the now long vanished lobster coral. Have a jug of melted butter to pour over the fish.

Poached turbot with a good egg or parsley sauce or Eliza Acton's Shrimp or Crab Sauce (see page 119) makes an elegant and unusual luncheon dish, with Champs (see page 188), and a dry fruity white wine such as Sauvignon or Sancerre. It may be followed by Cold Chocolate Pudding (see page 246).

Keep the milky fish stock, and let it simmer with the discarded skin, bones, head and so on of the turbot. It makes excellent fish stock which sets in a jelly when cold.

Whitebait

Until 1895 Ministers of the Crown used to go to Greenwich at the end of the summer parliamentary session for a whitebait dinner at the Trafalgar Tavern. The Opposition dined on whitebait at the Old Ship Tavern. There was a fair too and you could get tea with shrimps, saucers of fresh boiled whelks and pots of jellied eels. From 1845 until the end of the century Swigg's Hotel in King William Walk, Greenwich, was known for its whitebait dinners as well as hot joints, poultry and chops, and its tea with shrimps in the gardens. River pollution had killed off the abundant fresh and salt-water fish towards the end of the last century and gradually all this died out but the Cockney taste for eels and shellfish, eaten on high days and holidays since time immemorial, has not vanished entirely. The eel jelliers still flourish round Billingsgate market, and a few of the old fashioned shops selling pies or hot eels and mash are still to be found in the back streets of Bermondsey as well as Greenwich.

To Cook Whitebait

Rinse them in iced water, pat them dry in a tea towel, shake a few at a time in a bag containing flour, salt and pepper just before they are fried as they become soggy if they have to wait. Fry a few at a time in a pan of hot oil in a wire sieve. There is no need to have a large pan with a great deal of oil for deep frying, use a small saucepan. Remove the fish when crisp, serve them with lemon wedges, pepper, thin brown bread and butter.

Grilled Whiting

'Skin clean and dry and fasten the tails in the mouths of 6 whiting about a quarter of a pound each. Dip them in clarified butter, pepper and salt them. Put them on a gridiron and broil [grill] over a clear fire, turning them frequently, they should

223

take about 20 minutes to broil [grill] if the fire is nice and clear. Rub a little cold butter on each. Put in a hot entrée dish and serve.'   From *The Pytchley Cookery Book*, 1886.

Chapter 8

Puddings

Ices

In Restoration England the aristocracy had begun to have ice houses built in the garden in the Italian manner. They were usually sunk some way into the ground and had hollow walls filled with straw, short barley straw was thought best, and were then covered with a mound of earth. In winter they were filled with ice and snow, the door was then closed and packed with straw, until the hot weather when the ice was used. Some ice houses still exist in the grounds of English country houses.

Ice Creams and Sorbets

Not so long ago the kitchens of large country houses used to rattle in summer with the noise of little kitchen maids clanking ice cream buckets as if all hell were after them. These fantastic machines were filled with crushed ice and freezing salt and had a handle which was turned for hours until the stuff in the middle had set. If, unlike the wretched kitchen maids you were on the receiving end, Victorian iced puddings and custard ices were delicious. They appeared on the table smothered in Maidenhair Fern (see page 263) and brandy snaps.

Nowadays, with refrigerators and freezers readily available, they are very simple to make. One can also buy a small electric machine, or *sorbetière*, which is placed in the freezing compartment of the refrigerator and plugged in. A handle turns and whips and stirs the mixture as it sets. If no *sorbetière* is available however ice creams, ice bombes and sorbets are still very easily made. They have a different flavour and texture from the commercial ones.

225

Sorbets, Sherbets and Water Ices

In Victorian England sherbets, or sorbets, were served in the middle of dinner in large wine glasses to refresh the palate. Even to-day a lemon sherbet or champagne sherbet is sometimes served in the middle of Christmas dinner, after the roast beef or goose and before the Stilton cheese, plum pudding and dessert. Victorian sherbets were mostly wine flavoured, or spirit flavoured water ices which were only frozen just enough to be piled into a glass. Though some were made with champagne or sparkling hock, other less distinguished white wines were used, with good effect. Indeed much of the delicate flavour and nose of a fine wine is lost when it is frozen. Fruit sorbets, or sherbets, are less filling than ice cream and have recently returned to fashion. They are usually cheaper to make too and, if there is a freezer, provide a good way of using the soft fruit of summer and are simpler and quicker to make than jam.

Ice Bombes

In the second half of the 19th century there were very fancy moulds for ice puddings. Water was frozen in special moulds shaped like wine goblets or glasses, they were then filled with champagne sorbet and were popular at ball suppers, tennis parties and garden parties. Sometimes these goblet moulds were filled with a coloured mixture to imitate marble. There were pewter ice cream moulds shaped like beehives, quart-sized strawberries, hens on nests, swans and cauliflowers, cucumbers or cabbage roses.

Ice bombes were so called because they were made in a "bomb-shaped" copper mould with a lid – something like a shell case from the First World War. In those days – when the Anarchists were said to be everywhere attempting to blow up the mighty – they perhaps had a macabre fascination.

Charles Elmé Francatelli even gives a recipe for a Bombe Glacée à la Robert Peel, after the head of the police. The bombe shape was however an especially convenient one for burying in the ice and freezing salt mixture.

Nowadays if the freezer is used one does not need a mould with a lid, the top can be covered in foil. Ices can also be frozen in a cake tin or jelly mould. The ice has to be frozen really firm and to have been whipped before it is packed into the chilled mould. To turn it out draw the tin two or three times through a bowl of cold water to loosen the ice cream inside. Dry the mould, take off the foil, turn it out on a dish and decorate it. Cold Melba Sauce and Hot Chocolate Sauce are suitable accompaniments (see pages 126 and 231).

Champagne Sorbet
This is a recipe given to me by Christophers the wine merchants in Jermyn Street. It is really a sort of frozen Buck's Fizz.

Simmer 4 oz of sugar in a little water for 5 minutes to make a syrup. Add the juice of an orange and a lemon and ½ pint of champagne or sparkling white wine. Set the fridge at maximum cold. Put it in the freezer top of the refrigerator. Stir occasionally as ice crystals form so as to have a sort of champagne snow rather than a block of ice. After about 2 hours crush the frozen snow and fold in two very stiffly whipped egg whites. Freeze again until dinner time.

Raspberry or Strawberry Water Ice
Purée 8 oz of raspberries (or strawberries) with 3 oz of caster sugar, the juice of half a lemon and two or three drops of cochineal. Press the mixture through a fine sieve, adding ½ pint of water. Freeze, whip and freeze as usual. It may be garnished if liked with whole raspberries, either fresh or those which have been frozen. Raspberries freeze very well, but strawberries do not and frozen strawberries are not recommended as a garnish.

Rum Sherbet
This is a lemon water ice which has 1 wineglass of rum added to the ½ pint of it when nearly frozen. The rum should be stirred in when the ice is taken out of the freezer to whip it. It is then re-frozen. All ices containing alcohol take a long time to freeze.

Victorian Currant Water Ice
Strip the stalks off the red currants, reduce the fruit to a purée in the mixer, and then let the juice drip through a fine sieve.

227

Mix the juice with sugar, allowing 1 lb of sugar per 2 pints of juice. When well mixed, freeze, whipping the mixture when half frozen, then re-freezing it.

Black currants can be used in the same way to make a superb purple water ice. Wild blackberries are also suitable.

Apricot Ice
Use 8 oz of stoned apricots or $\frac{1}{2}$ pint apricot purée, $5\frac{1}{2}$ oz sugar, the juice of a lemon, $\frac{1}{4}$ pint of cream. Freeze as usual.

Banana Ice Cream (*a lovely ice*)
Peel and mash two ripe bananas, mix them with $3\frac{1}{2}$ oz of sugar, the juice of half a lemon or half an orange and $\frac{1}{4}$ pint of milk. Freeze as usual.

Edwardian Brown Bread Ice Cream
This was a forgotten English dish that I revived some years ago.

A recipe for it appeared in Frederick Nutt's *Complete Confectioner* in 1789 — though it may be older.

Mix 4 oz of *stale* brown breadcrumbs from a rough whole-wheat loaf (fine factory made brown bread will not do) with $\frac{1}{2}$ pint of stiffly whipped double cream, 3 oz of caster sugar flavoured with vanilla. Add 1 tablespoon of rum when half set.

Brown bread ice cream may be served on a chilled dish with Raspberry Sauce or Melba Sauce; 8 oz of fresh or unsweetened frozen raspberries should be rubbed through a fine sieve or strainer (when thawed). Then beat in 4 tablespoons of sifted icing sugar one after the other.

For **Ginger Ice cream** add 2 oz of chopped crystallized ginger and leave out the vanilla.

For **Mocca Ice Cream** (delicious with meringues) mix $2\frac{1}{2}$ oz of sugar with 1 teaspoon of cocoa. Add two egg yolks stirring till very frothy then stir in 1 tablespoon of instant coffee and $\frac{1}{4}$ pint of cream. Freeze as before.

Dark Red Cherry Ice Cream
Put 1 lb of cherries, stoned weight, in a fireproof dish with the

juice of a lemon and 4 tablespoons of coarse brown (Demerara) sugar. Leave them in a very moderate oven (325°F, 170°C, Mark 3) until they are soft and a brilliant red juice runs out. Purée them, add ½ pint of stiffly whipped double cream. Freeze, whip and re-freeze. Grant's Morello cherry brandy may be poured on the ice before serving.

Ginger Ice Cream
The familiar blue and white jars of ginger preserved in thick syrup had been coming here for some time in the holds of East Indiamen, it is a flavour which has long been popular in England much used here in cooking, less well understood abroad. Fancy jars of ginger are still sold, especially at Christmas, but it is much cheaper when packed in ordinary glass jars or bottles. From *The Complete Confectioner* by Frederick Nutt, 1789.
'Take four ounces of Ginger preserved. Pound it and put it in a basin with two gills [½ pint] of syrup; a lemon squeezed and one pint of cream; then freeze it.'

Gooseberry Ice Cream
An unusual ice cream which looks even cooler if one adds three or four drops of green confectioners' colouring to it.
Put 1 lb of fruit and 5 oz of sugar in a covered dish in a very moderate oven (325°F, 170°C, Mark 3) until the juice runs out. The gooseberries need not be topped and tailed. When they are soft and juicy press them through a sieve to make a purée without the pips and stalks and so on. When cold mix the purée with ½ pint of stiffly whipped double cream, adding two or three drops of green colouring and a little more sugar if liked. Freeze and whip. The same mixture can be served unfrozen as a gooseberry fool.

Lemon Ice Cream
Squeeze the juice from one lemon and cut another across in very very thin slices. Add both to 5 oz of icing sugar and let the mixture stand for an hour, stirring from time to time until all the sugar has melted. Whip 1 pint of double cream absolutely stiff, add 1 pint of milk and chill. Then add the lemon and sugar mixed

together with the white of an egg whipped so stiff the basin may be turned upside down without it falling out. Freeze as usual.

Macaroon Ice Cream
Crumble 1 lb of macaroons and soak them in about ¼ pint of old brown sherry or Madeira. Add ¾ pint of stiffly whipped double cream with sugar to your taste. Put it in a basin, leave it in the freezer for 30 minutes, beat it up with a fork then put it back in the freezer for another 30 minutes to freeze with wax paper to cover it. Chill until ready to serve it. The sherry in the cream takes longer to freeze than ordinary ices – about 3 hours.

Peach Melba
In Auguste Escoffier's *Ma Cuisine*, which was translated into English by Oscar Wilde's son, the late Vyvyan Holland, one can find the kind of meals which Lily Langtry and King Edward VII enjoyed, and there are dishes dedicated to Sarah Bernhardt and Adelina Patti. It was Escoffier too who invented the Peach Melba. The peach was brought to her one night after she had sung Elsa in *Lohengrin*. It nestled in an enormous swan carved from ice and was so huge that it took four footmen to carry it into the dining room.

A true Peach Melba consists in half a fresh peach peeled and then poached lightly in wine. It is then laid on a rich vanilla ice cream. This is to be made by whipping ½ pint of single and ½ pint of double cream with 6 oz of vanilla flavoured sugar. The mixture is then frozen, whipped when half set and re-frozen.

The peach on the vanilla ice is then covered with raspberry purée, decorated with whipped cream and split almonds. Nowadays it is frequently prepared with inferior material and with tinned fruit. The real thing is excellent. (For Melba Sauce see page 126.)

My Raspberry Ice
Press 1 lb of raspberries, or better still of raspberries and red currants, through a sieve with 3 oz of sugar. Add ¼ pint of stiffly whipped double cream, freeze, whip it at half time, re-freeze.

Victorian Tea Ice Cream

Beat up 4 egg yolks with 8 oz of sugar until they trickle off the spoon in ribbons. Heat ½ pint of milk with ¼ pint of very strong tea and stir this gradually into the eggs. Heat stirring in the top of a double pan with hot, but not quite boiling, water in the lower pan. When the tea-custard is thick enough to coat the spoon remove it from the heat. Freeze it when cold, whip and re-freeze it.

Hokey Pokey with Hot Chocolate Sauce

The old fashioned and, I think, absolutely delicious Hokey Pokey that children once bought from painted Italian ice cream carts was really a frozen egg custard, flavoured with vanilla and of varying degrees of richness according to where you bought it. The name is apparently a corruption of *Ecco un poco* "Here is a little" a phrase used constantly by the wandering ice cream sellers who, like the men with the barrel organs and performing dogs and monkeys, and the German street bands, came here because of political trouble in their native lands in the 19th century.

Hot Chocolate Sauce is very good with well frozen Hokey Pokey. But unless the ice cream is very hard the whole thing will melt.

Sauce: Break 8 oz of plain block chocolate in pieces. Melt it in the top of a double saucepan, adding about ⅓ pint of water. Heat it stirring all the time till the chocolate melts and the sauce is smooth and thick. Then add one or two teaspoons of instant coffee powder and a little sugar too if you like, though I myself prefer it without.

Tipsy Parson

Beat two large egg yolks with 1 oz of sugar, add two jiggers of rum and 1 jigger of whisky. Let it stand, stirring occasionally. Whip the whites of the two eggs so stiffly the basin may be turned upside down without them falling out, gradually add another ½ oz of sugar.

Whip ½ pint of double cream and mix all together. Freeze. It never freezes very stiff.

231

Apple Dumplings with Brown Sugar
Large Bramley cooking apples which become soft and fluffy
when cooked are the best apples to use.

For boiled or steamed apple dumplings: Stir 4 tablespoons of
grated or shredded suet into 8 tablespoons of self-raising flour
(or plain flour, but then add 1 teaspoon of bicarbonate of soda).
Add a pinch of salt and enough water to make a stiff dough
(about half a cup). Roll it out gently on a floured surface about
$\frac{1}{4}$ inch thick. Cut it in pieces (squares or rounds) big enough to
cover the whole apple. Place 4 peeled, cored, but whole apples
on the pastry. Fill the centres with brown sugar and a little
grated lemon peel, with a pinch of ground cloves. Or with
mincemeat, sugar, and a little whisky or rum. Fold the pastry
round the apples, moistening the edges and pinching them together, so that each apple is in a rolled-up parcel of pastry. Press
it firmly on to them. Then cover each completely in foil to keep
out the water. Put them in a pan of boiling water. If a lot of
dumplings are made a fish kettle is convenient. Let them bubble
gently, the water never ceasing to boil, for $1\frac{1}{2}$ hours according
to size.

To be served with more brown sugar and cream or with a
Devonshire Junket (see page 241), removing the foil and sending
the dumplings, hot and quickly, to table. Some cooks make the
dumplings without sugar, then when these are baked they slice
them through and sprinkle them with sugar and eat them as hot
as can be. The apple, they say, stays fluffier when cooked without
sugar.

Newton Abbot Dumplings
The apples are wrapped in puff pastry, baked in the oven and are
to be eaten hot with clotted cream and warm golden syrup.

Chill 12 oz of rough puff pastry before using it. Then roll it
out about $\frac{1}{4}$ inch thick on a floured surface, cut out 6 equal
squares of pastry, place a peeled cored apple in the centre of each,
filling the holes in the middle with a spoonful of caster sugar
mixed with a little ground cinnamon. Fold the pastry round the
apples, moistening the edges and pinching them together, so

each apple is completely enclosed. Place them, the other way up on a baking sheet, sprinkle the tops lightly with a little sugar. Bake in a hot oven (400°F, 200°C, Mark 6) for about 10 minutes until the pastry has risen then reduce the heat to moderate (350°F, 180°C, Mark 4) for another 20 minutes.

Apple and other Fritters
Peel and core the apples which may be sliced or diced but the pieces should be roughly the same thickness. If liked put them in a shallow dish and cover them with a sweet cider or some cooking sherry for some hours till ready to cook them. Drain them well. Dip them in the batter and drop them by spoonsful into deep hot oil. Fry them until crisp and brown. Drain them well, keep them hot.

The fritters may be dusted with caster sugar and powdered cinnamon.

Other fruits, stoned ripe plums, peeled bananas cut in chunks, rings of pineapple can be used for making fritters. They should not be soaked in wine or cider.

A bunch of sweet ripe cherries can be tied together in bunches of five or six, by the stalks. Dip them in fritter batter and fry them as before.

For the batter, beat up one egg with 4 oz of flour, add a pinch of salt, 1 tablespoon of sugar and gradually beat in ½ pint of milk. Double the quantity if there are a lot of apples.

Osborne House Apple Charlotte *(As made for Queen Victoria)*
When cooked and turned out of the dish, it may be flamed with warm brandy and served with cream. The Charlotte appears to have originated with Carème, sometime chef to George IV, when Prince Regent. It may well have been called after the Princess Charlotte, heir to the throne and daughter of King George IV, who died so young in childbirth.

There are of course other and richer Charlottes, but they all seem to have originated from the same famous chef and all pay the same compliment to his royal patron.

Osborne House Apple Charlotte is made with dessert apples.

Peel, core and slice 2 lb of dessert apples and cook them gently

233

in a casserole in a moderate oven (350°F, 180°C, Mark 4) with 3 oz of butter, 2 tablespoons of caster sugar and ½ teaspoon of ground ginger or ground cinnamon. When the apples are soft beat them to a pulp with a wooden spoon. Butter the inside of a 1½ pint pie dish very thickly. Mix 1 tablespoon of caster sugar with ½ teaspoon of ground cinnamon or ground ginger, use most of this to coat the butter in the pie dish. Cut the crusts off some thin bread and butter and cut it in fingers. With these, line the sides and bottom of the dish completely, butter side down. There must be no spaces between. Pour in the apple pulp. Cover it with more bread and butter fingers, butter side up, and with no spaces between. Sift another spoonful of spiced sugar over them. Bake the Apple Charlotte in a moderate oven (350°F, 180°C, Mark 4) for about 45 minutes. This is to be turned out and eaten hot.

With it one might drink a well chilled but luscious Rhine wine, or hock as it is called in Britain. The word is said to be an abbreviation of Hockamore which was the British pronunciation of *Hochheimer*, a Rhine wine of which Queen Victoria was so fond that one of the vineyards, *Hochheimer Koenigin Viktoriaberg*, was called after her. She appears to have acquired a taste for it at the time she became engaged to Prince Albert.

Yorkshire Apple Batter

In some parts of Yorkshire this simple pudding is served either as a sweet – when it is sprinkled with powdered cinnamon and sugar, or served with a little jam – or as a savoury dish to make an excellent accompaniment for grilled gammon and sausages.

Melt 3 oz of butter, use some to grease a Yorkshire pudding tin. Sift 4 oz of self-raising flour with 2 oz of sugar and a pinch of salt. Mix it with ½ pint of tepid milk to make a smooth batter, adding a beaten egg.

Stir in 1 lb of peeled, cored and sliced apples and the rest of the melted butter. Pour this into the buttery tin. Bake in a hot oven (400°F, 200°C, Mark 6) for 20 minutes. Then reduce the heat to moderate (350°F, 180°C, Mark 4) and bake for a further 20 minutes.

Barley Kernel Pudding et al

Though sago pudding is still made, tapioca pudding has almost vanished. It used to be made with the large grained tapioca of thirty or forty years ago, known as "frog's eggs pudding" to generations of children. This is now almost impossible to buy, flake tapioca being the kind now offered for sale. Packets of Farola with charming Edwardian labels were sold too in pharmacies and grocers' shops and used to make a very good pudding with a rich smooth texture and a creamy yellow colour. These too have vanished.

Barley Kernel Pudding had a thick nutty flavour which is forgotten, but, though the barley kernels are seldom found in grocers' shops, a very similar product is sold in packets in health food shops and used for making *muesli*. It is labelled "organically grown flaked barley" (*frische biologische Gerseflocken*) looks not unlike porridge oats and makes a very good pudding.

Put 2 oz of barley kernels, 1 oz of butter and 2 oz of sugar into a pie dish. Stir in 1 pint of milk. Bake it in a very moderate oven (325°F, 170°C, Mark 3) for 2 hours.

Welsh Rice Pudding

This is the thick creamy kind with the grains just slightly chewy and separate, it is to be eaten hot with raspberry jam, or the kind of home made Greengage Jam which has whole almonds in it (see page 272), or with a jug of warm golden syrup. It is almost traditional in Wales after roast mutton and is also very good cold with clotted cream.

Put a little less than 1 inch of hot water into a pie dish. Add about 1 oz of round grained pudding rice, to 1 pint of hot water. Put it in a moderate oven (350°F, 180°C, Mark 4) for 30 minutes until the rice has swelled and the water has vanished. Then add 1 pint of milk, 2 oz of Demerara sugar, 1 oz of butter, a pinch of salt, $\frac{1}{2}$ teaspoon of grated nutmeg and 1 bayleaf. Stir it from time to time. Then when it is cooked and comes out of the oven add two beaten egg yolks and, just before serving, fold in the two egg whites so stiffly whipped the basin may be turned upside down without them falling out. The bayleaf may be removed or not, it looks quite pretty in the pudding.

Thick cream might also be stirred into the pudding before serving, but then one leaves out the eggs.

Escoffier's Figs
As served at the Carlton Hotel in London
The now vanished Carlton Hotel is especially associated with Escoffier, 'the father of modern cooking', as almost all his working life was spent in London, first at the Savoy then at the Carlton Hotel from 1898. People said he was one of the greatest chefs the world has ever known, the Kaiser remarked that though he was Emperor of Germany Escoffier was Emperor of cooks. Many of his *entremêts* seem over-decorated, sickly and rather vulgar to modern tastes. Some are also very sweet like the rich egg custard for which he suggested adding 1 lb of sugar to 1¾ pints of milk. But the figs are delightful. It is the very breath of Edwardian England.

Peel some fresh figs. Cut them in two lengthways and put them in a silver or glass dish and keep them on ice. Prepare a raspberry purée, add double the quantity of Chantilly cream and cover the figs completely with the mixture.

One can still find waiters in the older and statelier hotels who are prepared to peel a fresh fig for one at table and serve it with thick cream. Escoffier also commends **Figs Baked in the Oven like Apples,** which 'served cold and accompanied by Chantilly cream constitute a very delicate dessert.'

'To do this take some figs with unblemished skins and place them in an earthenware dish with a few tablespoons of water, sprinkle them with sugar and bake them in the oven like apples. The sugar caramelizes during the cooking of the fruit and has an excellent taste which syrup, usually too sweet, does not possess.'

Luscious green figs from the Near East are sold here inexpensively by the pound in late summer, usually in districts where Greeks and Cypriots are living.

Queen Anne's Pears
Hard cooking pears need long and gentle cooking with dark brown sugar and just enough water to cover. They used to be laid in big earthenware crocks with greaseproof paper tied over

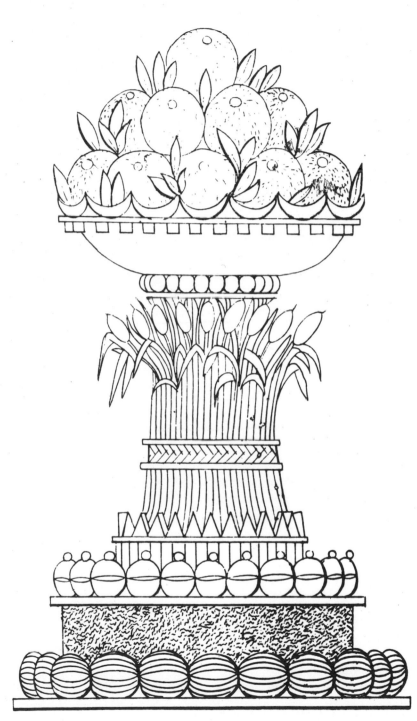

the top and then left in the old brick bread oven until the pears were soft. Damsons were cooked in the same gentle heat with plenty of brown sugar, and eaten hot in Suffolk farmhouses with a jug of cream and sometimes a piece of cheese as well. Whole peeled pears, when cooked gently in red wine, or red wine and water, with a little honey or sugar become stained a deep dressing gown red. The recipe, now more usually associated with France, was popular in this country in Queen Anne's day and during a great part of the 18th century. A recipe for them, differing little from the fashionable French *poires au vin rouge*, appears in *The Queen's Royal Cookery*, 1707, by T. Hall, Free Cook of London.

'Pare them (but leave them whole with the stalks on). Put them in a pipkin with so much red or claret wine and water, of each as much as will near reach the top of the pears. Stew or boil them gently till they grow tender, which may be in two hours [*in a moderate oven* 350°F, 180°C, Mark 4]. After a while put in some sticks of cinnamon bruised and a few cloves when they are almost done. Put in sugar enough to season them well and their syrup which you pour out upon them in a deep plate.'

Pears and Pastry
This is a cottage recipe from the Welsh Border Counties. The pears are served hot from the pan with cream and the suet pastry. Conference pears are ready in October and November.

Peel, halve and core, 1 lb of Conference pears, laying them flat in a heavy saucepan with a big pinch of nutmeg and 1 table-spoon of soft brown "pieces" sugar. Barely cover them with water, which bring gently to the boil. Reduce the heat to simmer. Meanwhile mix 2 oz of plain flour, a pinch of salt and 1 oz of grated suet. Stir in about 2 tablespoons of water, to make a light suet crust pastry. Shape it, with floury hands, to fit the top of the pan as a "lid". Cook it, simmering, over the pears for 30 minutes.

Strawberries
Strawberries and cream were first made fashionable by Cardinal Wolsey who gave great feasts to Henry VIII at Hampton Court

as well as at his palace in Whitehall. Strawberries and cream seem to have been served there in 1509 at an official banquet, following a dish of porpoise and mustard sauce which was then considered a great delicacy.

Strawberries, figs and cherries flourished on London soil in those days. Their prices varied according to the season. In the year of the Armada for example, strawberries dropped from 1s per pint on May 23rd to 3d per pint on June 7th. These early strawberries were small and more like wood strawberries in flavour – the *fragole di bosce* still so popular in Italy – than the modern fruit which is hybridized with Chilean and Virginian plants. They were, in Wolsey's day, similar to the hautboys (*Fragaria elatior*) shown in medieval manuscripts.

Strawberry Mess

Strawberry Mess is a dish consumed at Eton College, on the Fourth of June to celebrate King George III's birthday. He took great interest in the College and decreed that the scholars were to have a holiday on this day for ever after. The Glorious Fourth of June is a time of general jollification with visits from parents and sisters, speeches in the Upper School, people strolling about watching the cricket and rowing, eating Strawberry Mess and enjoying the procession of boats at 6.30 in the evening. There is also a cricket club at Eton College called Strawberry Mess the members of which wear strawberry pink and white cricket caps.

The Mess itself is mainly prepared in the Tuck Shop. We have it on good authority that it consists in 'plain ice cream with a lot of strawberries dolloped all round it and over the top, very thickly. Then with lots of strawberry jam over that, and a great deal of whipped cream on top.'

Old Etonians, we are told, have another secret version 'with quantities of rum sloshed over it as well.'

Raspberries or strawberries are delectable with a real Devonshire Junket (see page 241), a dish few people make now. They are best served with sifted icing sugar as a sweetener.

Strawberries in Red Wine Jelly *(A Victorian delicacy)*

Soak 1 lb of strawberries in a little brandy and caster sugar.

Make the jelly by melting 6 level teaspoons of powdered gelatine in 5 tablespoons of hot water. Stir, heating, until thoroughly dissolved. Then stir in 3 oz of caster sugar and 1 bottle of red wine. Let the jelly cool and when almost setting pour some into a wetted mould or pudding basin, let it set, then add a layer of strawberries in brandy. Then more wine jelly. Repeat until all is used. When set turn it out, decorate with whipped cream.

Summer or Hydropathic Pudding
So called because apparently it was made in summer for people who were taking the waters at Bath, but were not allowed the richer, fruitier and more alcoholic puddings.

Bilberries or black currants; raspberries and black currants; blackberries, raspberries and red currants may be used.

Line a pudding basin with thin slices of white bread with the crusts cut off. Cook about $1\frac{1}{2}$ lb blackberries or other fruit, as available, with sugar to your taste and enough liquid for there to be plenty of juice. Black currants with half water and half bottled black currant syrup, make a delicious pudding.

Pour all this hot into the lined basin, cover the fruit completely with a "lid" of white crustless bread. Press the pudding down with a weighted saucer. Leave it 24 hours or longer before turning it out on to a dish and bringing it, cool and refreshing, to table. It can be made in winter too with frozen fruit.

Milk and Cream Puddings
In the 18th century there were cows in Saint James's Park in London to which the fashionable went to drink milk, just as at Bath they drank the waters; eight cows in summer and four in winter for which the milk sellers had to obtain permission from the Home Secretary. Milk warm from the cow was thought particularly healthy, and at least if you had it milked into your cup you knew that it was fresh and clean and had not been watered. Some of the milk being cried in the streets was of very poor quality, often blue. One suspects that the large quantities of fresh cream specified in some 18th century recipes really refer to what we should now describe as full cream milk.

The great country houses had ornamental dairies some way from the house, such as those at Kenwood House, Hampstead, and at Ashburnham Place, Sussex, where countesses could play at being pretty milkmaids, with their gentlemen, in the Watteau-esque manner.

Butter was usually sold by the yard in the 18th century.

Clotted Cream, or Clouted Cream, or Devonshire Cream

This is not often made on Devon farms for sale nowadays. Most of that which is offered comes from creameries and is less good than the original which was clotted in great pans on the kitchen stove. Those bottles of gold top Channel Islands' milk produce superb clotted cream.

Pour 2 quarts of milk into a wide shallow pan and leave it for 24 hours until the cream rises to the top. Then very gently and steadily lift the pan on to the warm stove, do not shake it for this will break up the cream. Then leave it on a very low heat for the cream to clot. The lower the heat the better, it must not boil for then there would be a thick skin on it.

Exactly how long it takes to clot depends on the width of the pan, the heat of the cooker and so on, but when it has clotted a solid ring begins to form round the edge and the cream will look all wrinkled and ribbed on top. Now lift it off the stove as gently as possible, leave the pan in a cool place for 24 hours before skimming off the clotted cream into a dish.

Devonshire Junket

This is known as a *Cold Velvet Cream* in Scotland. Warm 1 pint of fresh unboiled milk to blood heat (it will feel neither hot nor cold when tested with the finger). Boiled or scalded milk should not be used and the milk must not be brought to the boil for then the junket will not set.

Add 1 tablespoon of sugar and 1 teaspoon of rennet essence (sold in bottles by good grocers). Add a tablespoon of rum or whisky or the grated rind of half a lemon to flavour the junket. Leave it at room temperature, not in the refrigerator, to set.

When set spread clotted cream gently and carefully over the top. Sprinkle this with grated nutmeg and Demerara sugar.

Brandy snaps or Honiton fairings may be served with it. Or, when set, the top may be sprinkled thickly with crushed macaroons or ratafias.

Syllabubs

Syllabubs, for which the cow was milked direct into the tall glasses in which the delicacy was to be served, on to a measure of sherry or white wine – or sometimes rough cider – were fashionable in the 18th century as part of the then popular cult of rustic simplicity.

Other good syllabubs were made by more conventional means, though it seems that some were made, on occasion, by climbing a step ladder so as to pour the warm milk or cream from a great height into the wine glasses containing sherry and so on. This apparently makes the milk froth, much as it does when milked into them straight from the cow. The traditional Lancashire Stone Cream was made in this way.

Victorian syllabubs, though they were still served in tall wine glasses or custard glasses, were very different.

I. Whip up 1 pint of double cream stiffly. Then, add the grated rind of a lemon and add a glass of Bual Madeira or of Marsala, with sugar to your liking. Spoon it into glasses, garnish with ratafias.

II. Stir the strained juice and grated rind of two large lemons into 6 oz of caster sugar and two wine glasses of brown sherry. Then, little by little, and whipping all the time with a piano wire egg whisk, add 1 pint of double cream. Go on whipping the mixture until it is thick and frothy. This is sometimes served chilled in a glass dish.

Atholl Brose

Whipped cream is mixed with a little sugar and whisky to your liking and served in custard glasses or wine glasses and eaten with a spoon. The "Edinburgh Fog" now popular in some Scottish hotels is Atholl Brose mixed with broken shortbread or crushed ratafias and garnished either with toasted almonds or toasted oatmeal.

Boodle's Orange Fool

A speciality of the club in St James's, London. Mr. Boodle, Mr. Brooks and Mr. White all kept coffee houses in St James's in the days of the Prince Regent. Brooks' was frequented by the politicians; the gambling horse-racing "bloods" went mostly to White's and the landed gentry to Boodle's. When the owners died the coffee houses became clubs.

Lay 6 sliced sponge cakes in a dish, or nearly fill it with chopped sandwich cake. Mix the juice and grated rind of one lemon and two oranges with 2 tablespoons of caster sugar. Stir this into 1 pint of thick cream. Pour it over the sponge cake. Chill it for some hours before serving, so that the cream may soak into the cake. It is to be served chilled.

Mrs. Rundell's Orange Fool (1806)

'Mix the juice of three Seville oranges, three eggs well beaten, a pint of cream, a little nutmeg and cinnamon and sweeten to your taste. Set the whole over a slow fire, and stir till it becomes as thick as good melted butter*, but it must not be boiled; then pour it into a dish for eating cold.'

This is best cooked like a conventional egg custard in the top of a double saucepan, very gently, with hot but not quite boiling water in the pan below. Stir it all the time until it is thick enough just to coat the back of the spoon, it thickens more when cold. It is not difficult to make but if it boils or almost boils the egg will form lumps and the juice might curdle the cream.

* By "melted butter" Mrs. Rundell meant the old English Butter Sauce (see page 115).

Burnt Cream

Known variously as Burnt Cream, *Crème Brûlée* or Cambridge Cream, this lovely cold pudding really seems to have originated at Cambridge University. Various colleges claim it as their own, Trinity College bases its claim on a recipe left to the college in manuscript by a 19th century pastrycook who worked there for many years.

Take 1 pint of single cream, 6 fresh egg yolks and 8 oz of

caster sugar. Beat up the egg yolks with $\frac{1}{2}$ oz of sugar, bring the cream to the boil and pour it gradually over the beaten yolks stirring all the time. Add 2 bayleaves and a blade of mace and heat the mixture gently stirring continuously until it is thick enough to coat the back of the spoon. It is safest to do this in the top of a double saucepan with hot, but not quite boiling, water in the pan below. If it boils it will curdle and be quite spoiled. When thickened strain it into a shallow fireproof serving dish. If liked, place it for a moment in a very hot oven (450°F, 230°C, Mark 8) to set.

When cold sprinkle it evenly all over with the remaining sugar to form a thick layer. Make the grill really hot. Stand the dish in another one with chunks of ice round it. Put the whole thing under the griller, until the sugar melts, bubbles and toasts lightly to form a kind of caramel top, which sets hard and crisp when cold. Watch it all the time, and remove the dish before the sugar burns.

It is served very cold.

Nanny's Pink Marbled Pudding
A delicate cold dish of the very palest pink. It tastes faintly of roses and looks pretty in a glass dish, embedded in cracked ice.

Mix 4 tablespoons of plain (bottled) rosehip syrup with $\frac{1}{2}$ pint of hot water, stir in $\frac{1}{4}$ oz of powdered gelatine over a low heat so as to be sure it has melted completely. Pour it into a suitable dish and put it in the refrigerator for 2–3 hours to set. When nearly set stir in 2 tablespoons of thick, unwhipped cream, so that the mixture is marbled, snow white and rose red.

A Cold Brown Bread Soufflé
Whip three egg yolks with 3 tablespoons of caster sugar and 4 tablespoons of brown sherry or Madeira over a low heat until the mixture becomes pale and frothy like a zabaglione. Melt $\frac{1}{2}$ oz of gelatine in 3 tablespoons of hot water, when cool whip it into the egg mixture together with 2 tablespoons of stale brown breadcrumbs (from a coarse grained wheaten or granary loaf). When almost set add $\frac{1}{4}$ pint of stiffly whipped double cream and three egg whites so stiffly whipped the basin may be turned

upside down without them falling out. Pour the whole thing into a white china soufflé dish or other suitable bowl and leave it in the refrigerator for 2–3 hours to set.

This is sometimes served with strawberries or other fruit in brandy.

A Cold Ginger Soufflé

A feather-light pudding which may be eaten with brandy snaps, or ginger biscuits.

Beat three egg yolks and 1 tablespoon of caster sugar until the mixture trickles off the spoon in "ribbons", then stir or fold in $\frac{1}{2}$ pint of stiffly whipped double cream together with about 3 tablespoons of finely chopped stem ginger. Melt $\frac{1}{2}$ oz of gelatine in 3 tablespoons of the warmed ginger syrup. When cool stir this in gently. Then, having whipped the three egg whites so stiffly the basin may be turned upside down without them falling out, stir or fold these in also. Pour the whole into a white china soufflé dish and leave it in the refrigerator for 2–3 hours to set.

It may be sprinkled with chopped walnuts and brown sugar before serving, or with chopped walnuts and brown sugar roasted in the oven.

A Cold Raspberry Soufflé

Press enough raspberries through a sieve to make 1 pint of purée. Add 2–3 tablespoons of caster sugar or sifted icing sugar and, if liked, a dash of lemon juice to bring out the flavour. Melt $\frac{1}{2}$ oz of powdered gelatine in 3 tablespoons of hot water. See that it is completely dissolved, add it to the fruit purée which pour into a white china soufflé dish or other suitable bowl to set, in 2 to 3 hours in the refrigerator. When more than half set, stir in two egg whites, so stiffly whipped the basin may be turned upside down without them falling out.

Then stir in, very gently, $\frac{1}{4}$ pint of stiffly whipped double cream, leave it to set. It may also be garnished with cream and sprigs of angelica.

Lemon Solid

This is an old fashioned country "set cream", which may be

turned out of the basin when set. It is still popular in Suffolk villages for tea with treacle tart, or some of the soft fruit.

Warm 1 pint of milk with 6 oz of sugar, stir in $\frac{1}{2}$ oz of gelatine and the grated rind of two lemons. Heat the mixture gently, stirring it until both the gelatine and the sugar have melted properly. Now add the strained juice of the two lemons and stir it for a moment over the low heat until the curd separates. Pour it into a bowl and turn it out when set. It may be garnished with sweetened raspberry purée, or with the Uncooked Raspberry Jam (see page 281).

'You Cannot Leave Me Alone'

This pudding with the plaintive name was well liked in the 18th century; it is flavoured with lemon.

Beat the yolks of 6 eggs with 4 oz of caster sugar, adding the grated rind and strained juice of two lemons. Melt $\frac{1}{2}$ oz of powdered gelatine in $\frac{1}{2}$ pint of hot water. When cool and thoroughly melted add this to the beaten egg yolks.

Now whip the 6 egg whites so stiff that the basin may be turned upside down without them falling out. Mix everything together lightly and pour the mixture into a glass dish, and let it set in 2–3 hours in the refrigerator.

When set the bottom goes all cool and lemonish, the top delicately frothy. If liked it may be covered with Greengage Jam and whipped cream, but it is also excellent plain.

Cold Chocolate Pudding

Very rich, and probably fattening, it may also be garnished with whipped cream.

Melt two 4 oz blocks of plain bitter chocolate gently in a pan over a low heat, stirring. When cool stir in 5 egg yolks, 4 oz of melted butter and 3 oz of caster sugar.

Whip the 5 egg whites so stiff the basin may be turned upside down without them falling out, stir them gently into the mixture. Dip 8 oz of Savoy fingers (sometimes sold in packets as boudoir biscuits) briefly and rapidly into very strong black coffee. Press them round the sides and over the bottom of a large china soufflé dish, or a cake tin or Charlotte mould. Being wet, they will stick, but they must not be so soggy that they disintegrate. Pour in the chocolate mixture, cover it with an appropriate sized plate with a weight on top. Chill for 24 hours, then turn it out and garnish with whipped cream.

Iced Fruit Pies

Until about the turn of the century when everyone began to have coal-fired kitchen ranges complete with oven, pies were usually sent round to the baker. He baked them for a small fee in the bread oven. Savoury pies containing meat, game, poultry and so on were decorated with patterns of roses and rose leaves, or with acorns and oak leaves, in pastry. This looked very handsome and also made the pie easier for its owner to recognize. Sweet pies were not decorated, however, probably because until a generation or so ago they were usually iced when they came out of the oven. This is especially good if the pie is made with sour fruit and has a very sweet icing. There were several ices and glazes for pies which were all quite common in Victorian England. It is strange that they should have been forgotten. One of the most effective is made with simple Royal Icing.

Royal Icing for a Fruit Pie: Sift 4 oz of icing sugar into a little whipped egg white. Beat it till smooth, making a mixture stiff enough to stand in peaks. Cover it with a cloth until you are ready. Take the pie out of the oven 10 minutes before it is cooked. When it has cooled a little, spread the pastry thickly and roughly all over with the icing using a palette knife.

Put the pie back in a moderate oven (350°F, 180°C, Mark 4) for about 10 minutes until the icing hardens and toasts lightly on top. The underneath part is soft and rather like marshmallow.

Apple, damson, rhubarb, gooseberry and black currant pies may all be iced in this manner.

Apple Pie

Apple-and-quince pie is a traditional English dish. For this peeled, cored and sliced quinces were mixed with the apples — with good effect. 'A few slices of quince are an improvement in our judgment,' as Mrs. Beeton wrote in 1861. 'Some say 2 or 3

247

tablespoonfuls of beer, others the same quantity of sherry; whilst the old-fashioned addition of a few cloves is, by many persons, preferred to anything else.' Sugar would also be necessary.

In Lancashire a much enjoyed apple pie filling is made by peeling coring and chopping 6 apples and mixing them with sugar, spices, two beaten eggs, ¼ pint of thick cream and enough currants and stoned raisins to make a firm filling for a nice family sized pie dish. These quantities can, of course, be halved.

Yorkshire Apple and Cheese Pie
In the North of England they believe that 'an apple pie without some cheese, is like a kiss without a squeeze'. And in Lancashire and Yorkshire, Blue Wensleydale, Red Cheshire and Lancashire cheeses have been eaten with apple pie for generations, sometimes with cream as well but often without. In the West Riding the cheese is sometimes put under the pie crust.

Fill a pie dish with about 1½ lb of sliced apples. Put 2 tablespoons of sugar in the middle, add 2 tablespoons of water. Lay three or four slices of farmhouse cheese on top, then cover the pie with short crust pastry made with 8 oz of flour. Bake it in a hot oven (375°F, 190°C, Mark 5) for about 45 minutes.

Apple Pie with Marmalade
Peel, core and slice 1½ lb of apples dropping them as you do so into a basin of cold water to prevent discolouration. Put them wet into a pie dish. Neither sugar nor extra liquid is necessary. Simply spread the contents of about half a jar of dark chunky marmalade over the top. Cover with short crust pastry and bake as usual.

'Apple pie is often eaten in Yorkshire with cheese. The two blend happily. Another associate of cheese is the thin flat oatcake, sold in large flat sheets about the size of a pancake, and just as soft. My grandmother used to hang them over a string in front of the fire to dry, but I preferred them soft, covered with butter and treacle, and rolled up like a truncheon. A famous regiment is called after these oatcakes, the Roll-up Havercake Lads.'   From Donald Boyd's *On Foot in Yorkshire*, 1932.

Damson or Plum Pie

A damson pie is especially good when sweetened with honey instead of sugar. The fruit could if liked be mixed with a few peeled cored and sliced apples to take off a little of the tartness. The big Magnum Bonum plums or Warwickshire Droopers and Yellow Pershores all make excellent pies too and should be well sweetened.

The greengage with its delicious and subtle flavour makes a very good pie but is now scarce. Many of those on sale are greengage-plums, hybrids without the true flavour. The fruit is called after the 18th century Sir William Gage who brought it home from France, (where it is known as the *Reine Claude*) and cultivated it on his estate at Firle Place, Firle, near Lewes, Sussex. He had it specially from a Carthusian Monastery in Paris.

The pie is delicious when iced after it is taken from the oven.

Gooseberry and Elderflower Pie

Elderflowers are those sprays of creamy white, heavily scented blossom flowering almost everywhere in English hedgerows when gooseberries are in season. They have an unattractive musty smell when raw, but cooked with the gooseberries they give the pie a warm hothouse smell of crushed geraniums. They are excellent too in gooseberry jam.

Hairy gooseberries make the best pie, remove the stalks and snouts and put them in a pie dish with 4—5 oz of brown sugar per 1 lb of gooseberries. Add a little water and put a few sprigs of elderflowers with the gooseberries. Cover the dish with short crust pastry, sprinkle the top with sugar (or leave it plain and ice the pie as it comes out of the oven, see page 247). Bake it in a hot oven (400°F, 200°C, Mark 6) for about 30 minutes.

If the pie is to be eaten cold open the oven door, turn off the heat, and let the pie and oven cool together. Some gooseberries then turn bright red.

Fresh raw gooseberries freeze very well, but they should have their stalks and snouts removed before they are put in the freezer, as it will be impossible to do this later unless one uses Mrs. McNair's method (page 270). When elderflowers are unavailable the gooseberry pie may be cooked with beer. Add a little light ale or draught bitter to the fruit and sugar in the pie dish instead of water, and proceed as usual. The flavour of the beer mingling with that of the gooseberries is quite delicious.

Rhubarb and Beer Pie

Rhubarb was brought here in the 16th century, probably by Andrew Boorde, and was first used as a decorative plant to grow at the edge of ponds, perhaps rather like *Gunnera monstrosa*. It is known as "spring fruit" in Gloucestershire.

Much of the pale forced rhubarb on sale in spring is grown in glasshouses in South Yorkshire. Rhubarb leaves contain oxalic acid and are poisonous, but not of course the stalks though even these are very indigestible for people with ulcers etc.

The beer takes the acidity from the rhubarb, though of course the pie still needs sweetening. The flavour is most delicate. If liked the rhubarb may be mixed with peeled chopped apple.

Slice about 1½ lb of rhubarb into a pie dish with 4 oz of Demerara sugar. Add a small teacupful of light ale or draught bitter instead of water. Top the pie with short crust pastry which sprinkle lightly with sugar. Bake in a moderate oven (350°F, 180°C, Mark 4) for about 30 minutes.

Dorset Apple Cake

This is eaten hot with cream in the West Country, and is really a country pudding, though (in Somerset) it is also popular for High Tea. It is not unlike the now more famous *clafoutis* which used to be served in French farmhouses at harvest suppers.

Put 8 oz of self-raising flour into a mixing bowl with 4 oz of sugar, then 4 oz of chopped-up butter, which is not to be creamed or rubbed in, just chopped in lumps. Peel and slice three or four cooking apples into the mixture and stir in a beaten egg, then if necessary a very little milk to make a stiff batter. It must not be too wet.

This may look very lumpy but do not worry. Put it in a greased or buttered baking tin or cake tin, sprinkle a little sugar on it and bake it in a moderate oven (350°F, 180°C, Mark 4) for an hour. To be eaten hot from the oven.

Brown Bread Pudding *(To be eaten hot with whipped cream)*
This superb pudding is filled with Black Bucks cherries, or, if unavailable, with Morello cherries and is from a recipe of Charles Elmé Francatelli, Chief-Cook-in-Ordinary to Queen Victoria and the inventor of Brown Windsor Soup, which in its original version is in fact excellent.

Mix 3 oz of fresh brown crumbs from a coarse grained wheaten or granary loaf (the fine textured proprietary breads are unsuitable) with $1\frac{1}{2}$ oz of caster sugar, a very large pinch of ground cinnamon and the grated rind of half a lemon. Add two egg yolks and about 3 tablespoons of whipped cream. Mix well. Butter a large pudding basin (or pie dish or large soufflé dish) thickly and, as Francatelli says 'strew some brown breadcrumbs therein' tilting and turning it so the buttered surface is coated with crumbs. Whip the whites of two eggs so stiffly the basin may be turned upside down without them falling out. Fold these into the mixture and spoon it into the buttered basin in layers with 4 oz of Oven-Baked Cherries. Do not fill the basin more than three quarters to allow room for the pudding to rise. Cover the top with foil, bake in a moderate oven (350°F, 180°C, Mark 4) for about 40 minutes.

Turn It out to serve, shake some cinnamon sugar over it and garnish the pudding with whipped cream.

Oven-Baked Cherries: Put 4 tablespoons of brown sugar, the juice of a lemon and 1 lb of dark red cherries in a fireproof dish, cover with foil and let them simmer in a moderate oven (350°F, 180°C, Mark 4) until the juice runs out. This will be a deep vermilion colour. No water is added. The cherries are excellent hot or cold and delicious with Welsh Rice Pudding (see page 235).

A Canary's Pudding
A Canary's Pudding is one of those light and fluffy affairs, yellow as a goose egg or a young duckling; once popular in English nurseries, it rises a great deal in cooking, is best cooked rather gently and is excellent with warm home made Lemon Curd (see page 272) or hot Sherry Sauce (page 252) poured over it.

There are several variations in flavour and in the sauces

served with it. The pudding can be steamed in a pan, or steamed in a casserole in the oven, or it can be baked in the oven, at will.

First butter a 1½ pint pudding basin. Then put 3 oz of sultanas or some marrow and ginger jam, or some sliced stem ginger in the bottom.

Then cream 4 oz of butter and 4 oz of sugar until pale straw coloured and fluffy, add the juice and grated rind of a lemon. Then having sifted 3 oz of plain flour with 1 oz of cornflour and 1 level teaspoon of baking powder, fold this into the butter/sugar mixture alternately with two beaten eggs. The best way is to fold in a tablespoon of the flour mixture with each beaten egg. one at a time then fold in the rest adding about 2 tablespoons of milk to make a smooth mixture which just drops from the spoon. Tip it into the buttered and garnished pudding basin. Tie a piece of foil, pleated in the middle to let the pudding rise, over the basin, tying it on firmly so no steam can get under the paper and wet the pudding.

Now, *either* stand the basin on an upturned saucer in a large saucepan with boiling water to come half way up. Let the water bubble away gently, with a lid on the pan, for 1½–2 hours until the pudding is cooked. When adding more water to the pan be sure it is boiling water otherwise the pudding will be soggy.

Or, *alternatively*, the pudding may be steamed in the oven by standing the basin in a casserole containing enough boiling water to come half way up it, as before. Cook it in a moderate oven (350°F, 180°C, Mark 4) for 1½–2 hours, with a lid on the casserole. Fill up with boiling water as before. The result will be a *steamed* not a baked pudding.

Turn the Steamed Canary's Pudding out carefully and send it piping hot to table with the **Sherry Sauce**. This is made simply by heating and stirring 2 tablespoons of honey in a saucepan with some cooking sherry so as to make a smooth hot mixture.

Canary's Pudding Variations

The buttered 1½ pint pudding basin may be lined with golden syrup before the pudding mixture is poured in. Alternatively 3 oz of sultanas may be stirred into the pudding mixture, together with some stoned raisins and currants, instead of being used to line the basin. Sometimes chopped candied peel or chopped dried dates are stirred into the pudding.

It may also be *baked*. Use the same Canary's Pudding mixture as before but tip it into a well buttered pie dish. Bake it near the top of a moderate oven (350°F, 180°C, Mark 4) for 30–40 minutes. It should be well risen, golden on top but will be different from a steamed Canary's Pudding.

Banana Sauce is pleasant with it. Beat together 3 oz of sugar, the grated rind and strained juice of a lemon and one egg. Add 1 tablespoon of butter, and stir the mixture over a low heat until slightly thickened. Then fold in 1 tablespoon of strained fresh orange juice and two mashed bananas.

Individual Castle Puddings with Raspberry Sauce *(An old nursery favourite)*
These are made with the same mixture as the Canary's Pudding. Half fill buttered dariole moulds or little individual buttered pudding tins with this mixture. Bake them for 15–20 minutes in a moderate oven (350°F, 180°C, Mark 4). Turn them out and serve with **Raspberry Sauce**: Mix 2 tablespoons of raspberry jam in a pan with 1 oz of sugar, ¼ pint of water, heat slowly, stirring. Mix 1 dessertspoon of cornflour with a little cold water. Strain the contents of the pan into it, pour it back into the warm pan. Bring it to the boil gently, stirring, and boil it for about 3 minutes, stirring until it thickens.

These were called Kassel Puddings a hundred years ago, after the German town; many Victorian puddings had German names probably due to the influence of the Prince Consort.

Christmas or Plum Pudding
English Christmas puddings are now almost as fashionable in Paris and Vienna as they are in Britain, one of our exports. A few Austrian families make their own — amazed at the use of suet with sugar — but many buy them ready made in pudding basins from Demels' famous pastry shop in Vienna.

Plum puddings take a long time to prepare and cook, but they mature like wine, are easy to do, and always improve with keeping. Some families or groups of friends therefore make a batch of puddings every other November and have some that Christmas and keep the rest for the following year. It can be great fun, especially if there are enough basins and boiling facilities are available. In the old days puddings were mostly boiled in the kitchen copper where the laundry used to be done. A solid fuel cooker is helpful.

This recipe is for a rich dark pudding laced with rum and sherry, it should fill about five pudding basins of the $1\frac{1}{2}$–2 pint capacity which is a good size for modern families as it yields eight and more ample portions. The puddings are best made around November 21st, or Stir Up Sunday, when the Collect in church begins with the words: 'Stir up we beseech Thee, O Lord . . .' Puddings need a lot of stirring and all available should be invited into the kitchen to stir the pudding – for luck and to wish as they do so.

You need 4 oz flour, $1\frac{1}{2}$ lb stoned raisins, 1 lb sultanas, 8 oz glacé fruits, 8 oz cooking apples, 1 lb dark brown moist Barbados sugar, $\frac{1}{2}$ teaspoon ground mace, $\frac{1}{2}$ teaspoon ground cinnamon, $\frac{1}{2}$ teaspoon ground ginger, $\frac{1}{2}$ teaspoon salt, $\frac{1}{2}$ nutmeg grated, 2 tablespoons black treacle, 2 glasses of Jamaica rum (about $\frac{1}{4}$ pint), 4 oz currants, 12 oz breadcrumbs (or sponge cake crumbs, if liked, this makes an even richer pudding), 8 oz mixed candied peel (which should be soft and moist looking), 8 oz shredded beef suet, 4 oz ground almonds, 1 carrot, 8 eggs, the juice of a lemon, sherry to mix.

Clean the dried fruit by tipping it into a bowl and sprinkling it well with flour, then rub it through the fingers as if making pastry, tip it on to a sieve and shake vigorously. Not all fruit needs cleaning nowadays, though it is usual to do so.

Wash and scrape and grate the carrot, peel and core the apples and put them through a mincer with the candied peel, raisins, and glacé fruits. Sift the flour, salt, mace, cinnamon, ginger and nutmeg into a bowl and stir in the breadcrumbs, the prepared fruit, the ground almonds, shredded suet, sugar, grated carrot and then the beaten eggs. Mix them in well with your hand. Now stir in the black treacle, rum, lemon juice and a glass of sherry with a wooden spoon. The mixture should drop fairly easily from the spoon but not be too runny. Add the sherry little by little to get the right texture. Cover the bowl with a clean tea cloth and let it stand for 24 hours.

Meanwhile prepare the pudding basins. Butter them well, cut small rounds of greaseproof paper to fit the bottom of the pudding basins, butter these, put them in place. Cut double rounds of foil or greaseproof paper a little bigger than the tops of the pudding basins and large enough to be folded in a pleat. Butter them well on both sides. Over these some people put pudding cloths which should be scalded, wrung out well and sprinkled inside with flour.

Now stir the pudding mixture, thoroughly and well. Get helpers to do some stirring. Pack it into the prepared basins filling them to within an inch of the top, smooth over the tops, making a very slight hollow in the middle. Cover them with the two thicknesses of buttered foil or greaseproof paper pleated in the middle to allow room for the pudding to rise, and tied down firmly with string. Then if liked cover the top of each with a pudding cloth. Tie it on and knot the ends over to make a handle (by which the cooked puddings can be fished out of the pan with the end of a wooden spoon handle).

Put the puddings on a rack in a large pan, or fish kettle, with boiling water to come half way up the basins. Put a lid on top and when topping up as the water boils away be sure to add boiling water. Boil the 2 pint puddings for 8 hours and for 2–3 hours more on Christmas day.

When cooked let them cool, then cover them with fresh clean foil tied on firmly and with pudding cloths if used. When quite cold put them in a dark airy cupboard until wanted.

On Christmas day the pudding — stuck with holly and flaming with lighted brandy or rum — is served with Hard Sauce or Ullswater Rum Butter, or Brandy Butter and perhaps thick cream as well. Do not forget the lucky sixpence or silver pudding charms, these should be embedded in the hot pudding before serving. Then the pudding must come in lapped in flames, warm the rum or brandy before you try to set light to it. It is convenient to warm it in a metal soup ladle over the kitchen stove.

To make a dramatic entrance to the dining room with your

flaming pudding held high a little cunning is helpful. Scoop a small hole out of the top of the hot pudding. In this put half an empty upturned eggshell. Fill the shell with the warm spirits, set light to them. Move the dish about to spill the flaming spirits as you enter the dining room (by candlelight, hopefully) . . . to all the compliments of the season.

Cold Christmas Pudding is usually sliced and fried in butter and served with soft white sugar and brandy sauce. In Yorkshire a slice of Blue Wensleydale is often laid on a slice of cold Christmas pudding and the two are eaten together, usually with a glass of port.

Guards' Pudding

Butter a 2 pint pudding basin thickly. Or use a buttered pudding mould if available.

Mix 5 oz of soft white breadcrumbs with 3 oz of caster sugar, 5 tablespoons of raspberry jam, 3 oz of melted butter. Add a saltspoon of baking powder melted in a few drops of water. Stir in three well beaten eggs. Pour it into the basin, cover the top with two layers of kitchen foil pleated in the middle to allow the pudding to rise and tied on firmly. Place it in a pan of boiling water to come half way up. Boil for 2 hours, filling up when necessary with boiling water.

Turn it out to serve with Raspberry Sauce, Ullswater Rum Butter, cream or a Banana Sauce (see pages 261 and 253).

Steamed Apple Pudding

This splendid pudding was one of the mainstays of English sporting squires throughout the 18th and 19th centuries and is still sometimes served hot at shooting lunches and sheep dog trials. It should be eaten with a jug of warm cream and a piece of crumbly Cheshire cheese, preferably Blue Cheshire, to go with it. Either or both.

Butter a 2 pint pudding basin (or old fashioned pudding mould) thickly all over the inside. Line it with suet pastry. Fill it with about 1½ lb of peeled, cored and quartered apples. As you peel them drop the apples into a basin of cold water to stop them going brown. Then put them damp into the pudding basin. No water is added, simply the grated rind and juice of a lemon, or one or two tablespoons of bitter orange marmalade. The old cooks never added sugar to an apple pudding, it stops the apples going fluffy when cooked. They just heaped the sugar over the pudding at table, together with a slice of unsalted butter and a little grated nutmeg. Demerara sugar, or the very dark "pieces" sugar are excellent with it.

Make a "lid" of the remaining suet pastry, pinching the edges together to seal it. Cover the basin with two layers of foil, tied on and pleated in the middle to leave room for the pudding to rise. Put it in a pan with boiling water to come half way up, standing the basin on an upturned saucer so that it will not crack. Boil for about 2 hours making sure the water boils all the time. Fill up the pan when necessary with *boiling* water.

Turn out the pudding onto a hot dish, very gently as it might burst. Cut a small hole in the top to let the steam out. Garnish with the butter, nutmeg and sugar as above.

Steamed Fruit Pudding
The wall fruit from cottage gardens, ripe greengages or apricots or plums as well as damsons, makes excellent steamed puddings, sweet and hot and smelling of country gardens. Stoned fruit used to be halved; the stones were then cracked and the kernels were added to the pudding to give a faint almond flavour. Black currants, or gooseberries with brown sugar, or raspberries, red currants and icing sugar, may all be used for steamed puddings. Damsons are best left whole, they will need a great deal of sweetening and the pudding, when done, had better be turned out and topped with a layer of brown sugar.

The young Yorkshire rhubarb, once known as "spring fruit" makes a delicious pudding. A little chopped candied angelica is sometimes added to it.

Line a thickly buttered pudding basin with suet pastry. Put the fruit in the middle just with honey, sugar or golden syrup — no liquid. Juicy plums are best cut in half. Top the pudding with a "lid" of suet pastry, moisten the edges and pinch them together. Tie two layers of foil over the top, pleated in the middle to allow

room for the pudding to rise. Proceed as for Steamed Apple
Pudding (see page 256).

Spotted Dick or Plum Bolster

A man's dish, this was a great favourite of the late Duke of Marlborough for shooting lunches. "Suety Jack", popular in the
Potteries, is a plain roly-poly pudding.

Mix 3 oz of plain flour with 3 oz of soft white breadcrumbs
and 3 oz of shredded or grated beef suet, adding enough cold
water to make it into a firm paste or dough which leaves the
basin quite clean. Not much water is required, add it gradually.
Roll the suet pastry out at once about $\frac{1}{2}$ inch thick, on a lightly
floured surface. Sprinkle it thickly with stoned raisins, sultanas
and currants before rolling it up in a Swiss roll or sausage shape.
Wrap it completely and closely in foil which must overlap so the
water cannot get into the pudding. Tie it in a cloth. Lower it into
a pan of boiling water, let it boil continuously for $1\frac{1}{2}$–2 hours.
As the water evaporates fill up with boiling water, otherwise the
pudding may be soggy. Turn it out onto a hot dish.

Serve it with butter and brown sugar. Or with rum butter. Or
with black treacle sauce. Or golden syrup. These are easily made
by warming 9 tablespoons of black treacle (or of golden syrup)
with 6 tablespoons of water. Heat, stirring and letting it simmer
for a few minutes, then add the strained juice of half a lemon.

A Christmas Trifle

The secret of a good trifle is to pour the custard, while hot, over
the sponge cakes and leave it till next day before finishing it.

Slice half a dozen sponge cakes and sandwich them with raspberry jam. Lay them in a suitable dish for your trifle, in two
layers if need be. Pour some cooking sherry over, but not
enough to make them soggy.

Now, in a double saucepan, make an egg custard by mixing
6 egg yolks with 2 tablespoons of granulated sugar. Add $1\frac{1}{2}$ pints
of warm milk and a vanilla pod, gradually mixing and heating,
and stirring all the time in the top of a double saucepan with hot,
but not quite boiling, water in the pan below. Continue heating
gently and stirring all the time until the custard is thick enough

4. *Jelly of two Colours.*   1. *Chantilly Basket.*   6. *Open Jelly with*

5. *Oranges & Jelly.*   2. *Trifle*   *whipped Cream*

                                3. *Ices*   7. *Blanc Mange*

Standidge & Cᵒ London.

259

to coat the back of the spoon. The custard must not boil as it would then become lumpy and "curdled". If it begins to do so it may sometimes be restored by *immediately* stirring in 2 table-spoons of cold milk. Remove the vanilla pod and strain it over the sponge cakes, leave it for 24 hours.

Then decorate it with whipped sweetened cream and garnish it with peeled almonds and ratafia biscuits.

Trifle decorations have recently become so boring it is as well to keep them as restrained as possible. Some cooks flavour the sponge cakes with Irish whiskey as well as the sherry.

Mince Pies

For winter parties, very small very hot mince pies, to be eaten in the fingers, are sometimes piled high on a silver tray and handed round with the mulled wine or hot punch. They should be no bigger than the top of an egg cup and made with short crust pastry. Larger ones will need a plate and a fork and are best kept warm on the electric hot plate, for example, in silver entrée dishes. They should be sprinkled with caster sugar, and cream or rum butter are often handed separately.

When mince pies are served at table, hot from the oven, it is pleasant to lift the lids and put a spoonful of thick cream under each.

The **Royal Mince Pies** recipe is about a hundred and fifty years old, something which may well have been munched by the Prince Regent when he went down to Brighton with Mrs. Fitzherbert.

Line about 12 patty tins with 1 lb thinly rolled short crust pastry. Fill them three quarters full with a mixture of 1 oz of melted butter, $1\frac{1}{2}$ oz of sugar, 4 egg yolks, the grated rind and juice of a lemon and 7 oz of mincemeat. Put no pastry lids on them. Bake the pies in a moderate oven (350°F, 180°C, Mark 4) for about 30 minutes. Beat 4 egg whites so stiff they stand in peaks and fold or stir 4 good tablespoons of caster sugar gently into them. Take your pies from the oven, reduce the heat. Top each with a spoonful of the meringue mixture. Bake them in a slow oven (300°F, 150°C, Mark 2) until they are faintly coloured.

The Duke of Bedford's Christmas Omelette

Alfred Suzanne, who was chef at Woburn Abbey to a 19th century Duke of Bedford used to make delicious flaming mincemeat omelettes. The mincemeat at Woburn was made in large quantities in stoneware crocks, tightly sealed and stored in the cellars for a month before Christmas but, except that it contained a quantity of rum, Cognac and Madeira and 1 lb of chopped roast beef, was not unlike that which is made today.

'Make an omelette with 6 eggs, 1 tablespoon rum, 1 tablespoon cream, a little grated lemon peel and fill this omelette with the mincemeat. After turning it onto the platter, powder it with sugar and baste it with the hot rum. Set the rum aflame when sending the omelette to the table.' From *La Cuisine et la Pâtisserie Anglaise et Américaine* by Alfred Suzanne.

Ullswater Rum Butter and Brandy Butter

These are very good with most steamed puddings, not simply a Christmas pudding. Brandy butter makes a good filling for a Victoria sponge sandwich cake and, when orange flavoured, for pancakes, which can be flamed with brandy if liked. It is also a good stuffing for baked apples. Cold Christmas pudding is delicious when eaten with rum butter. A glass of brown sherry or a glass of very old Madeira, such as Bual Solera 1878, would be excellent with it.

Dutch Advocaat served cold and plain, just as it is, makes a good sauce for Christmas pudding and other hot steamed puddings.

Ullswater Rum Butter: Mix 8 oz of melted butter, 12 oz of soft dark brown "pieces" sugar, a wine glass of rum with $1\frac{1}{2}$ teaspoons of allspice, $1\frac{1}{2}$ teaspoons of grated nutmeg. Mix it very thoroughly, stirring until it stiffens. It is served very cold sprinkled with sugar.

Brandy Butter or Senior Wrangler Sauce: Cream 4 oz of unsalted butter gradually beating in 3–4 oz of icing sugar. Then, drop by drop add 3 tablespoons of brandy beating until the mixture is light and fluffy. Nowadays most people prefer brandy butter when it is made rather soft, so one should add a few drops of hot water to get it to the right modern consistency, rather than in the form of a Victorian "Hard Sauce". A good teaspoon of grated orange rind is an enormous improvement.

Brandy Butter is also known as Senior Wrangler Sauce, or Hard Sauce.

Ratafias

A ratafia was a liqueur or cordial and thence the name came to mean the little almond biscuits eaten with it. These round biscuits, about the size of a large button, are made from sugar, egg white and ground almonds, as are macaroons. They were once fashionable for decorating cakes or puddings and are also used in a Victorian trifle and as an ingredient in some other recipes. Though preferable to the ubiquitous glacé cherry, they are seldom used to-day. Mrs. Beeton in the original 1861 edition of *Household Management* does give a recipe for them but says it is more practical to buy them. They are still made, and sold in 4 oz boxes by Atkinsons of Windermere.

Earlier the word "ratafia" was used for all kinds of household cordials or liqueurs made by steeping fruit in brandy or other spirits, as is still done in making sloe gin and farmhouse cherry brandy. They were made by steeping the fruit, or spices and herbs, the carnations, or violets, or angelica, or crushed cherry or apricot stones in alcohol or spirits, preferably about 70° proof, as opposed to distilling the herbs and fruits as is done in making Bénédictine for instance.

The word came into use because in the 17th century business contracts were signed under the words *ut rata fiat*, meaning 'when the bargain is made', and a little glass of spirits was drunk to seal the bargain. In France, in the Champagne district, this drink itself became known as a *ratafiat*, and later a *ratafia*. The house of Veuve Clicquot still sells these things.

They went out of fashion in Britain in the late 19th century and the high duty on spirits has undoubtedly contributed to their decline. 'Ratafias or household liqueurs, which were very popular, are no longer fashionable nowadays,' as Escoffier wrote in *Ma Cuisine*, 'which is very regrettable.' They can be made with all sorts of fruit.

'Put the chosen fruit into a wide-mouthed jar and cover it with colourless brandy. Cover the jar tightly and expose it to the sun for 40 days. Decant and add ½ pint of syrup boiled to 219° to each 1¾ pints of fruit juice. Filter and put it into stoppered jars.'

Maidenhair Fern

This was used in the 19th and early 20th centuries to decorate ice creams, jellies and blancmanges. For dinner parties it was also laid on the damask cloth together with the brilliantly coloured satin ribbon table runners and the heavy silver candlesticks.

It grows wild in damp shady places near springs and wells in some parts of Europe but is usually thought of as a greenhouse plant.

It can also be boiled to make a sticky liquid or jelly which, mixed with sugar and water, forms a syrup called capillaire. Dr. Johnson is said to have drunk capillaire in his port, and in the early part of the 19th century it was also an ingredient of Oxford Punch. The drink is still to be found in old fashioned bars in Switzerland and the French provinces and was one of the drinks which were given to young girls as a cure for stomach ache.

Vanilla Sugar

This is invaluable for flavouring rich cakes and puddings, it has a better, more subtle flavour than the bottled essences and is also cheaper. Simply insert one or two vanilla pods into a jar of caster sugar, and store closely covered. Use the delicately flavoured sugar as required. Keep filling up the jar with more sugar until the vanilla pods finally lose their smell.

Cinnamon sugar can be prepared in the same way by storing cinnamon sticks in a jar of sugar.

Finger Bowls

Mrs. Beeton's *Book of Household Management*, edited by Mrs. Isabella Beeton, published by S. O. Beeton, 18 Bouverie Street, E.C. 1861 edition.

Item 37 'When dinner is finished, the dessert is placed on the table accompanied with finger glasses. It is the custom of some gentlemen to wet a corner of the napkin; but the hostess, whose behaviour will set the tone to all the ladies present, will merely wet the tips of her fingers, which will serve all the purposes required. The French and other continentals have the habit of gargling the mouth; but it is a custom which no English gentlewoman should, in the slightest degree, imitate.'

Chapter 9

The Still Room

Barley Water

Cheap and refreshing, this old country drink used to be served at hay-making and in the garden in summer in old fashioned bedroom water jugs.

Rinse 2 oz of pearl barley in a strainer. Tip it into 1 pint of cold water and boil it for about 15 minutes, strain it once more throwing the water away.

Meanwhile peel two lemons thinly and squeeze out the juice. Put the peel in a pan with 1 oz of sugar and 1 pint of cold water. Simmer until it is well flavoured of lemon, add the lemon juice. Boil up 2 quarts of water, add the pearl barley and boil until the liquid is reduced by half. You will now have one quart of barley water, which strain and add to the lemon-flavoured liquid and chill.

Resist the temptation to make it with oranges when lemons are not to hand. The barley water does not taste so fresh and is the most peculiar colour.

Lady Clark's Barley Water

"A pleasant and safe beverage"

'Wash a tablespoon of pearl barley well in spring water. Pour over it a quart of boiling water, the juice of a lemon, and half the rind peeled very thin. When cold pour the barley water off the dregs, strain it, and add 2 wineglassfuls of sherry or Madeira; sweeten with sugar to your taste.' From *The Cookery Book of Lady Clark of Tillypronie*.

265

Bilberry Jelly

A purple jelly which is sometimes served in Derbyshire with roast grouse, lamb and mutton. Though the bilberries grow wild, nowadays they are mostly imported from Poland.

Put the bilberries in a pan with water to cover, simmering till soft. Strain the juice through a cloth without pressing the fruit as this makes the jelly cloudy. Add 1 lb of sugar per 1 pint of juice and a handful of chopped mint. Heat it gently, stirring, until the sugar melts then boil rapidly till setting point is reached. Strain and bottle it in warm jars and cover it when cold.

Bilberry and Rhubarb Jam

Bilberries are also called "hurts" in some parts of the country, blaeberries in Scotland and whortleberries in the Cotswolds.

Rhubarb for cooking is at its best in early spring when it has been forced. The delicate pink stalks are delicious when simmered in syrup and served cold with cream.

The later, garden rhubarb is green and red and often needs peeling. The leaves *must* be thrown away as they are poisonous. **For the jam:** 1 lb of thin red Yorkshire rhubarb cut in inch lengths. Put it in the jam pan. Add 5 lb of sugar, heat gently until the sugar melts. Boil for 10 minutes. Add 7 lb of bilberries having first picked them over to remove any bits of stalk or leaf. Simmer, skimming off the froth, until the fruit is tender and setting point is reached. Bottle in warm jars. Cover when cold.

Spiced Bramble (or Blackberry) Jelly

This is an old Lancashire recipe, and the jelly is delicious not only with venison, wild duck or a boiled leg of lamb, but also on hot buttered crumpets.

Rinse the brambles (or blackberries) and put them in a pan with water to cover. Add one small teaspoon of mixed spices per lb of blackberries, and do see that the spices are fresh. One has the habit of keeping little boxes of seasoning at the back of the kitchen cupboard and using them about once every seven or eight months, when they are so stale they are tasteless.

Bring it all gently to the boil and let it simmer till all the juice runs out. Strain the mixture overnight through a tea towel, old pillowcase, or proper jellybag. Next day add 1 lb of sugar to every 1 pint of juice. Bring it slowly to the boil, stirring until the sugar has melted. Now boil it rapidly and fiercely until setting point is reached in about 30 minutes. Bottle in warm jars and cover when cold.

Blackberry, or Damson, and Apple Cheese
This is stored in little pots. It is sliced at table and may be eaten with poultry and game, cold meat, or with creamy cheese, bread and butter. The pots should preferably be brushed with cooking oil before they are filled with the fruit "cheese" to make it easy to turn them out.

Mix 2 lb of blackberries with 1 lb of roughly chopped windfall or other apples. Simmer both together in $\frac{1}{4}$ pint of water till soft, this may conveniently be done in a slow oven (300°F, 150°C, Mark 2); when damsons are cooked in this way the stones eventually rise to the top.

Rub the cooked fruit through a sieve (pips, cores, skins and stones will be left behind in the sieve). Add 1 lb of sugar per 1 lb of pulp. Heat gently stirring until the sugar melts then bring the mixture to the boil and heat, stirring, until it goes solid. As it thickens it should be stirred frequently to prevent it sticking to the bottom of the pan. It is done when so thick that if a spoon be drawn across the bottom of the pan it will leave a clear line. Cover like jam. Keep it four months before eating to allow the flavours to mature and develop. Blackberries freeze well, plain, raw, in polythene bags without sugar. They have less flavour of course than when fresh but are very welcome as a basis for blackberry and apple pie or Summer Pudding (see page 240) in winter.

Black Currant Jam *(A simple recipe)*
There is, I think, nothing quite so evocative of country gardens, as the flavour of black currant jam with Cornish cream, eaten either by themselves or with the traditional "splits".

Pick over the fruit then put it into the jam pan with $\frac{3}{4}$ lb of sugar per 1 lb of black currants. Do not add water. Heat the mixture slowly and gently so that it does not burn. Stir it gently,

plenty of juice will run out of the black currants, go on stirring
and heating until you can see the jam pan distinctly as you stir.
The jam will then have reached setting point. Bottle in warm
jars, cover when cold.

The old fashioned brass and copper preserving pans are
excellent for jam making, but they need a lot of cleaning. Orange
juice is one old fashioned scouring material still used by some
people to bring up the surface.

Chutney
Chetney – from the Hindustani *Chatni*, a strong sweet dish; relic
of the British Raj
If stored in bottles use plastic tops. Metal covers can be used if
protected from the action of the vinegar by several thicknesses of
greaseproof paper. Ketchups – catchups – catsups (from the
Malay *Kechup* in turn from the Chinese *Koe-chiap*) are firmer in
texture than chutneys, the fruit or vegetables are put through a
sieve after cooking to make a sauce – popular with sea faring
men to relieve the monotony of pickled pork and ship's biscuits.
Stem ginger and curry paste from the Far East were already
well known in the 18th century.

Cherry Brandy *(A household recipe)*
Use ripe dark (Morello) cherries, wash and dry them, cut the
stalks to within ¼ inch of the fruit. Prick the cherries here and
there with a thin skewer or fork. Allow 6 oz of caster sugar to
2 lb of cherries. Put alternate layers of sugar and cherries in a
wide mouthed bottle. Add 1 pint or more of brandy so that the
cherries are properly covered. Cork the bottle tightly. Store it in
a cool dark place for 2 to 3 months shaking it at intervals.
When ready, strain off the liqueur and re-bottle.

The brandied cherries will of course be delicious to eat, for
instance, with a Welsh Rice Pudding (page 235), or as a garnish
for ice cream, or with junket or Highland crowdie.

Eliza Acton's Damson Jam *(very good)*
'The fruit for this jam should be freshly gathered and quite ripe.

269

Split, stone, weigh and boil it quickly for forty minutes; then stir in half its weight of good sugar . . . , and when it is dissolved, give the preserve fifteen minutes additional boiling, keeping it stirred, and thoroughly skimmed.

Damsons, stoned, 6 lb: 40 minutes. Sugar, 3 lb: 15 minutes. *Obs.* – A more refined preserve is made by pressing the fruit through a sieve after it is boiled tender; but the jam is excellent without.' From *Modern Cookery for Private Families*, 1845.

White Currant Jam *(A beautiful preserve)*

'Boil together quickly for seven minutes an equal weight of fine white currants, stalked with the greatest nicety, and of the best sugar . . Stir the preserve gently the whole time, and be careful to skim it thoroughly. White currants, 4 lb; best sugar, 4 lb; 7 minutes.' *Ibid.*

Note: The omissions in Miss Acton's recipes for preserves above thus . . . refer to her instructions for pounding and preparing the old sugar loaves which have not been sold in this country for a couple of generations at least though Messrs. Tate & Lyle do still make a few for export to Ethiopia. They are not obtainable here.

Elderflower Bubbly

A midsummer drink, cool and refreshing and very slightly sparkling. It is perfect for hot summer days, cheap and simple to make. It is also very good chilled and laced with a little gin.

Put 2 tablespoons of white wine vinegar or white distilled vinegar in a large basin with a gallon of cold water, $1\frac{1}{2}$ lb of sugar and 4 heads of elderflowers. Add two squeezed and quartered lemons. Let it stand for 24 hours stirring occasionally. Then strain and bottle it in screw topped bottles. It will be ready to drink in a couple of weeks' time.

It keeps for about three months, though some people manage to keep it successfully for about a year.

Frozen Gooseberries

Gooseberries freeze very well. If you follow the method closely explained to me by a correspondent who lives on a fruit farm in Swanley, Kent, there is no need to top and tail them first.

Freeze the fruit dry (no sugar) in plastic bags that are about twice as big as necessary. When required for use re-tie the bag at the end being sure to keep out all the air. Then roll the gooseberries across the draining board for a few minutes. Shake the bag and all the tops and tails will be in the bottom of the bag. This must be done when the fruit is still frozen hard. It works just as well with red or black currants.

Mrs. McNair says she has done this very successfully for years but, like myself, she has never seen it mentioned in print anywhere.

Gooseberry Chutney
Top and tail 2 quarts of green gooseberries, chop up 1 lb of stoned raisins, peel and slice 1½ lb of onions and put them all in a large jar with 1½ oz of ground ginger, 8 oz of brown sugar, a bare teaspoon of Cayenne pepper, 1 dessertspoon of salt and one quart of vinegar. Put the jar in a very slow oven (250°F, 130°C, Mark ½). Leave for 4 hours, stirring occasionally. Store the chutney somewhere cool and dry.

Gooseberry and Elderflower Jelly
This has a delicate flavour of muscats and is particularly delicious with roast mutton.
Just cover the washed gooseberries with water − no need to top and tail them − simmer gently for 2 hours and strain off the juice through a cloth. Let it drip overnight if you like but do not try to push the pulp through, it makes the jelly cloudy. Then to each pint of juice add 1 lb of sugar, heating and stirring gently. When it has melted add the heads of 12 elderflowers tied in a bunch in a muslin bag. Bring it to the boil and boil for 10 minutes until setting point is reached. Skim, pour it into warmed jars and cover while it is still hot.

Elderflowers are those flat white heavily scented clusters of flowers which cover the hedgerows when gooseberries are in season.

The gooseberry is a native plant. There are many different kinds from hairy cooking gooseberries to red, white or green dessert gooseberries. Aluminium pans should not be used, they change the colour of the fruit. Because the bush is so prickly in some parts of Britain the birds do not touch the fruit and it needs no netting.

Greengage Jam
Cut the greengages in half, take out the stones. Put them in a bowl in layers with 12 oz of sugar per lb of fruit weighed after stoning. Leave them for 12 hours with a cloth over the bowl. The fruit will be found to be swimming in a fragrant syrup. Tip it into a pan, heat, stirring, to dissolve any unmelted sugar at the bottom of the basin, bring it to the boil, stirring, and when the sugar has melted boil rapidly until setting point is reached, skimming off the froth meanwhile. They need short fierce cooking to preserve their delicate green colour. Bottle in warm jars. Add some blanched split almonds instead of the greengage kernels.

Plums and apricots can be prepared in the same way but the apricots should be soaked in sugar for longer than the greengages – about 24 hours.

Horseradish and Beet Relish (*Monmouthshire*)
A Welsh store sauce of a beautiful red colour
Wash, scrape and grate two sticks of horseradish, straight across the sticks so it does not become stringy. Peel three large cooked beetroots, grate and mix them with the horseradish. Add caster sugar to your taste. Then pour on as much good cold malt vinegar as the mixture will take. This is important, for if there is not enough vinegar the relish loses its beautiful red colour. Place in jars and seal.

Lemon Curd
This delicate English speciality is perhaps at its most irresistible when freshly made, to eat with rough brown bread and pale unsalted butter. The home made kind tastes creamier and more strongly of lemon than that from the factories.

Beat up 6 eggs and gradually whip in 12 oz of caster sugar. Use the mixer if possible to whip it. Gradually whip in the grated rind of three large lemons and then, little by little, their strained juice. When perfectly blended whip in 6 oz of just liquid butter. Go on whipping the mixture. Then let it thicken, stirring all the time, in a pan over a low heat like a conventional custard. It must not boil or it will be ruined, some cooks find it safer to use a double saucepan.

Bottle the lemon curd in warm jars and cover it when cold.

Marmalade
There must be scores of old family recipes for making marmalade, each slightly different, some dark and thick and chunky, others as clear as a stained glass window.

Marmalade has been made in Scotland with bitter oranges since the early part of the 18th century, that of Dundee is especially famous, but there are others. Nowadays Britain takes 98% of the whole Spanish bitter orange crop for marmalade, which is mostly made in factories, and there is a Scottish steamship line which exists especially to ship fruit from Seville.

A Seville orange has a rougher skin than other bitter oranges and is always a reddish colour. The Moors planted them round Seville for the exquisite scent of the blossom, which is stronger and sweeter than that of the sweet China, or Valencia, orange. They were used in perfumery and for years most of the fruit was thrown away. Some of it is still used for pickling the enormous black olives which are sold in Seville.

Bitter oranges may be sliced and put into a plastic bag and frozen successfully, for use later in marmalade or in orange sauce for roast lamb and roast duck.

A Simple Orange Marmalade
Wash 2 lb of bitter oranges and two lemons, cut them all in half and take out the pips. Pass the fruit through the mincer's coarse plates before putting it in a basin and covering it with 6 pints of cold water. Leave it for at least 24 hours. Meanwhile soak the pips in 1 pint of cold water. Next day boil the fruit for 1 hour with the pips tied in a muslin bag or clean handkerchief together with the covering water. Then add 8 lb of sugar, and boil the marmalade for another 45 minutes or until setting point is reached. Bottle it in warm jars. Cover it at once.

273

Note: When making marmalade, by whatever recipe, let the marmalade cool in the pan when setting point is reached until a "skin" forms over it, then stir it and pour it into warm jars.

Dark Chunky Marmalade
Wash two lemons and $1\frac{1}{2}$ lb of Seville oranges. Then let them simmer gently for 2 hours in water just to cover. When soft take out the fruit, let it cool and chop it in coarse chunks, returning any juice to the pan – together with the pips. Boil these for about 15 minutes. Strain the liquor into a jam pan, add 1 tablespoon of black treacle and 3 lb of sugar, stir this until it melts. Add the chopped fruit and boil fast until setting point is reached. Bottle in warm jars, cover when cold.

Mrs. Trott's Apricot and Orange Marmalade
Dark plump dried apricots have been used for generations for jam making. They go very well with Seville oranges.

Wash 1 lb of dried apricots, chop them in pieces and cover them with 2 pints of cold water. Wipe four Seville oranges and one grapefruit. Cut them in coarse slices removing all the pips and put these in a basin. Add the sliced oranges and grapefruit to the apricots with another $2\frac{1}{2}$ pints of water. Pour a little water over the pips in the basin. Leave everything overnight. Next day strain the water from the pips into the mixture. Boil the fruit gently for 30 minutes. Add 2 lb of sugar and boil gently for another 30 minutes or until setting point is reached. Bottle in warm jars and cover when cold.

Marrow and Ginger Jam
Peel your marrows, take out the seeds and cut about 5 lb of the rest in 1 inch chunks. Allow 1 lb of marrow per 1 lb of sugar, put both in the jam pan in layers and leave it covered with a tea towel for 24 hours. Then add 6 oz of crystallized ginger and the grated rind and the juice of three lemons. Simmer for 3–5 hours stirring occasionally until setting point. Bottle in warm jars.

Medlar Jelly
From the fruit of the medlar tree, sometimes found in old gar-

dens, though it also grows wild in Southern England. The fruit has a brown dry skin and must be gathered and stored until the fruit is "bletted" – very ripe and beginning to disintegrate – in November or December. Well bletted medlars were once popular as dessert with the new season's walnuts and a glass of tawny port, and medlar comfits were sometimes eaten to sweeten the breath after drinking, or eating "gross meats".

Medlar jelly is served with game, cold ham and other cold meats and has a unique flavour. To make it follow the recipe for Bilberry Jelly (see page 266) but omit the mint.

Medlar Gin

Simmer ¾ lb of sugar with ½ pint of water gently stirring, to make a syrup. Fill a bottling jar with ripe bletted medlars, add the syrup up to between a third and half the height of the jar. Top it with gin. The fruit must be covered. Close the top tightly and wait for two months to a year before using.

Melon and Ginger Jam

In July and August one can sometimes buy large damaged melons cheaply enough for it to be worth making jam from them.

Peel the melons removing any over-ripe parts together with the seeds and pithy bits. Weigh all the rest, cutting it in chunks. Put it in an ovenproof dish with a lid adding 1 lb of sugar to 4 lb of melon. Leave it for about 10 minutes in a cool oven (300°F, 150°C, Mark 2) until the melon is soft but not entirely broken up. The exact time depends on the kind of melon. Now turn it all into a preserving pan with 8 oz of crystallized ginger cut in chunks, the juice of 4 lemons and another 3 lb of sugar per 4 lb of melon. Boil it until setting point is reached in about 25 minutes adding the grated rinds of the lemons just before it is finished.

Mulberry Jam

From the fruit of the mulberry tree now little grown in England, and very rarely to be bought. The fruit looks like a large black-berry but has more flavour. It is unwise to sit under a mulberry tree as the ripe falling fruit makes purple stains.

The mulberry was introduced into England in 1548 with the

intention of establishing a silk industry as the leaves are used to feed silk worms; the first tree was planted at Sion House.

Put 3 lb of mulberries and 3 lb of sugar in a bowl and leave them for 24 hours with a cloth over the bowl. Next day the mulberries will be covered in their own sweet purple juice. Put the whole thing into a jam pan, without adding any water. Heat gently stirring to melt any surplus sugar which was left at the bottom of the bowl. When it has all dissolved boil rapidly until setting point is reached in about 20 minutes. Bottle in warm jars.

Mushroom Ketchup
Any edible mushrooms may be used, but fully developed well opened field mushrooms were the most popular.

Break them in pieces, put them in a basin and sprinkle them with 2 oz of salt per 1 lb of mushrooms. Leave them for 3 or 4 days and stir them at least once every day.

Put the bowl in a slow oven (300°F, 150°C, Mark 2) and let them cook gently for about 60 minutes before straining off the liquor. To each quart of mushroom liquor add 1 level teaspoon each of peppercorns and whole allspice. Add also a small piece of root ginger, a few cloves and a little cinnamon. If ground spices are used add about one quarter of the quantities while cooking the mushrooms in the oven. Boil the ketchup until it is reduced to about half the original quantity. Strain the ketchup while still hot and pour it into warm bottles and seal it at once.

Some cooks omit the spices and add a small onion and some herbs instead.

Orange Pickle (Cheshire)
Very good with cheese or cold duck
Peel six oranges and slice them thickly removing the pips and pith. Steam in a double pan till clear, soft and translucent. In another saucepan simmer two cups of distilled white vinegar with some pieces of stick cinnamon, cloves and mace and also a strip of lemon peel tied in a muslin bag. Add three cups of white sugar, bring to the boil gradually, stirring, until the sugar has melted. Boil 25 minutes before removing the spice bag. Add

the fruit, simmer for at least an hour. Bottle as usual and leave it at least 3 weeks before using it.

Passion Flowers

The passion flower is grown as a creeper on house walls in Southern England and in fine summers often bears fruit. I have often been asked if it can be used to make jam, though according to the Royal Horticultural Society, 'the fruit of the passion flower, *passiflora caerulea*, which is grown out of doors in this country is not poisonous, it contains a very large number of seeds and very little pulp, so that the fruits are not really edible.'

'The edible passion fruit comes from a species which can only be grown in a greenhouse in this country, but is cultivated in tropical regions for the fruit.'

Spiced Pears

An excellent mild pickle which is eaten with cold meat or curry and very good with the cold ham and turkey on Boxing Day.

Peel some Conference pears but leave them whole, drop them into a large pan of sweetened water, allowing 2 oz of sugar per quart of water. Heat this stirring until the sugar melts then simmer the pears in it until they are tender.

Meanwhile, in another pan, make a spiced vinegary syrup by heating $1\frac{1}{2}$ lb of sugar to every $4\frac{1}{2}$ pints of white distilled vinegar. Add one or two sticks of cinnamon and a few cloves tied up in a clean handkerchief, or fastened in a tea infuser which may be hung over the side of the pan. Stir, heating gently, until the sugar has melted. Then let the mixture boil for a few minutes to become syrupy. Now add the pears. Bring the liquid back to the boil, let it cool. Bring it to the boil and cool again, repeat three times more. Then, when cold, bottle the spiced pears in their vinegar, having removed the spices.

This method ensures that the pears are soft, well flavoured with the spicy syrup, but not cooked to pieces, as they might be if allowed to boil continuously.

Boozy Prunes

These are popular in some country pubs where the landlord has a screw topped jar of best quality prunes on the bar top. Bottle ends are poured into it, wines, spirits, beer, everything. Some of the regulars order "one for the prunes" from time to time, and are usually given some of the contents of the jar for Christmas. After about six months of being marinated in this alcoholic mixture a jar of once plain desiccated prunes has a unique flavour.

Mixed dried fruits (prunes with dried apples and pears and apricots) are also very good when prepared in this way.

Quince Jelly and Quince Cheese
This is a pale yellow fruit, not unlike a pear, with a delicious honeyed fragrance, not widely grown now but found in old gardens.

Peel and quarter the quinces, squeeze lemon juice on them and, having kept the quince pips, tie these in a piece of muslin or clean handkerchief. Put the fruit in a pan with water to cover, add the bag of pips (to make the jelly set) boil the fruit until it is tender and pulpy. Strain off the clear juice through a sieve or cloth. Weigh the juice and add an equal weight of sugar. Boil the juice and the sugar for ten minutes or until setting point is reached. Skim off the scum as it rises. Bottle the jelly in warm jars, cover when cold.

From the pulp left over after making the jelly one can make **Quince Cheese**, this will keep for months in a biscuit tin.
Press the left-over fruit pulp through a muslin, or fine sieve. Put the resulting purée into a pan with $1\frac{1}{2}$ lb of sugar for every 1 lb of pulp. Simmer gently for some time, stirring – almost scraping – the bottom until the mixture begins to come away from the sides and you see the bottom of the pan as you stir. It is better to over- rather than under-cook it. Sprinkle a handful of sugar on a cool marble table top. Tip the paste on to it. spread it to an even thickness, sprinkle sugar on top. When cold cut it in slices. Dry these in the air before storing them in a tin.

The Queen's Preserving Woman's Fine White Jelly of Quinces
The Queen's Royal Cookery has a delightful picture of Queen Anne and also of some kitchens, presumably the royal ones, on the

278

frontispiece. It was published in 1710 and is by T. Hall, Free Cook of London. Free cooks were those engaged on a temporary basis, perhaps for a big dinner or a party, and Mr. Hall seems to have cooked at Court over a long period. Among others he gives recipes for Clouted Cream, Almond Custards, A Gooseberry Tart Baked Green and Clear as Crystal, for Scotch Collups of Mutton, Rabbets Roasted, Lobsters Fried, and Pickled Oysters. His book was printed at Pye Corner, Cheapside, and perhaps he sold pies in one of the famous cooked meat shops there when not cooking for royalty. The pies in his book are excellent.

For The Queen's Preserving Woman's Fine White Jelly of Quinces, 'Take Quinces newly from the Tree, wipe them clean, and boil them whole in a large Quantity of Water, the more the better till the Quinces crack and are soft; then press out their juice hard, but so, that only the Liquor runs out, but none of the Pap; take three pound of this strained liquor, being settled, and one pound of fine Sugar, and boil them up to a jelly, with a moderate fire; they may require near an hour's boiling to come to a jelly, the Tryal of that is to take a thin plate and wet it with fair Water, and drop a little of it upon the wet Plate, if it stick to the plate it is not enough, but if it falls off (when you stop the Plate) without sticking at all to it, then it is enough; then put it into flat, shallow Tin Forms, first melted with cold water, and let it stand in them four or five hours; then reverse the Plates that it may shale and fall out, and so put the Parcels up in Boxes.'

Raspberry Vinegar

This is served with batter puddings in some parts of England and in Anjou is sometimes sprinkled over fresh sweetened strawberries.

Bruise 1 quart of fresh raspberries, pour 1 pint of white wine vinegar or cider over them. Cover the basin and leave the mixture to stand for a few days, stirring from time to time. Then strain the raspberry liquor through a tea towel or a jellybag without squeezing the mixture at all for this will make it cloudy.

Add 1 lb of sugar per 1 pint of liquor, stir, and boil for 15 minutes. Skim. Bottle when cold.

Uncooked Raspberry Jam

One needs two ovenproof basins. Put 2 lb of raspberries in one basin and 2 lb of granulated sugar in the other. Then stand them in a moderate oven (350°F, 180°C, Mark 4) for half an hour or a little longer so they become really hot but do not let them boil. Mix the fruit and sugar together in a large basin stirring with a wooden spoon until the sugar has quite melted and is well mixed with the fruit. Now pack it in warm jars and seal.

It will not keep very long, even in the refrigerator and does not always set very well but it tastes deliciously of fresh warm summer raspberries. Some cooks make it with $1\frac{1}{4}$ lb of sugar to 1 lb of fruit and say that it keeps a little longer.

Raspberries can also be frozen very successfully whole, raw, in cartons or polythene bags, with or without sugar. Over-ripe squashy raspberries are best puréed, then pressed through a sieve. It makes a thick raspberry purée which may be sweetened and frozen and is very useful for making raspberry water ices, raspberry ice cream or sauces.

Wild raspberries grow in Yorkshire and were once used to stuff grouse for roasting.

Rhubarb and Ginger Jam

Wipe, trim and cut 4 lb of rhubarb in chunks, lay these in a fireproof dish with 1 lb of sugar, leave it in a slow oven (300°F, 150°C, Mark 2) for 20–30 minutes, long enough for the juice to run and the fruit to soften but not break up. Tip it into the jam pan adding a further 3 lb of sugar, 8 oz of chopped crystallized ginger and the juice and grated rind of 4 lemons.

Put the pan on a low heat and cook the fruit gently, stirring, until the sugar melts, then boil it rapidly for about 30 minutes until setting point is reached. Pour it into warm jars, cover when cold. If liked, 8 oz of chopped mixed peel could be used instead of the ginger. This makes 5–6 lb of jam.

Wash $\frac{1}{2}$ pint of sloes or damsons, pricking each with a darning needle. Put them in an empty gin or other spirits bottle if the opening is wide enough, otherwise use a preserving jar. Add 6 oz of sugar, 3 drops of almond essence, a few blanched bruised almonds and $\frac{3}{4}$ pint of gin. Leave the sloe gin for at least 3 months before decanting it; this, properly speaking, is a ratafia.

Strawberry Jam
Small strawberries usually have the most flavour. The perfect fruit for preserving whether one picks it or buys it in a shop should not be under-ripe for then it has no flavour. On the other hand, over-ripe fruit is often mushy and sets with difficulty.

This is a very favourite old recipe of mine which came originally from France. It is tedious to make but the strawberries remain whole and fragrant in it.

Allow $\frac{3}{4}$ lb of sugar per 1 lb of strawberries. First put the sugar in the pan with only a couple of tablespoonsful of cold water. Stir it, heating gently until it froths. Then tip in the hulled strawberries and let them boil over a low heat for about 10 minutes. Most people go to endless trouble skimming off the froth from jam, but I just add a coffee spoon of butter to the jam mixture. This dispenses with froth and skimming.

Now tip the strawberries into a sieve to drain and let them drip well into a basin. The syrup may have become diluted with the juice from the strawberries so it must now be boiled up again (without the fruit but with the juice which has dripped from it) until it thickens again. Then put back the strawberries for another 15 minutes of gentle bubbling until the syrup is thick enough to pour off the spoon in ribbons, or until setting point is reached. The juice should be slightly thinner than for ordinary English jam. Put it all in a big bowl until next day, then bottle and seal it cold. If you bottle the jam when hot the strawberries bob up to the top of the jars.

King Charles II's Surfeit Water
The following recipe for King Charles II's Surfeit Water is probably for a hangover cure. It appeared in Eliza Smith's *The Compleat Housewife* a work of uncertain date, for no first editions are known. Bitting cites the fourth edition dated 1727, but the original work may well have been contemporary with the Merry Monarch.

'Take a gallon of the best aqua-vitae, a quart of brandy, a

quart of aniseed-water, a pint of poppy water, and a pint of damask rose-water, put these in a large glass jar, adding to it a pound of fine powder'd sugar, a pound and a half of raisins stoned, a quarter of a pound of dates stoned and sliced, one ounce of cinnamon bruised, cloves one ounce, four nutmegs bruised, one stick of liquorice scrap'd and sliced; let all there stand nine days close cover'd stirring it three or four times a day; then add to it three pounds of fresh poppies, or three handfulls of dry'd poppies, a sprig of angelica, two or three of balm; so let it stand a week longer, then strain it out and bottle it.'

We have not of course tried it ourselves but felt it was of interest rather for its associates than its flavour.

Vinegar
One can make Tarragon Vinegar for salads by stuffing some sprigs of fresh green tarragon into a bottle and filling it up with white wine vinegar. Basil Vinegar can be prepared in the same way.

Onion, Garlic or Eschallot Vinegar is, according to Mrs. Esther Copley, 'to be made between Midsummer and Michaelmas.'

Peel and chop 2 oz of whichever bulb is desired. 'Pour over them a quart of best vinegar, stopping close the jar or bottle, and well shaking everyday. Let it steep ten days then pour off the liquor into small bottles.'
(Mrs. Copley was a 19th century "do-gooder" who was married successively to two parsons, twice widowed and the author of many improving books for the "labouring classes" such as *Mother Encouraged, Hints to Christian Females on Dress, The Master and Mistress, The Working Man's Wife,* and *The Passing Bell.*)

Vinegar itself can also be made at home by using a vinegar plant, or what in Italy is known as "mother of vinegar", a rather unattractive fungus-like mass which is plunged into a large jar of sweetened water turning it into mild vinegar.

Pickled Walnuts
These are prepared with fresh green walnuts which are still soft right through. One should be able to run a darning needle

through them easily. There is, however, no need to prick the walnuts all over with a pin as is sometimes recommended, before pickling them.

Buy some rock salt and make a brine solution with 6 oz of salt to a quart of water. Leave the walnuts in it for nine days. Change the brine twice and stir it up, night and morning. Then drain the walnuts into a colander and rinse them by pouring hot water over them. Stand them in the sun, or air, on trays till they become black. Put one tablespoonful of mixed pickling spice and two freshly grated nutmegs in a muslin bag or white handkerchief. Boil this in an enamel or stainless steel pan in enough vinegar to cover them. One needs about a quart for 50 walnuts. Pack them into warm jars and strain the hot vinegar over them. Screw down the tops when cold, but put a piece of paper between them and the vinegar, so that it doesn't attack the metal covers.

Index

285

287

288